ATARI ST™

3-D Graphic Programming

By Uwe Braun

A Data Becker Book

Published by

Abacus ▦ Software

Table of Contents

Appendices

Introduction

1. Introduction

The possibilities of computer graphics are some of the most challenging reasons for working with a computer today. Dazzling computer-generated images are showing up almost everywhere--in medicine, engineering, motion pictures, music videos, television advertising, and even in newspapers like USA Today. The public is fascinated by the unlimited forms that computer graphics are taking. Some of the more sophisticated of these works are the three-dimensional, computer-animated videos used in television advertisements.

One major application of computer graphics in industry is for CAD (Computer-Aided Design) systems. The integration of CAD systems into the manufacturing process is of increasing importance. Known as CAD-CAM (Computer-Aided Design - Computer-Aided Manufacturing), these systems are making significant inroads in automating many of the manufactured, assembled, and processed goods such as machine tools, automobiles, electronics, and agricultural products. Without advanced graphic data processing, the latest medical processes such as CAT scans would be difficult, if not impossible. Furthermore, three-dimensional graphic data processing has made it possible to visually represent complicated scientific relationships and to make them comprehensible (like atomic and molecular models and the DNA helix). Eventually these graphics will be integrated with advanced teaching and simulation methods, and are bound to have a profound impact on the way we think and learn.

The enormous strides made in the production of integrated circuits and the increase in processing speeds of relatively new microprocessors such as the Motorola MC68000 has made it possible for the home and personal computers to enter application areas that were formerly the domain of large mainframe computers costing several hundred thousand dollars. Even now, an affordable 32-bit personal computer is just around the corner. The traditional distinctions between microcomputers, minicomputers, and mainframes are becoming increasingly blurred.

Of course, even the largest mainframes are getting faster as well. The fastest computer at this time, the Cray II, has a throughput capacity of 2000 megaflops (200 million floating-point operations per second). Such high computing speeds are needed to closely simulate natural world processes with computer models. Examples are the simulation of ecological problems (acid rain), simulation of the human physiology, weather prediction, nuclear fusion and fission, origin of the solar system, simulation of star systems, space travel, etc.

This book is intended to explore some of the possibilities of creating two- and three-dimensional computer graphics on the Atari ST computer series. To obtain a good understanding of the program sections, you should have some fundamental knowledge of MC68000 machine language.

Machine language represents the lowest level of communication with the computer and contains a small number of rather simple instructions that are consequently easy to learn. For the hobbyist, knowing machine language programming makes it easier to understand the data structure of higher-level languages such as Pascal and C. However, most problems and algorithms are easier to program in a higher-level language than in machine language.

For the problem of depicting and representing the 3-D wire models presented here, maximum processor speed is crucial. Machine language is clearly superior to any higher-level language in fulfilling this requirement. With these applications for the Atari ST, real-time three-dimensional graphics can be achieved. The removal of hidden lines and the shading of areas requires a considerable amount of processor time. The Cray II requires 8 minutes to create a single picture with a resolution of 2000 by 3000 pixels, with up to 30 bits of color information per picture point. In contrast, the ST manages only 640 by 400 pixels and only one bit of color information. Of course, it is possible to increase the computational capabilities of the ST with programming tricks, fast mass storage (hard disk) and large amounts of memory to solve more complex graphic problems.

This book provides you with help in solving the complex programming problems of three-dimensional graphics. While the sample programs are directly tailored for the Atari ST, the techniques can be used without too much difficulty on other computers. Only the routines for hardware communication and display control (keyboard input, line drawing, surface shading (if possible) and switching between two screens) need to be tailored to another computer using an MC68000 CPU (i.e., the Apple Macintosh and Commodore's Amiga). The subroutines for generating and handling three-dimensional graphic objects can be run on any computer with an MC68000 microprocessor.

Mathematical Basis of
Graphic Programming

2. Mathematical Basis of Graphic Programming

This chapter serves as the mathematical foundation of computer-generated, three-dimensional graphics. As a result, the explanations are very extensive. For this reason we ask readers who are already familiar with these topics for a little patience and understanding.

All computer graphic problems can ultimately be reduced to the problem of drawing points on a graphic output device (monitor screen, plotter, or printer) and to connect these points with lines. There may also be the task of shading the area delineated by the lines. For a demonstration, we will use a two-dimensional plane with one Cartesian coordinate system, familiar to everybody, whose origin lies in the lower left hand corner of the screen.

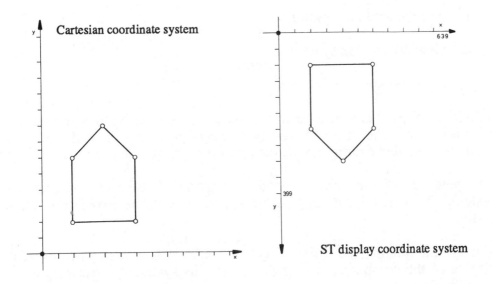

Fig. 2.1: coordinate system and ST display coordinate system

In Figure 2.1, the first problem of representing graphics becomes clear. The Cartesian coordinate system and the display coordinate system used by the ST's software and hardware are not the same. The directions of the y-axis are opposite, and the coordinate origin is displaced. Consequently, an object defined in the first system is inverted in the system on the right, and is also displaced on the y-axis.

At first, you might be tempted to define objects to be represented using the ST's coordinate system. But doing this does not solve the second problem--that the display surface of every computer is limited. The ST can display only 640x400 points at its highest resolution. So, to avoid defining objects with these limitations of 640x400 points, we must be able to define an object in any desired coordinate system before displaying it on the monitor screen. In other words, we must be able to scale the object in any of the coordinate systems, i.e., change its size. All points of the defined object can then be transformed using graphics operations.

This operation is called *windowing*. We now introduce three coordinate systems. They are:

1. world coordinate system

2. view coordinate system

3. picture coordinate system

Individual objects are defined in the *world coordinate system*, where the calibration of the coordinate axis may be any desired unit of measurement--for example, millimeters, kilometers, years, etc.

The *view coordinate system* accepts a portion of the world coordinate system. This is similar to an observation window in the world coordinate system.

Finally, the *picture coordinate system* represents the physical screen display of the computer, A single point in this system corresponds to an individual pixel on the screen.

This concept can be explained very simply with an example. Two objects are defined in a world coordinate system, the outlines of a house and of a church. The two outlines represent all objects that can be depicted on a plane. For example, an architect would use the outline of the house in a world coordinate system to define individual rooms and furniture.

Our task is to transform the observation window, together with the house that fills its surface, to the specific picture window for display on the ST's screen.

Here's the preferred solution to the problem, using the view coordinate system: The origin of the world coordinate system is moved to the lower left corner of the observation window and scaled by a suitable factor. It now represents all points in the picture coordinate system. If the points are in the field of picture coordinates, they can be drawn and connected with lines.

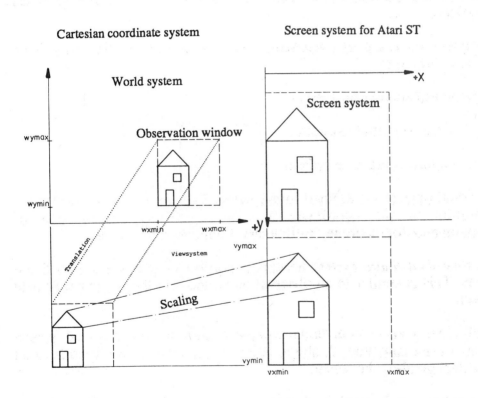

Fig. 2.2: Transformation of world coordinates to picture coordinates

2.1   Moving the coordinate base

Scaling and (as we shall see later) rotation are both related to the coordinate base. To scale an object in relation to another point, or to rotate it around an arbitrary point, the coordinate origin must first be moved to the relative origin. We can illustrate this again using the house example.

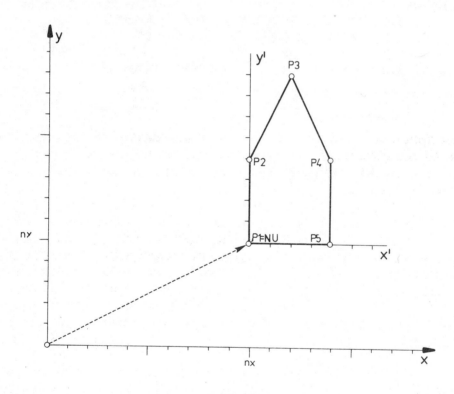

Fig. 2.1.1

One way to describe the house is to list the coordinates of the end points and to list the points which are connected with lines. For this example, the two lists are as follows:

End point list:

Point	X-coordinate	Y-coordinate
P1	100	50
P2	100	90
P3	120	130
P4	140	90
P5	140	50

Connection list:

Line from	Point A to	Point B
L1:	P1	P2
L2:	P2	P3
L3:	P3	P4
L4:	P4	P5
L5:	P5	P1

This description of a polygon, consists of a sequence of closed lines. It contains all the information necessary for representing it on the display screen. To draw the polygon, the lines' endpoints are passed to a subroutine for drawing.

As we shall see later, the polygon is also perfectly acceptable for the description of complex, three-dimensional objects. Any physical object can be closely approximated by chaining various polygons. Also, natural asymmetrical bodies such as mountains, forests, lakes and animals can be represented in a realistic manner with polygons created through fractional geometry, i.e. fractals. In addition, most man-made objects are constructed in a symmetrical manner and are easier to represent graphically.

In Figure 2.1.1 the coordinate origin of the world system is moved to point P1[100,50]. The new world coordinates (view coordinates) are obtained by subtracting the coordinates of point P1--the new origin--from the points that define the object. In general, the new world coordinates are equal to the old world coordinates, minus the coordinates of the new origin (in world coordinates). If we describe the old world coordinate axis with x and y, the new world coordinate axis with x' and y', the new origin point with NU[nx,ny] and the point to be moved with P1[x,y], we can write:

$$P1[x1',y1'] = P1[x1,y1] - NU[nx,ny]$$

11

For example, for point 5--the new origin is located at
P1(100,50) = NU(100,50). The coordinates of the point to be
moved P5(140,50) become in the new world coordinate system
P5x'=140-100 = 40,   P5y'=50-50 = 0.   The   point
P5(140,50) becomes point P5'(40,0). This translation must be
performed for every point of the object. It is possible to move the origin
of the world coordinate system to any point.

2.1.1   Scaling the Axis

As previously mentioned, scaling the axis refers to the coordinate origin.
This can be readily seen in Figure 2.1.2. The points of the house, i.e. the
X and Y coordinates, are scaled by the factor one half in the X and Y
axes. The result is the halving of the length of the edges, but also a
translation in the direction of the origin. If we want to avoid displacing
the direction of the origin, then before scaling the origin must be moved
to a point not affected by the scaling itself. The Figure 2.1.3 is an
example. If we want to leave the left lower corner of the house (the point
P1) in its place. The origin is moved to point P1. The picture is scaled by
multiplying the X and Y values by one half and finally moving the origin
to its original location. In this example this means:

1.   Subtract 100 from the X-values of points P1-P5

     Subtract 50 from the Y-values of points P1-P5

2.   Multiply all X- and Y-values of points P1-P5

     with the factor one half.

3.   Add 100 to all X-values of points P1-P5

     Add 50 to all Y-values of points P1-P5

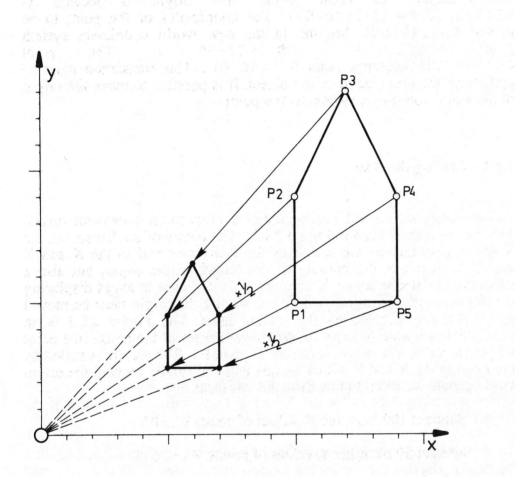

Figure 2.1.2

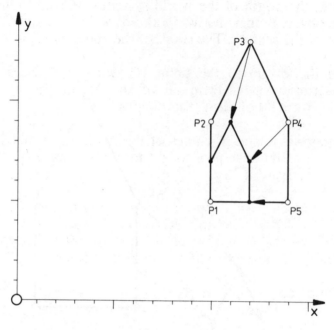

Figure 2.1.3

Scaling with factors greater than one enlarges the object. If we select different scaling factors for the X and Y axes, a distorted picture of the object results.

At this point let's briefly return to the example, at Figure 2.1, and alter the scaling factors for converting to view coordinates. With the maximum coordinates of the observation:

        [wxmin,wymin]; [wxmax,wymax],
and the display window
        [vxmin,vymin]; [vxmax,vymax]
one can give differing scaling factors for the two axes, Sx and Sy. In our example:

        Sx=(vxmax-vxmin)/(wxmax-wxmin)

        Sy=(vymax-vymin)/(wymax-wymin)

Before scaling, the origin of the world system is moved to the left lower corner of the observation window [wxmin, wymin], since this point is the data point of the scaling. The result of the conversions is therefore:

1. Move the origin to the point W1[wxmin, wymin] by subtracting wxmin from all of the X coordinates and wymin from all of the Y coordinates.

2. Multiply all X and Y values of the points with the factor Sx. If the relationship of height to width is equal for both windows, then Sx=Sy.

3. Convert to the display system by multiplying the Y values by -1 and adding of the maximum Y value to these Y values (for the monochrome ST this is 399). This moves the origin to the upper left corner of the screen.

The third step of converting the Y values to the screen display of the ST is always the same. During the description we shall limit ourselves to the view system. If during subsequent discussions no special reference is made to this step, you should remember that if it is not performed, all objects appear inverted on the screen after the drawing is completed.

The location of the picture window in the view system is not fixed to the origin, but is movable in the total view system. However, the three conversions must be followed by another conversion--moving the window to point V1[vxmin, vymin]. Basically the conversion of an object is the opposite of the conversion of a coordinate system. Therefore, when moving the picture window and the object to the point V1[vxmin, vymin], the coordinates of this point (vxmin and vymin) must be added to all object coordinates.

Summarizing the conversion of the world system into the view system:

1. Move the origin to the point W1[wxmin, wymin] by subtracting wxmin from all X coordinates, and wymin from all Y coordinates.

2. Multiply all X values of the points by the factor Sx=(vxmax-vxmin)/(wxmax-wxmin), the Y values with the factor Sy=(vymax-vymin)/(wymax-wymin).

3. Move the window and the object to the point
    V1[vxmin,vymin] by adding vxmin to all X values,
    and vymin to all Y values.

4. Convert to the display system by multiplying the Y values
    by -1 and adding the maximum Y-value to these Y values
    (for the highest resolution this value is always 399).

2.1.2   Rotation around one point

The rotation of an object is related to a single point, just as we found out
in the previous section on scaling. To start the conversion, a single point
is rotated around the origin. Since the rotation occurs around the single
origin point, the data point of the rotation angle is the connecting line
between coordinate source and the point to be rotated. See Figure 2.1.4.

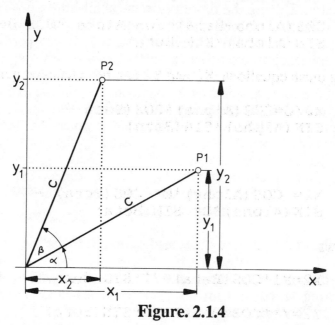

Figure. 2.1.4

The point P1(x1,y1) is moved by rotation around the angle β of the
origin to the point P2(x2,y2). We must define the sign of the angles α
and β as + or -. Following the conventions of mathematics, we designate

the angles as positive when the rotation moves the positive X axis to the positive Y axis. Expressed differently, positive angles are measured in the counterclockwise direction. For the angle between the connecting line from 0,0 to P1 and the X-axis, the relationships are:

    1)   SIN(alpha) = Y1/C

    2)   COS(alpha) = X1/C

    3)   SIN(alpha+beta)=Y2/C

    4)   COS(alpha+beta)=X2/C

with $C=\sqrt{(X1^2+Y1^2)}=\sqrt{(X2^2+Y2^2)}$. The addition theorems for the angle functions SIN and COS are as follow (we won't derive them here):

    5)   SIN(Alpha+Beta)=SIN(Alpha)*COS
            (Beta)+COS(Alpha)*SIN(Beta)

    6)   COS(Alpha+Beta)=COS(Alpha)*COS(Beta)-
            SIN(Alpha)*SIN(Beta)

By combining these equations, X2 and Y2 can be calculated quite easily:

    7)   X2/C=COS(Alpha)*COS(Beta)-
            SIN(Alpha)*SIN(Beta)

gives us

    8)   X2= COS(Alpha)*C* COS(Beta) -
            SIN(Alpha)*C* SIN(Beta)

from 1) follows

    9)   X2=X1*COS(Beta)-Y1*SIN(Beta)

    10)   Y2=Y1*COS(Beta)+X1*SIN(Beta)

As an example of rotation, we will rotate the house in Figure 2.1.5 by an angle of 30 degrees around the origin. The points P1-P5 become points R1-R5, as can be seen on the example at Point P1.

        R1X=P1X*COS(30)-P1Y*SIN(30)

        R1Y=P1Y*COS(30)+P1X*SIN(30)

From P1(100,50) follows R1(61.6,93.3). According to the same principle, the remaining points are likewise converted.

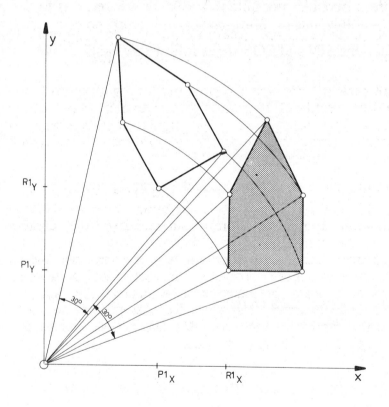

Figure 2.1.5

18

2.2   Plane conversion with matrix operations

After learning about the conversions, translations, scaling and rotations described in the previous chapter, we are now able to draw on the screen any object previously defined in a two dimensional coordinate system, in any selected size and viewing angle. One drawback to this method is that several arithmetic operations are required for each and every point of the object.

Right now we'll combine these conversion operations into a single matrix operation. (Explanations of matrix operations are found in the Appendix). Therefore it becomes possible to apply the conversions to the array and then to multiply the resulting array with every point of the object. To make the array operations usable for the point coordinates of the plane, the point coordinates are first converted to array form.

There are basically two ways to convert these: with column vectors (2,1), or with line vector (1,2) arrays. A conversion array (2,2) is used to multiply a line vector with the transformation array, where the transformation array must be multiplied with the column vector. (number of columns A = number of rows B).

In this book we shall write the point coordinates as line vectors P and the multiply this line vector with the transformation array. This sequence of multiplication simplifies, purely subjectively, the creation of the transformation matrices. If you multiply a line vector (1,2) with a quadratic array (2,2), you will obtain as a result another line vector (1,2), which represents point coordinates. The individual point operations can be expressed by a suitable transformation matrix T. For scaling the X axis by the factor 2, the array S1 is valid. It is also possible to quadruple the Y values using transformation array S2. The two scaling steps can be by multiplying S1 and S2 with array S3.

$$S_1 \quad \begin{array}{cc} 2 & 0 \\ 0 & 1 \end{array} \qquad S_2 = \begin{array}{cc} 1 & 0 \\ 0 & 4 \end{array}$$

$$S_3 = S_1 * S_2 = \begin{array}{cc} 2 & 0 \\ 0 & 1 \end{array} \quad * \quad \begin{array}{cc} 1 & 0 \\ 0 & 4 \end{array}$$

$$S_3 = \begin{array}{cc} 2 & 0 \\ 0 & 4 \end{array}$$

For rotation, R_1 is valid for one counter clockwise rotation; from trigonometry, a clockwise rotation occurs with R_2. From Figure 2.1.5, the movement of point P1 [x1, y1] to point P2 [x2, y2], results from multiplying P1 with R.

```
R1 =      cos(b)        sin(b)
         -sin(b)        cos(b)
```

```
R2 =     cos(-b)       sin(-b)     =     cos(b)      -sin(b)
        -sin(-b        cos(-b)           sin(b)       cos(b)
```

```
P2[X2,Y2] = [X1,Y1] *          cos(30)      -sin(30)
                               sin(30)       cos(30)
```

Several rotations in succession can be carried out by multiplying the rotation matrices. Unfortunately, this array form does not permit translation (origin relocation). For this you can add a dimension to the vectors. Every n-dimensional object can be represented in a (n+1) space in innumerable many ways.

In a three dimensional space there are infinite possibilities for laying out the X-Y plane we have just observed. The additional dimension is known as Z coordinate of the X-Y plane. For two dimensional objects, its value is always one. The X and Y coordinates remain unchanged: the line vector [x,y] becomes the line vector [x,y,1]. The array for the translation of the source at point D is as follows:

```
         1      1      0
T =      0      1      0
       -DX    -DY      1
```

Every point of the object must be multiplied with this array to move the origin of the world coordinate system to the point (DX, DY). For the point P [x, y, 1] the result is: new point in world coordinates P' =P * T

```
                                  1     0     0
P'[x',y',1] = [x,y,1]    *        0     1     0 = [x-dx,y-dy,1]
                                -DX   -DY     1
```

You can combine two displacements by using array multiplications. First the origin is moved to the point [DX, DY, 1] and then to the point [AX, AY, 1] of the new coordinate system. The two translation matrices T1 and T2 are as follows:

$$
T_1 = \begin{array}{ccc} 1 & 0 & 0 \\ 0 & 1 & 0 \\ DX & -DY & 1 \end{array}
\qquad
T_2 = \begin{array}{ccc} 1 & 0 & 0 \\ 0 & 1 & 0 \\ -AX & -AY & 1 \end{array}
$$

Multiplication of the matrices results in T_3:

$$
T_3 = T_1 * T_2 = \begin{array}{ccc} 1 & 0 & 0 \\ 0 & 1 & 0 \\ -DX & -DY & 1 \end{array} * \begin{array}{ccc} 1 & 0 & 0 \\ 0 & 1 & 0 \\ -AX & -AY & 1 \end{array}
$$

$$
T_3 = \begin{array}{ccc} 1 & 0 & 0 \\ 0 & 1 & 0 \\ -DX-AX & -DY-AY & 1 \end{array}
$$

P' [x', y', 1]= P [x, y, 1]*T_3 = [x-DX-AX, Y-DY-AY, 1]

The scaling array S can be defined in the new system:

$$
S = \begin{array}{ccc} SX & 0 & 0 \\ 0 & SY & 0 \\ 0 & 0 & 1 \end{array} \quad \text{and} \quad P' = P * S
$$

and finally the rotation array R

$$
R(a) = \begin{array}{ccc} \cos(a) & \sin(a) & 0 \\ -\sin(a) & \cos(a) & 0 \\ 0 & 0 & 1 \end{array}
$$

Scaling as well as rotation, viewed individually, may be carried out in a series through array multiplications. The array multiplication is normally not commutative, i.e. $T_1 * T_2$ is not necessarily identical with $T_2 * T_1$. However, the multiplication of the following array types is commutative:

```
1)    Translation    *    Translation
2)    Scaling         *    Scaling
3)    Rotation        *    Rotation around
                            the same axis
4)    Scaling         *    Rotating
```

Type 4 (scaling and rotating) is only valid when both scale factors (Sx, Sy) are identical.

These fundamentals enable us, through a combination of several array operations, to rotate an object around a selected point V[vx, vy, 1] using a series of several array operations. The various operations are:

1. Shifting the origin to point V

2. Rotation around point V by an angle of alpha

3. Shifting of the origin to the original point

Three matrices T_1, R_1 and T_2 are required:

$$T_1 = \begin{matrix} 1 & 0 & 0 \\ 0 & 1 & 0 \\ -vx & -vy & 1 \end{matrix} \qquad R_1 = \begin{matrix} \cos(a) & \sin(a) & 0 \\ -\sin(a) & \cos(a) & 0 \\ 0 & 0 & 1 \end{matrix}$$

$$T_2 = \begin{matrix} 1 & 0 & 0 \\ 0 & 1 & 0 \\ vx & vy & 1 \end{matrix}$$

For the multiplication array M_1, the result is:

$$M_1 = T_1 * R_1 * T_2 \text{ and for every point follows:}$$
$$P' = P * M_1$$

The sequence of matrices is decisive in these operations and must occur from left to right. It is possible however, to first calculate intermediate results, but these must be used in the "right" sequence. In this example, there are two possible ways to proceed:

1. First calculate from $Z_1 = T_1 * R_1$ and then $M_1 = Z_1 * T_2$

2. First calculate from $Z_2 = R_1 * T_2$ and then $M_2 = T_1 * Z_2$

The first case is explained in detail. $Z_1 = T_1 * R_1$:

$$Z_1 = \begin{bmatrix} 1 & 0 & 0 \\ 0 & 1 & 0 \\ -vx & -vy & 1 \end{bmatrix} * \begin{bmatrix} \cos(a) & \sin(a) & 0 \\ -\sin(a) & \cos(a) & 0 \\ 0 & 0 & 1 \end{bmatrix}$$

$$Z_1 = \begin{bmatrix} \cos(a) & \sin(a) & 0 \\ -\sin(a) & \cos(a) & 0 \\ -vx*\cos(a)+vy*\sin(a) & -vx*\sin(a)-vy*\cos(a) & 1 \end{bmatrix}$$

and now $M_1 = Z_1 * T_2$:

$$M_1 = \begin{bmatrix} \cos(a) & \sin(a) & 0 \\ -\sin(a) & \cos(a) & 0 \\ -vx*\cos(a)+vy*\sin(a) & -vx*\sin(a)-vy*\cos(a) & 1 \end{bmatrix} *$$

$$\begin{bmatrix} 1 & 0 & 0 \\ 0 & 1 & 0 \\ vx & vy & 1 \end{bmatrix} =$$

$$\begin{bmatrix} \cos(a) & \sin(a) & 0 \\ -\sin(a) & \cos(a) & 0 \\ -vx*\cos(a)+vy*\sin(a)+vx & -vx*\sin(a)-vy*\cos(a)+vy & 1 \end{bmatrix}$$

If point P1 [x,y,1] is multiplied with this array, the result is point
P1′ [x′,y′,1], the point P1 which was rotated around the angle
alpha at point V1 [vx,vy,1]. This connection can be recognized in
Figure 2.2.1 and should be performed as example for point P1.
P1[x,y,1] * M1 =

```
                          cos(a)                      sin(a)              0
[x,y,1] *                 -sin(a)                     cos(a)              0
              -vx*cos(a)+vy*sin(a)+vx      -vx*sin(a)-vy*cos(a)+vy        1
```

```
P1[x,y,z]=      [[x*cos(a)-y*sin(a)-vx*cos(a)+vy*sin(a)+vx],
                 [x*sin(a)+y*cos(a)-vx*sin(a)-vy*cos(a)+vy], [1]]
```

You can see that when the rotation point and the point to be rotated are
identical, therefore x=vx and y=vy, the expression for the line vector of
the point at [vx,vy,1] = [x,y,1] degenerates. That means that the
point coordinates do not change.

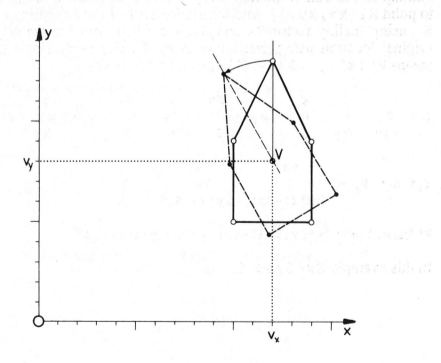

Figure 2.2.1

The house already familiar in Figure 2.2.1 shall be rotated by the angle alpha=30 degrees around the point V1[vx,vy,1]=[120,80,1]. As an example this is carried out on point P2[100,90,1].

$$P2x'=100*\cos(30)-90*\sin(30)-120*\cos(30)+80*\sin(a)+120$$

$$P2y'=100*\sin(30)+90*\cos(30)-120*\sin(30)-80*\cos(30)+80$$

P2'=[97.68,78.66,1] and finally for the remaining points P1-P5.

```
P1'=[117.68,44.02,1]
P2'=[97.68,78.66,1]
P3'=[95,123.30,1]
P4'=[132,32,98,66,1]
P5'=[143.66,59.02,1]
```

This procedure also permits you to change the point for scaling to any location in the coordinate system. In the following, you can see the buildup of the transformation array. First the coordinate origin is moved to point K1[kx,ky,1] with translation array T_1, then scaling with array S_1, using scaling factor Sx and Sy, and finally moving the origin to its original location using translation array T_2. For every single point this means P'[x',y',1] = P[x,y,1]*T_1*S_1*T_2.

$$T_1 = \begin{bmatrix} 1 & 0 & 0 \\ 0 & 1 & 0 \\ -kx & -ky & 1 \end{bmatrix} \quad S_1 = \begin{bmatrix} Sx & 0 & 0 \\ 0 & Sy & 0 \\ 0 & 0 & 1 \end{bmatrix} \quad T_2 = \begin{bmatrix} 1 & 0 & 0 \\ 0 & 1 & 0 \\ kx & ky & 1 \end{bmatrix}$$

$$T_1*S_1*T_2 = \begin{bmatrix} Sx & 0 & 0 \\ 0 & Sy & 0 \\ kx*(1-Sx) & ky*(1-Sy) & 1 \end{bmatrix}$$

P'[x,y,1]=P'[x*Sx+kx(1-Sx),y*Sy+ky(1-Sy),1]

In this example Sx=Sy=0.5.

2.3 Clipping

As we transformed the object coordinates to the display coordinate system, we assumed that all points in the object can be represented in the picture coordinate system. When we define a window in the world system, some objects may be completely pushed out of the view of the window, or objects are cut in half by the window. This means that one or several connecting lines of the points cut the corners of the observation window.

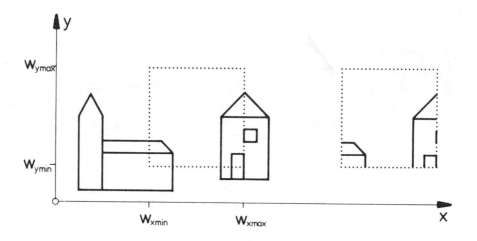

Figure 2.3.1

To avoid these incomplete objects, we can test the coordinates to make sure they lie within the borders of the window. This method slows down the drawing procedures considerably. Therefore it is better to determine before drawing a line if the line is completely visible, partially visible, or not visible at all. The window is surrounded by eight equally large surfaces to determine the exact position of the line to the window. Now the exact location of a line can be determined by comparing its coordinates to the window borders. A code containing four bits can be used to represent the relative position of a line outside of the window.

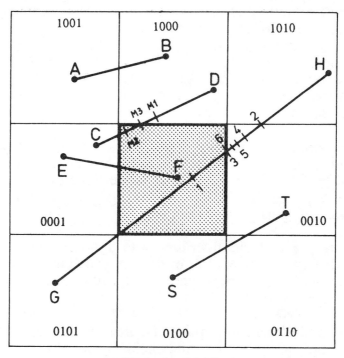

Bit number 3 2 1 0

Figure 2.3.2:Clip-Window

In the Figure 2.3.2 the position of a point outside a window is repeated by a set bit as follows:

    bit   position

    0 =   Point is left of the window

    1 =   Point is right of the window

    2 =   Point is below the window

    3 =   Point is above the window

The code [0,1,0,1] means the following: the point is to the left and below the window. With this information, it is possible to calculate the points of intersection of the lines with the window edges by including them in the equation. This leads to a quadratic equation system whose solution requires several multiplications and divisions. For our purposes, we want to limit the number of multiplications and to replace them when possible with other mathematical operations. We do this for two reasons. The first is for speed since multiplication requires about eight to ten times the calculation time of addition. The second is the fact that the result of multiplication, with the same number of significant positions of the operands, has a larger relative error.

To get an optimal solution of the line-clipping problem requires a programming language which permits bit manipulation. This was developed by Cohen and Sutherland. Since the efficiency of the Cohen-Sutherland clipping algorithm is so great, it is sometimes implemented in the hardware of some graphic terminals.

The starting point of the algorithm is to divide the plane into the nine areas previously illustrated. For every line which is to be "clipped", you must determine a center point and on the basis of its position relative to the window.

The calculation of the center point of a line AB is simple. Just add the X and Y coordinates of the end points and divide them by two. $Mx=(ax+bx)/2$, $My=(ay+by)/2$. Division by two is performed by microcomputers easily by a single right shift and this explains the speed of the algorithm.

The 8 different positions of the end points relative to the window are illustrated in Figure 2.3.2. Before calling the clip-routine, you must first test to see if the two end points are visible. If any of the bits are set, then some portion of the line is not visible. In Figure 2.3.2 both A and B are above the upper window edge, and therefore the line AB is not visible and no longer needs to be considered. You can calculate the position of the points by "ANDing" their codes and then testing for a "not zero" condition. For lines which have no common position parameter, for example the line CD, positions are determined with two separate procedures. First the right and then the left intersecting points with the clip-window.

First calculate the midpoint M1 of line CD. After determining the position code of the point M1, it is compared with the code of the right endpoint D. If a single bit of these codes is the same, then the partial line M1D does not have to be considered further, and the right endpoint D is replaced with the point M1 which was just determined. Now the midpoint of line CM1 (M2), is calculated and tested again with the right endpoint, this time M1. If both points are not on one side, M2 becomes the new left endpoint and the right endpoint remains M1. Next search the midpoint of the line M2M1. This procedure is continued until a new calculated midpoint is equal to one of the two end points used for calculation.

After completing the algorithm, the last left endpoint is the desired intersecting point with the window. The intersecting point is stored and the two starting points C and D are interchanged. With the same procedure the intersection with the left window edge is determined. At the start of the routine, if you find that an endpoint is already inside the window, this endpoint must be stored. The line ST causes a problem. The two end points S and T are not on the same window side and the line does not intersect the window. A comparison of the first center point T1 shows it matching both end points. The points T1 and T are both to the right of the window and point S below the window. You can thus define a new ending criteria--if a new midpoint lies outside of the window and matches both end points of the line, then the line is not visible.

2.4 Transformations in three dimensional space

A small warning before we start: Thinking in three dimensions requires a period of adjustment for the non-mathematically oriented reader. It may be necessary to read this chapter several times before the concepts can be fully understood.

Starting with the two dimensional X-Y-coordinate system, there are two ways to introduce a right angle coordinate system to describe three dimensional space. They are the *right-hand* and the *left-hand* coordinate system which differ only in the orientation of the negative Z axis.

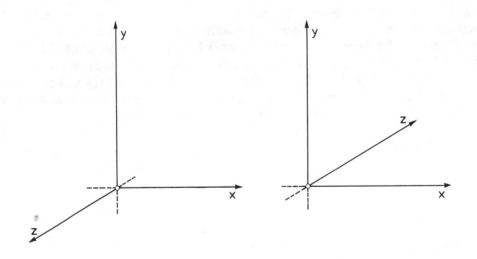

Figure 2.4.1

A coordinate system is called a *right-hand* coordinate system when a screw with a right-handed thread (a normal wood screw) moves in the direction of the positive Z axis when it is turned from the positive X axis in the direction of the positive Y axis. See Figure 2.4.2. The *right-hand* coordinate system is used extensively in mathematics while some computer graphic books select the *left-hand* coordinate system.

Mathematical problems can be solved in either system and one system can easily be turned into the other. We shall use both systems. The transformations in three dimensional space will be explained on a *right-hand* coordinate system, the perspective transformations on a *left-hand* coordinate system.

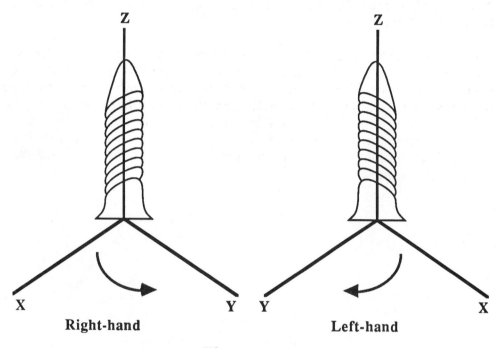

Right-hand   **Left-hand**

Figure 2.4.2

All operations in a two dimensional space are special cases of corresponding operations in three dimensional space. In the extended coordinate system, the line vector of a point is expressed as: $P[x,y,z,1]$. To move the origin to the point $V[vx,vy,vz,1]$, use the matrix T1:

$$T_1 = \begin{array}{cccc} 1 & 0 & 0 & 0 \\ 0 & 1 & 0 & 0 \\ 0 & 0 & 1 & 0 \\ -vx & -vy & -vz & 1 \end{array}$$

So for every point: $[x,y,z,1] \ast T_1 = [x-vx,y-vy,z-vz,1]$

The scaling matrix is similar. A scaling factor for the Z axis (Sz) is added:

$$
S_1 = \begin{array}{cccc}
Sx & 0 & 0 & 0 \\
0 & Sy & 0 & 0 \\
0 & 0 & Sz & 0 \\
0 & 0 & 0 & 1
\end{array}
$$

For every point: $[x,y,z,1] * S_1 = [x*Sx, y*Sy, z*Sz, 1]$

Rotation is limited to the three rotation axis: X,Y, and Z. We are already familiar with rotation about the Z axis from the earlier 2D description. The 3D description is derived by assuming that the positive Z axis projects from the drawing surface. The coordinates of the axis about which rotation takes place, does not change, in this case the Z coordinates retain their values.

$$
R_z = \begin{array}{cccc}
\cos(zw) & \sin(zw) & 0 & 0 \\
-\sin(zw) & \cos(zw) & 0 & 0 \\
0 & 0 & 1 & 0 \\
0 & 0 & 0 & 1
\end{array}
$$

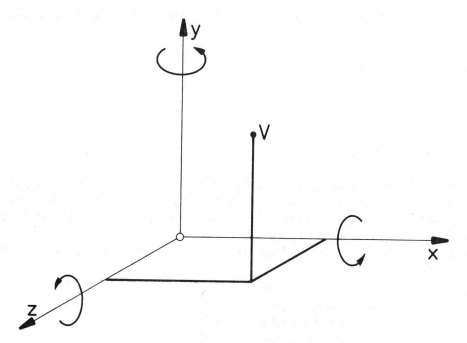

Figure 2.4.3

We must also allow for setting a positive turning angle for the rotation about the X and Y axes. A solution which can be applied to both the *left-hand* and *right-hand* coordinate systems uses the following definitions:

Rotation axis positive angles are measured from

    Z-axis   X- to Y-axis

    Y-axis   Z- to X-axis

    X-axis   Y- to Z-axis

From this follow the matrices for rotation around the X and Y axis R_x and R_y.

$$R_x = \begin{array}{cccc} 1 & 0 & 0 & 0 \\ 0 & \cos(xw) & \sin(xw) & 0 \\ 0 & -\sin(xw) & \cos(xw) & 0 \\ 0 & 0 & 0 & 1 \end{array}$$

$$R_y = \begin{array}{cccc} \cos(yw) & 0 & -\sin(yw) & 0 \\ 0 & 1 & 0 & 0 \\ \sin(yw) & 0 & \cos(yw) & 0 \\ 0 & 0 & 0 & 1 \end{array}$$

For the coordinate system this means that if you look from a positive axis in the direction of the coordinate origin, a positive angle describes a counterclockwise rotation. In a *left-hand* coordinate system a positive angle describes a rotation in the clockwise direction. This definition applies to a fixed coordinate system in which the objects are rotated. The other type of representation would be the fixed placement of the object and the rotation of the coordinate system. The two types differ only in the sign of the rotation angles. This means that if the object is rotated about the angle alpha, or the coordinate system is rotated about angle alpha, the result in both cases will be the same. In three dimensional space the point of the rotation, as in the two dimensional plane, is the origin. If you want to rotate an object around another point, it is first necessary to move the origin to that point. The required steps are:

1. Change the origin to the point B[bx,by,bz,1] using translation matrix T₁.

2. Rotate around the Z axis with rotation matrix R₁.

3. Retranslate the origin using translation matrix T₂

$$T_1 = \begin{array}{cccc} 1 & 0 & 0 & 0 \\ 0 & 1 & 0 & 0 \\ 0 & 0 & 1 & 0 \\ -bx & -by & -bz & 1 \end{array} \qquad R1 = \begin{array}{cccc} \cos(a) & -\sin(a) & 0 & 0 \\ -\sin(a) & \cos(a) & 0 & 0 \\ 0 & 0 & 1 & 0 \\ 0 & 0 & 0 & 1 \end{array}$$

$$T_2 = \begin{array}{cccc} 1 & 0 & 0 & 0 \\ 0 & 1 & 0 & 0 \\ 0 & 0 & 1 & 0 \\ bx & by & bz & 1 \end{array}$$

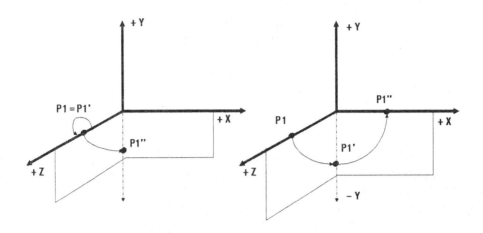

Figure 2.4.4

Let's assume that you want to rotate an object about around all three axes. It is then possible to combine the rotation matrices R_x, R_y and R_z by multiplying with R_g. In contrast with the combination of rotations about the same axis in this example the sequence of multiplications is important, i.e. $R_x*R_y*R_z$ yields a result different from $R_z*R_y*R_x$. A point with a positive Z value is rotated 90 degrees around both the Z and X axes. If the rotation is first made about the Z axis, the coordinates do not change, X- and Y-coordinates are equal to zero, and the subsequent rotation about the X axis rotates the point to the Z=0 level; which is the X-Y plane.

If the first rotation is about the X axis, the point is transferred to the Z=0 level and the subsequent rotation about the Z axis rotates the point into the Y=0 level, which is the level between the X and Z axes. This example shows why it is necessary to follow the sequence of rotations during program generation.

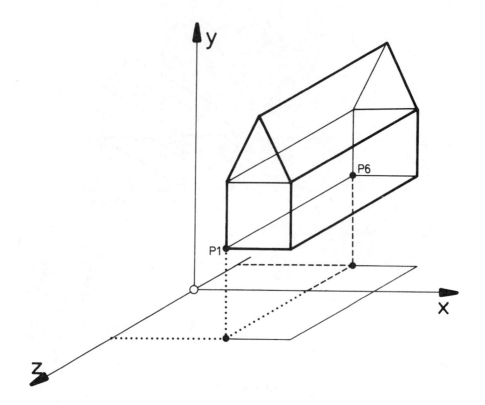

Figure 2.4.5

2.4.1   Rotation about any desired axis

Up to now we have only considered rotation about one of the coordinate
axes; with suitable combinations of various transformations we can turn
an object around any desired line in space. Two points `P1[x1,y1,z1]`
and `P2[x2,y2,z2]` are sufficient to describe a point in space. The
equation through these two points:

```
x = x1 + t*(x2-x1)
y = y1 + t*(y2-y1) with t elements from R
z = z1 + t*(z2-z1)
```

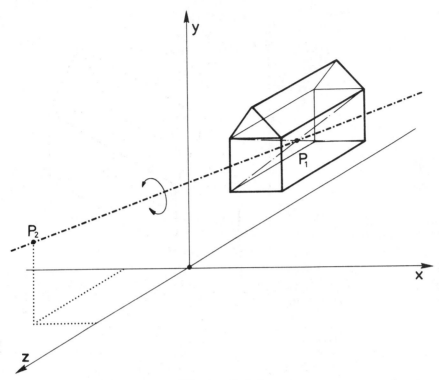

Figure 2.4.6

Since the problem for rotation about one coordinate axis has already been solved, we want to transform a rotation axis in such a way that it will coincide with the negative Z axis. The sequence of the transformation looks like this:

> Displacement of the coordinate origin to the point P1[x1,y1,z1] on the line.

> Rotation about the angle xw on the X axis, so that the rotation axis lies in the X-Z plane.

> Rotation of the angle yw about the Y-axis until the rotation axis coincides with the negative Z axis.

It is now possible to rotate the desired angle zw about the Z axis since it matches the rotation axis. If one looks from P1 to P2 a positive angle will rotate an object in a counterclockwise direction.

To transform back to the original we need:

Rotation of the angle $-yw$ around the Y axis

Rotation of the angle $-xw$ around the X axis

Displacement of the coordinate origin at the starting point.

The only problem is the determination of the angles xw, yw, which can be derived from the equation. As in Figure 2.4.7 we imagine that the coordinate origin is already moved to point P1. Then the coordinates of the point P2' [x2-x1,y2-y1,z2-z1] represent the direction vector of the lines. This vector is now projected on the Y-Z plane, whereby the term projection should be taken literally. In addition you should imagine the vector G[gx,gy,gz] = G[x2-x1,y2-y1,z2-z1] illuminated by light rays, parallel to the X axis and originating from the positive X axis. The shadow created in the Y-Z plane is the vector L[0,gy,gz] and the angle alpha between vector L and the positive axis Z is the desired angle xw.

In a rotation about the X axis, a positive angle describes the rotation of a point from the positive Y axis in the direction of the positive Z axis. The angle alpha is positive and the rotation matrix is as follows:

$$
R_x = \begin{array}{cccc}
1 & 0 & 0 & 0 \\
0 & \cos(a) & \sin(a) & 0 \\
0 & -\sin(a) & \cos(a) & 0 \\
0 & 0 & 0 & 1
\end{array}
$$

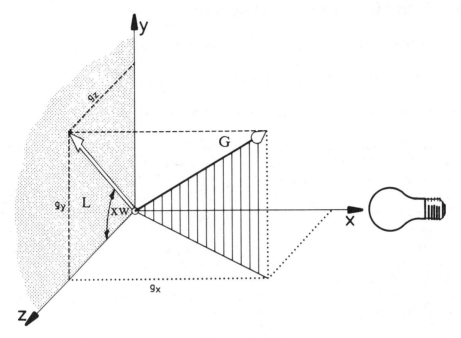

Figure 2.4.7

From Figure 2.4.7 we get, with the length of vector L, $l=\sqrt{(gy^2+gz^2)}$

$$\sin(a) = gy/l \text{ and } \cos(a) = gz/l$$

For the rotation matrix R_x this means:

$$
R_x = \begin{array}{cccc}
1 & 0 & 0 & 0 \\
0 & gz/l & gy/l & 0 \\
0 & -gy/l & gz/l & 0 \\
0 & 0 & 0 & 1
\end{array}
$$

After this transformation, the vector G (P1P2) lies in the plane located between the positive Y and positive X axis. The angle gamma, which we defined to be positive, is the desired angle (yw), which rotates the vector G with one rotation about the Y axis on the negative Z axis. The rotation matrix R_y:

$$R_y = \begin{matrix} \cos(g) & 0 & -\sin(g) & 0 \\ 0 & 1 & 0 & 0 \\ \sin(g) & 0 & \cos(g) & 0 \\ 0 & 0 & 0 & 1 \end{matrix}$$

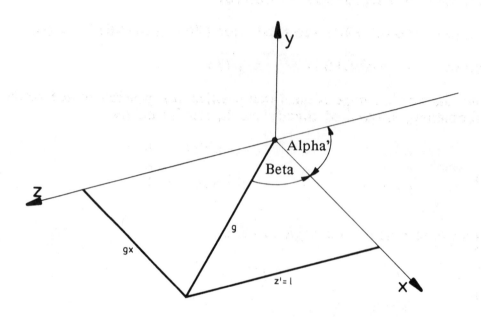

Figure 2.4.8

It is possible to divide the angle gamma into the partial angles beta and the right angle alpha' (90 degrees), between the positive X and negative Z axes. Through rotation about the X axis the X coordinate of the point P2 has not changed, whereas the Y coordinate has become zero. The sum of the vector $G[gx,gy,gz]$ $g = \sqrt{(gx^2+gy^2+gz^2)}$ is therefore identical to $g = \sqrt{(gx^2+z'^2)}$. From this follows $z' = \sqrt{(g^2-gx^2)}$ and from $1 = \sqrt{(gy^2+gz^2)} = \sqrt{(g^2-gx^2)}$ results in z' : $z' = 1$.

For the angle beta the following relationships result:

$$\sin(b) = 1/g \text{ and } \cos(b) = gx/g$$

The rotation angle gamma is composed of beta plus 90 degrees, $ga = b + 90$

From the addition theorems for sine and cosine we get:

```
sin(ga)=sin(b+90)=sin(b)*cos(90))+sin(90)*cos(b)

sin(ga)  =  sin(b+90)  =  cos(b)

cos(ga)=cos(b+90)=cos(b)*cos(90)-sin(90)*sin(b)

cos(ga)  =  cos(b+90)  =  -sin(b)
```

Since the rotation angle is measured positive, it is possible to include the information just acquired directly into the rotation matrix.

$$
R_y = \begin{array}{cccc}
-\sin(b) & 0 & -\cos(b) & 0 \\
0 & 1 & 0 & 0 \\
\cos(b) & 0 & -\sin(b) & 0 \\
0 & 0 & 0 & 1
\end{array}
$$

with the references to the angle functions:

$$
R_y = \begin{array}{cccc}
-1/g & 0 & -gx/g & 0 \\
0 & 1 & 0 & 0 \\
gx/g & 0 & -1/g & 0 \\
0 & 0 & 0 & 1
\end{array}
$$

After these preparatory transformations, the rotation takes place about the desired angle za about the rotation axis, which is the connecting line between P1 to P2. The matrix for this is:

$$
R_z = - \begin{array}{cccc}
\cos(zw) & \sin(zw) & 0 & 0 \\
\sin(zw) & \cos(zw) & 0 & 0 \\
0 & 0 & 1 & 0 \\
0 & 0 & 0 & 1
\end{array}
$$

The inverse transformation matrices:

The transformations for one point

$$R_y^{-1} = \begin{matrix} -1/g & 0 & gx/g & 0 \\ 0 & 1 & 0 & 0 \\ -gx/g & 0 & -1/g & 0 \\ 0 & 0 & 0 & 1 \end{matrix}$$

$$R_x^{-1} = \begin{matrix} 1 & 0 & 0 & 0 \\ 0 & gz/l & -gy/l & 0 \\ 0 & gy/l & gz/l & 0 \\ 0 & 0 & 0 & 1 \end{matrix}$$

$$T^{-1} = \begin{matrix} 1 & 0 & 0 & 0 \\ 0 & 1 & 0 & 0 \\ 0 & 0 & 1 & 0 \\ x1 & y1 & z1 & 1 \end{matrix}$$

$$P'[x',y',z',1] = [x,y,z,1]*T*R_x*R_y*R_z*R_y^{-1}*R_x^{-1}*T^{-1}$$

In these cases the rotation matrices R_x etc. are combined through multiplication. The translations are performed separately.

2.5   Projections from space to a two dimensional plane

A window can be made for observation in 3D space just as it can on a 2-dimensional plane. The position of the window and its orientation relative to the world system is purely arbitrary. For definition of this observation window you should imagine a second coordinate system, the view system inside the world system. Its origin lies in the left corner of the observation window.

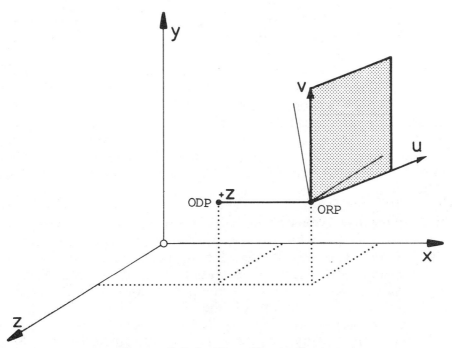

Figure 2.5.1: Coordinate Systems

As a position parameter which describes the position of the view system relative to the world system, the two points ORP (Observation reference point) and ODP (Observation direction point) are sufficient, both of which are defined in the world coordinate system, as well as perhaps an inclination angle between positive Y and positive V axis (za), which describes a rotation of the U-V plane about the Z axis. The view system, as illustrated in Figure 2.5.1 is a left system. The orientation of the positive Z axis is opposite to the world coordinate system.

For clarification: Every scene defined in the world coordinate system, such as an airport for a flight simulator, can be viewed from any point inside this scene. The only parameters required are the observation reference point (ORP), which in comparison with a camera, would represent the film, and the observation direction point (ODP), which determines the direction in which the observer (the camera) is looking. The additional angle used (za) between positive Y and positive V axes describes a rotation of the camera about the longitudinal axis of the objective. The focal point of the lens at which all light rays passing the objective meet, would in this example be on the negative Z axis. Keeping to the example of the camera, exposing a picture must transform the entire scene into the view system (U-V-Z').

This transformation, which appears complicated at first glance, has already been solved: it is the rotation about an arbitrary axis. The points P1 and P2 of the axis of rotation are replaced by the points ORP and ODP and the angle za describes the inclination of the V axis to the Y axis. All operations relate to the observation reference point (ORP [orx,ory,orz]), the positive axis of the observation coordinate system (view-system) points to the observation direction point (ODP [odx,ody,odz]). Both points are described in world coordinates and the rotation matrix rotates the vector G[odx-orx,ody-ory,odz-orz] to the negative Z axis of the world coordinate system. After fitting the V axis, the object, which was subjected to the same operations, is available in the view coordinates. Not quite, though, since the two coordinate systems still differ in the orientation of the Z axis. Therefore after fitting the V axis, all Z values must be multiplied by the factor -1 which corrects the orientation of the Z axis. The last step is a mathematical cosmetic which is required only because of the starting model of the positive Z axis of the *left-hand* coordinate system. If one views the result of the transformation as a *right-hand* system, the last step can be omitted.

Let us combine the steps again, considering the steps necessary for rotation around any desired axis.

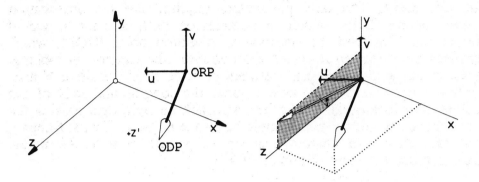

Figure 2.5.2

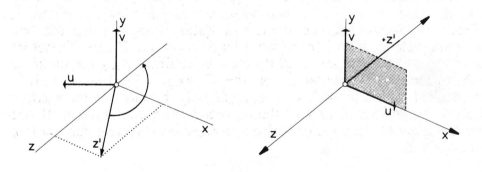

Figure 2.5.3

1. Shifting the origin to the observation reference point ORP via the translation matrix T_1

$$T_1 = \begin{bmatrix} 1 & 0 & 0 & 0 \\ 0 & 1 & 0 & 0 \\ 0 & 0 & 1 & 0 \\ -orx & -ory & -orz & 1 \end{bmatrix}$$

2. Rotation around the X axis until the vector G[odx-orx, ody-ory, odz-orz] = [gx, gy, gz] lies in the Y-Z-plane.

$$R_x = \begin{bmatrix} 1 & 0 & 0 & 0 \\ 0 & gz/l & gy/l & 0 \\ 0 & -gy/l & gz/l & 0 \\ 0 & 0 & 0 & 1 \end{bmatrix}$$

with $l = \sqrt{(gy^2 + gz^2)}$

3. Rotation about the Y axis until the vector G[gx, 0, z'] meets with the Z axis:

$$R_y = \begin{bmatrix} -l/g & 0 & -gx/g & 0 \\ 0 & 1 & 0 & 0 \\ gx/g & 0 & -l/g & 0 \\ 0 & 0 & 0 & 1 \end{bmatrix}$$

with $g = \sqrt{(gx^2 + gy^2 + gz^2)}$

$l = \sqrt{(gy^2 + gz^2)}$

$z' = l$

4. Rotation of the Z axis around the za angle for adaptation of the inclination of the V axis:

$$R_z = \begin{bmatrix} \cos(zw) & \sin(zw) & 0 & 0 \\ -\sin(zw) & \cos(zw) & 0 & 0 \\ 0 & 0 & 1 & 0 \\ 0 & 0 & 0 & 1 \end{bmatrix}$$

5. Multiplication of the Z coordinates with -1 to convert from the *right-hand* to the *left-hand* coordinate system.

$$M_1 = \begin{matrix} 1 & 0 & 0 & 0 \\ 0 & 1 & 0 & 0 \\ 0 & 0 & -1 & 0 \\ 0 & 0 & 0 & 1 \end{matrix}$$

The object now lies in the *left-hand* coordinate system U-V-Z' and can be projected on the display, the plane suspended between the U and V axis via a suitable perspective transformation.

2.6   Perspective transformation

Since the representation of objects on the screen is limited to two
dimensions, we have to simulate the third dimension, the Z coordinate, in
the two-dimensional plane. The method we used, the central projection,
defines a point in space (the focal point of a lens) at which visual rays
emanating from the object meet. The size of the objects represented on
the display screen is directly proportional to their distance from this focal
point. Equal size objects which are farther away are shown smaller than
objects which are closer to the observer.

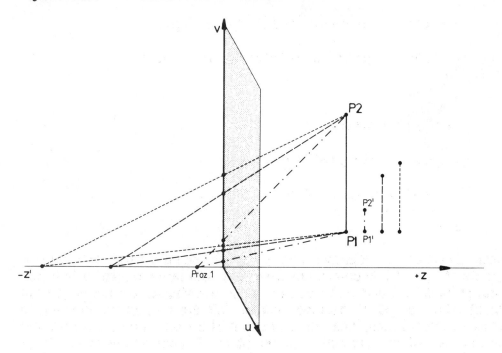

Figure 2.6.1: Perspective

The coordinate system from Figure 2.6.1 is, as already indicated, another
coordinate system and the plane suspended between the positive U and
the positive V axis at point z'=0 will represent the screen. The center of
the projection (focal point) is located on the negative Z axis at point
PROZ[prozx,prozy,prozz'] = [0,0,prozz']. The position of the
point to be viewed P[pu,pv,pz], appears to be located behind the

observation plane. The line through these two points is described by the following equation:

```
u = plu + (prozu-plu)*t

v = plv + (prozv-plv)*t

z' = plz' + (prozz'-plz')*t = 0 , the plane
lies at z'=0 =>

t = -plz'/(prozz'-plz')

u = plu - (prou-plu)*plz'/(prozz'-plz')

v = plv - (prozv-plv)*plz'/(prozz'-plz')

z' = 0

with prozu=prozv=0:

u = plu + plu*plz'/(prozz'-plz')

v = plv + plv*plz'/(prozz'-plz')

z = 0
```

Since `prozz'` is negative and `plz'` is positive, the denominator (`prozz'-plz'`) becomes negative, and with larger distances between focal point `PROZ` and point `P1`, the point coordinates (in the projection plane) `plu'` or `plv'` become smaller. We are now in the position to project a three-dimensional representation of the object on the screen and the distance of the projection-center object is comparable to the focal length of a camera lens. A short length corresponds to a wide-angle lens and a larger distance to a telephoto lens. The projections described are valid for the special case of the projection plane at the point z'=0. The project plane can be moved freely on the z' axis and can be behind the object or also behind the eye.

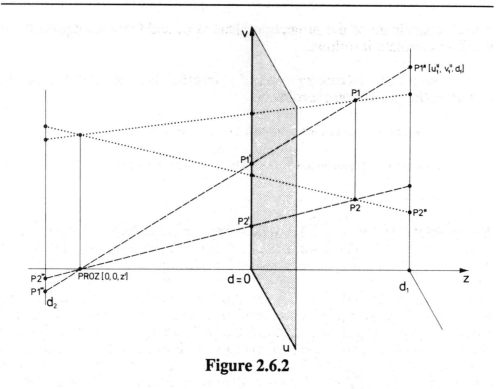

Figure 2.6.2

In this illustration the projection center is at the point PROZ, while the object to be projected is the connecting line between the points P1 P2. d designates the location of the projection plane on the Z'-axis, which can be moved arbitrarily in either direction. If the projection center and projection plane (d=PROZ) match, all objects degenerate to a single point, the center of the projection. The size of the projection can be changed by moving the projection plane. For the line between projection center PROZ and object point P1 the two point equation holds:

$$u = plu + (prozu-plu)*t$$

$$v = plv + (prozv-plv)*t$$

$$z' = plz' + (prozz'-plz')*t = d$$

The Z'-coordinate of the projection plane is d, and from the equation for the Z'-coordinate it follows:

`t = (d-plz')/(prozz'-plz')` inserted into the linear equation results in the projection coordinates:

```
u' = plx + [(prozu-plu) * (d-plz')] / (prozz'-plz')

v' = plv + [(prozv-plv) * (d-plz')] / (prozz'-plz')

z' = d
```

Every point `P[u,v,z',1]` is transformed into the display coordinates `P'[u',v',d,1]`. The coordinates `u'` and `v'` represent a point on the screen.

The equation derived from Figure 2.6.1 comes from the special case where the projection center lies on the Z axis `prozu=prozv=0` and when the projection plane is on the `z'=0` plane, `d=0`. The following illustrations show how the selection of the various observation parameters (`ORP`, `PROZ`, `d`) influence the appearance of the projection. The coordinate origin of the display is in the lower left corner of the screen.

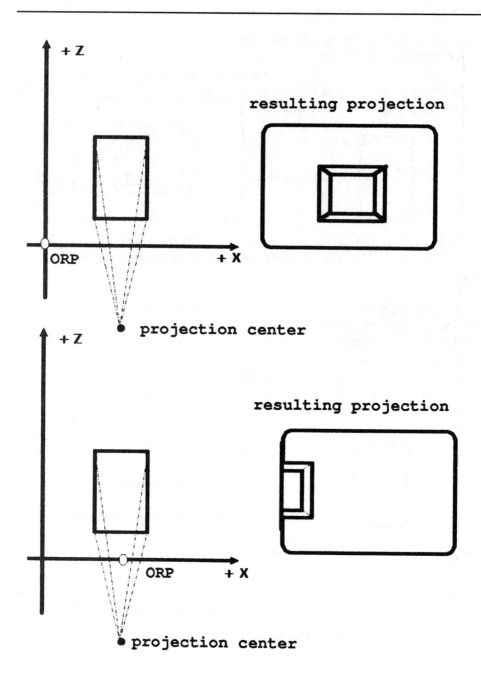

resulting projection

+ Z

ORP

+ X

projection center

+ Z

resulting projection

ORP

+ X

projection center

Figure 2.6.3

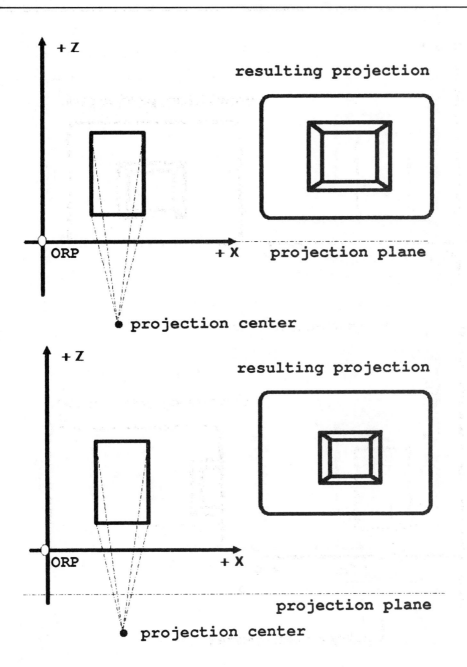

Figure 2.6.4

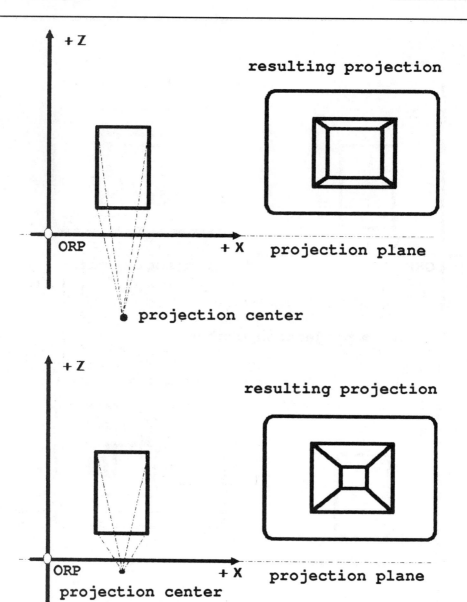

Figure 2.6.5

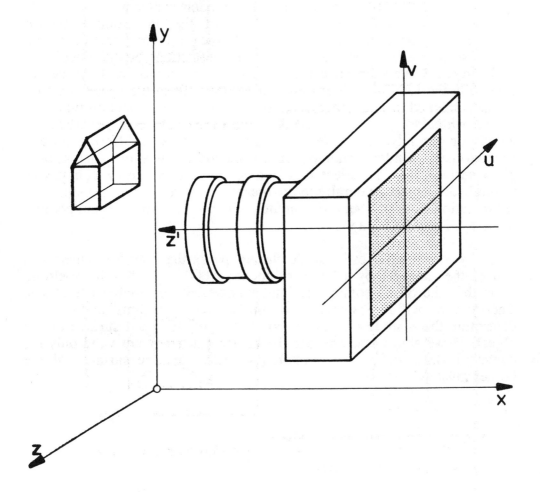

Figure 2.6.6

2.7   Hidden lines and hidden surfaces

Up to now we have been in the position to project wire models of objects on the screen. The action sequence of most any computer animation is set up with the help of 3-D wire models. Wire models can be handled in real-time and thus shorten the development of the animation sequence considerably. Once the sequence is set, the computer calculates the visible surface and color nuances and light reflections of the objects for every intermediate point of the movement, according to the illumination. Generally the scan line algorithm is used. Seen from the eye, the vision rays are tracked through each pixel of the display (= projection plane) to the individual objects. The visual ray is either reflected, absorbed, or wholly or partially transmitted by various objects with differing surface characteristics. Under certain conditions the visual ray splits, such as on a glass surface, into a reflected and a second visual ray which passes through the object, naturally both must be tracked. This explains the computation time of about 10 minutes which even super-computers like the Cray II require for a picture.

Since by conservative estimate the throughput of the Cray II is superior to that of the Atari ST by a factor of about 10,000 to 15,000, it should be clear that the ST is somewhat "under powered" for such calculations. Therefore we will limit ourselves to the "surface algorithms" and will not determine the visibility of every point, but just for each surface of the object. These algorithms are fast. To be accurate, they are valid only for convex bodies, and in the version presented here the surfaces of the bodies must also be convex.

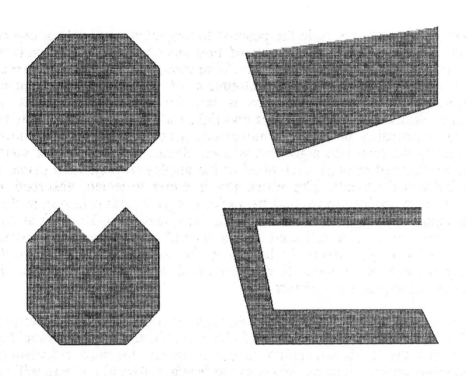

Figure 2.7.1: Convex and Concave Surfaces

With convex polygons the line connecting two points on the polygon lies within the polygon, whereas in convex bodies the connecting line between two points on the surface passes through the body or runs along the surface. Formulated differently, convex polygons have at least one inner angle which is larger than 180 degrees.

For these surface algorithms we must expand the object definition, which up to now consisted of the point and line list, to include a surface list. The surface list contains a description of each surface by the lines which border the surface.

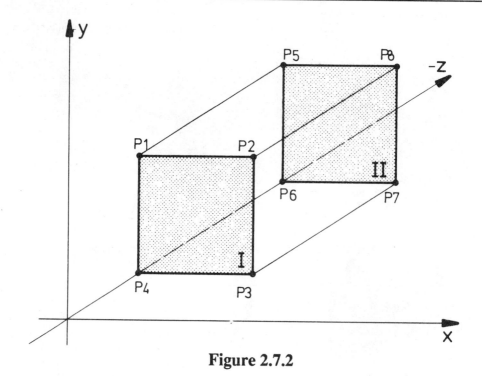

Figure 2.7.2

The two surfaces I and II would be described in the surface list as follows:

Surface	Line from point to point
I	P1,P4 P4,P3 P3,P2 P2,P1
II	P5,P6 P6,P7 P7,P8 P8,P1

You probably noticed that the line direction is reversed in the description of the surfaces. The line vectors of surface I describe the surface as seen from the negative Z axis in a clockwise direction, while surface II is described in a counterclockwise direction. This small difference contains the solution to the hidden-line-problem. If you imagine the surfaces I and II as outer surfaces of a block, then SI is the front surface and SII the rear surface of the block. The observation point is still on the negative Z axis. SII is not visible from the observation point since it is hidden by the other surfaces.

You can see that the description of the surface is always done in the clockwise direction from outside the cube and looking toward the current surface center. For the definition of the surface one wanders around the object to be described and determines the direction of the connection lines of the points belonging to the surface. As one can see in the next illustration, the visibility of the surfaces can be determined through the direction of the connection lines with a little vector algebra.

To do this, start from any point on the surface and form the vector to the next point

```
P=[px,py,pz]=[p2x-p1x,p2y-p1y,p2z-p1z],
```

and the vector to the next point

```
Q[qx,qy,qz]=[p3x-p1x,p3y-p1y,p3z-p1z],
```

as well as the projection vector from a point on the surface to observation point A. An appropriate selection is the point

```
P1,S[sx,sy,sz] = [ax-p1x,ay-p1y,az-p1z].
```

As explained in the appendix, the product of two vectors (a\b) (see App. B) forms a vertical vector

```
R=[rx,ry,rz]=[py*qz-pz*qy,pz*qx-px*qz,px*qy-
    py*qx].
```

The direction of this vector results from the system in which the vector product was performed. In the left coordinate system used here, the vector d points in the same direction in which a screw with a left-handed thread would move from P to Q when turned, that is, it points with surface I in the direction of the positive Z axis and with surface II in the direction of the negative Z axis.

Now we can say this about the visibility of surface I: if the vectors S and R are pointing in the same direction, the surface is visible from the observation point. If the vectors S and R point in different directions, the surface is not visible. As mentioned earlier, this process is limited to closed convex bodies, but the error is not very large with concave bodies.

Figure 2.7.3-4: Hardcopy of bodies before and after Hidden-Line-Algorithm

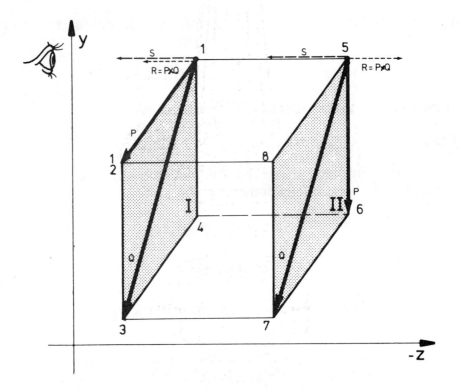

Figure 2.7.3

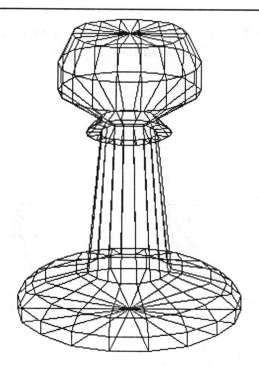

Figure 2.7.4

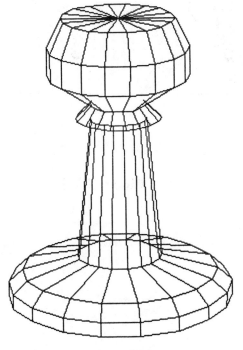

Figure 2.7.5

Figure 2.7.6

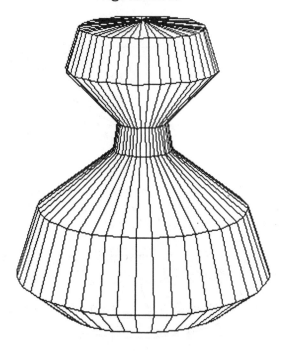

Figure 2.7.7

The error with concave bodies is that surfaces which are visible from the observation point are hidden by other surfaces but are not recognized. Now only the "direction comparison criterium" between two vectors is missing. This is accomplished by the scalar product of two vectors (S*R) which is defined as follows:

```
c = |S|*|R|*cos(Phi) = sx*rx+sy*ry+sz*rz
```

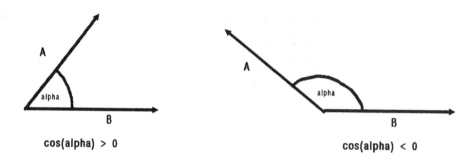

Figure 2.7.8

c is a real number and phi is the angle enclosed by S and R. From Figure 2.7.8 we can see that the vectors a and b point in the same direction when cos(phi) is positive. The recognition of hidden surfaces can be summarized as follows.

1. Creation of a surface list in which the points are listed in a clockwise direction.

2. Finding the vectors P and Q from three successive points for each surface.

3. Determination of the vector S[sx, sy, sz] from a point on the surface to the observation point.

4. Determination of the vector perpendicular to P and Q R[rx, ry, rz] through the vector product (P\Q).

5. Comparison of the direction of the vectors S and R by checking the sign of the scalar product (S*R) through multiplication of the single components from S and R (Scalar product = sx*rx+sy*ry+sz*rz)

6. Marking of surfaces which have positive scalar products as visible surfaces. (Applies to left coordinate systems. In right coordinate systems the surfaces with negative scalar products are visible surfaces.)

7. Drawing the visible surfaces.

2.8   Rembrandt and hidden surfaces

You probably want to know what computer graphics and a painter who died in 1669 have in common. An oil painting is created from back to the front, that is to say, the painter first draws the background and then objects are placed further to the front simply by covering the background with oil paint. This method, carried over to the computer, is another solution of the hidden surface problem. A middle Z coordinate is calculated for each surface and, as an example, all Z coordinates of the corner points can be added and divided by the number of corner points which are stored for the surface. Then the surfaces are sorted according to size and drawn from the largest to the smallest Z coordinates.

To insure that the surfaces which are painted over have really been covered, we can't just to draw the outer lines of the surface. It is necessary to fill the surfaces with color. The surface construction from the back to the front is shown in the following illustrations.

Figures 2.8.1-5: Hardcopy of the surface construction

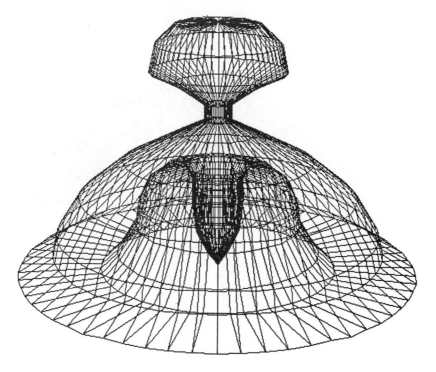

Figure 2.8.1

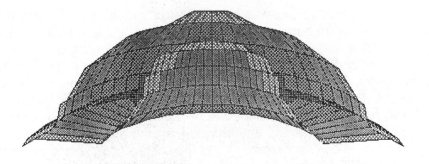

Figure 2.8.2

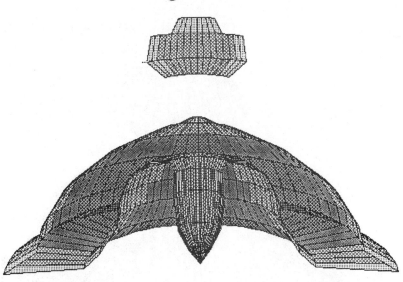

Figure 2.8.3

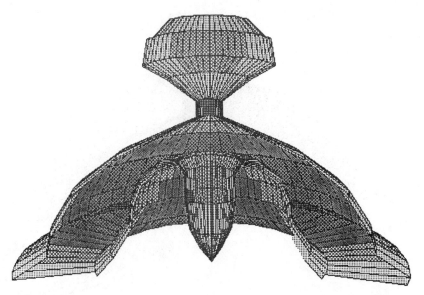

Figure 2.8.4

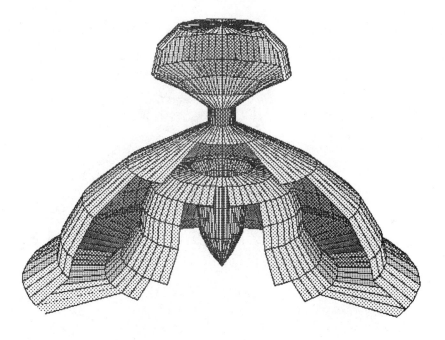

Figure 2.8.5

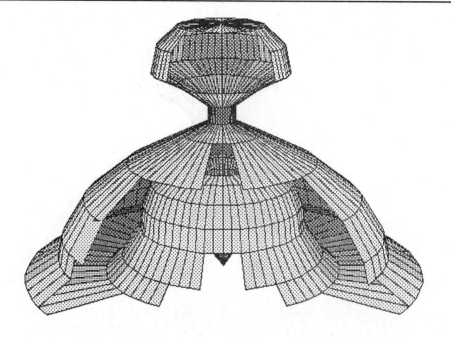

Figure 2.8.6

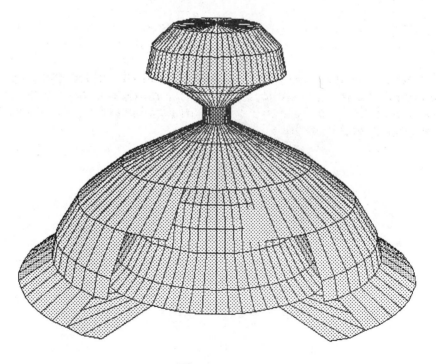

Figure 2.8.7

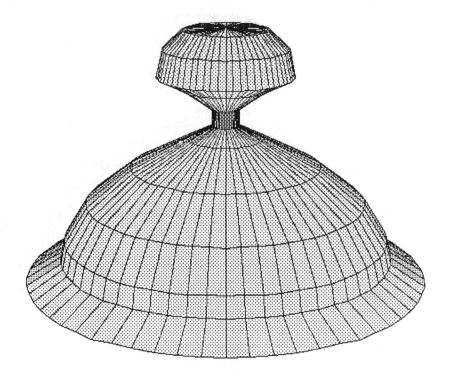

Figure 2.8.8

Of course, the two methods for the removal of hidden surfaces can be combined. First the visible surfaces can be determined through scalar products. Followed by sorting the surfaces according to descending Z coordinates, and then drawing them.

2.8.1   Light and Shadow

In general, there are two types of illumination, direct and indirect. With indirect illumination the intensity of the light is equal on all places in space. The indirect light is created through diffuse reflection from other objects, such as walls and ceilings. The appearance of an object in space under this illumination is dependent only on the reflection coefficient of the object. This reflection coefficient is the relationship of reflected light rays to the total striking the surface. Its value runs from zero for a black body (all light rays which strike are absorbed) and one for a white body (all light rays which strike are reflected). A body whose reflection coefficients are between zero and one is designated as a gray body. A reflection coefficient R can be given for every surface which determines the intensity of the surface.

Intensity = R * IL with IL = Intensity of available indirect light.

A more realistic representation results from the definition of one or more point light sources in the space. These point light sources, for example lamp, candle, or sunshine, have a certain position in the space and shine in the direction of the object. In this case, the orientation of the illuminated surface to the light source is of great importance. More light rays fall on a surface which is perpendicular to the light source than an equally large surface which is not perpendicular to the light source.

The orientation of the surface to the light source can be determined by comparing the normal vector of the surface (the vector perpendicular to it) with the vector to surface from the light source. If L and N are two vectors of length 1, the relation for the angle between L and N is:

```
L*N  =  lx*nx+ly*ny+lz*nz  =  cos(w)
```

For the gray value of the surface the result is then:

```
Intensity = R*IL  +  R*(L*N)*DL
```

with the reflection coefficient R and the intensity of the direct light source DL, which is between zero and one.

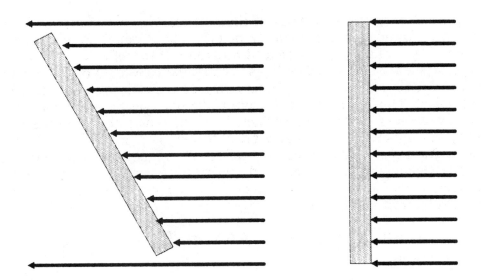

Figure 2.8.9: Surfaces with Light Rays

Machine Language Fundamentals
for Graphic Programming

3. Machine Language Fundamentals for Graphic Programming

All programs described in this book may be run on various ST computer/monitor combinations. To simplify the compatibility, all drawing functions for the 3-D graphics project were done with operating systems functions (line-A). To introduce you to machine language programming on the ST, we first have an explanation of some of the basic principles (sine) and then a small program for drawing random lines. This program illustrates the program interface to the operating system and a simple line-drawing algorithm which writes directly to the screen. The line-drawing algorithm is not necessary for the 3-D project coming later and is intended only as an example. The use of the algorithm is limited to monochrome monitors. Owners of color monitors can replace the call draw1 with ddraw1 (indicated in the listing) if they want to run the program main1.s.

3.1   Speed Advantages from tables

Before starting a project in machine language, you should think about the number format to be used. For all the following applications we can perform all calculations with 16-bit integers. Another problem is the sine function, whose function values can range from -1 and +1. The function values can be approximated on computers using the Taylor series, which approximates the exact function value through repeated summation of the terms of a sequence. In practice, the summation can be terminated after 3 or 4 terms. As an example, we have here the Taylor series for the sine function.

$$\sin(x) = x - x^3/3! + x^5/5! - x^7/7! + \ldots$$

The angle x is given in radians, and $3!$ means 3 factorial $= 1*2*3 = 6$. This method is not suitable for quick calculation of sine and cosine values because several multiplications must be performed for each function value. A rather unelegant but simple and common solution is to store all the necessary function values in a table in memory, which can then be accessed very quickly.

The accuracy can be set as desired since the function values are calculated before the actual program application and the time factor does not play a role. In our example, all sine values between 0 and 360 degrees are entered in steps of one degree. This is quite adequate for almost all applications which require trigonometric functions. Should an intermediate value be required, it can be interpolated from the table. Since the cosine function is the same as the sine function shifted by 90 degrees, the cosine functions can also be taken from the sine table.

The function values of the angle functions are real numbers which are floating point numbers with several places after the decimal point. Since all our calculations involve only integers, it is necessary to transform the values of the sine function. This is done by multiplying by a sufficiently large number--in our example with $2^{14} = 16384$.

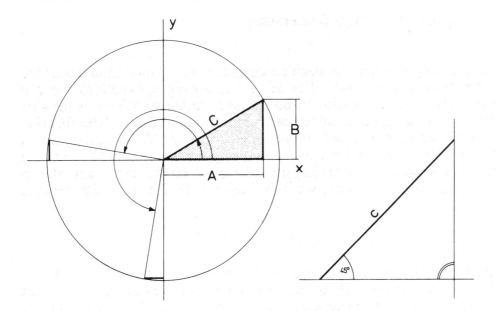

Figure 3.1.1: Triangle

The length of the line c and the angle alpha are already known, and we want to find the length of b. According to the definition of the angle function, the length of the distance =c*sin(a) = 20*sin(45). The sine of 45 degrees is 0.707106781 with nine-place precision. In our table we have the value 0.707106781 * 16384 = 11585 for 45 degrees. After multiplying by 20 we got the number 231700 as a result. We don't have to worry that this number will exceed the value range of 16-bit integer arithmetic because the processor always produces a 32-bit product as the result of a 16-bit multiplication. This 32-bit result, the number 231700, can now be adapted to the original value range by dividing by 16384, and we get 14 as the result.

You may ask yourself why 16384 was used for the multiplication: first of all the number is large enough to extend the range of the sine function. Numbers between -1 and 1 become numbers between -16384 and +16384. Second, the multiplication can be performed with two very fast commands of the processor. Multiplications by a multiple of two can be replaced in all microprocessors with shift commands which don't take much more time than an addition.

At this point I would like to briefly discuss the possibilities of the table representation in the computer. The sine table is the simplest form of a table, a linear list. The individual table values are stored sequentially in memory. Our sine table for the first values looks like this:

```
sintab: .dc.w   0,286,572,857,1143,1428,1713,1997,2280
        .dc.w   2563,2845,3126,3406,3686,3964,4240,4516
        .dc.w   4790,5063,5334,5604,5872,6138,6402,6664
```

Since the gradations of the angles are in 1 degree steps, the first table value gives the sine of 0 degrees, the second the sine of one degree, the third the sine of two degrees, etc. The 91st table value is the sine of 90. table value and the sine of 360 degrees is represented by the 361st value. Zero is chosen as the start to match the table numbers to the corresponding angle. This means that table value zero represents the sine of zero degrees. Value number 90 corresponds to 90 degrees and 180 to 180 degrees. The 68000 computer makes access to this table very easy through its excellent addressing capabilities. The initial address of the table is loaded into the address register. This is the address where the zero element is stored. With the number of the desired table value in a data register it is possible to access the location using the addressing mode "address register indirect with index." In this table format it is absolutely necessary to pay attention to the data length of individual entries. The address of the zero value is equal to the beginning address of the table plus zero, but the address of the first value is the beginning address of the table plus two, since each value occupies two bytes. This means that the index number in the data register must be multiplied by the number of bytes for one entry. In this case it is two bytes. This multiplication by two is very fast with one left shift of the bits in the index number.

3.2   Assembler routines for screen manipulation

The screen of the Atari ST is organized using what is called bit-mapped graphics. This means that bits which are set in the screen storage correspond directly to dots on the monitor and therefore there is no difference between text and graphics. Since the screen memory is part of the main memory of the CPU, it can be manipulated quickly, i.e. without waiting cycles. For monochrome display the resolution is 640*400 points, which are represented by 400 times 640 bits in RAM.

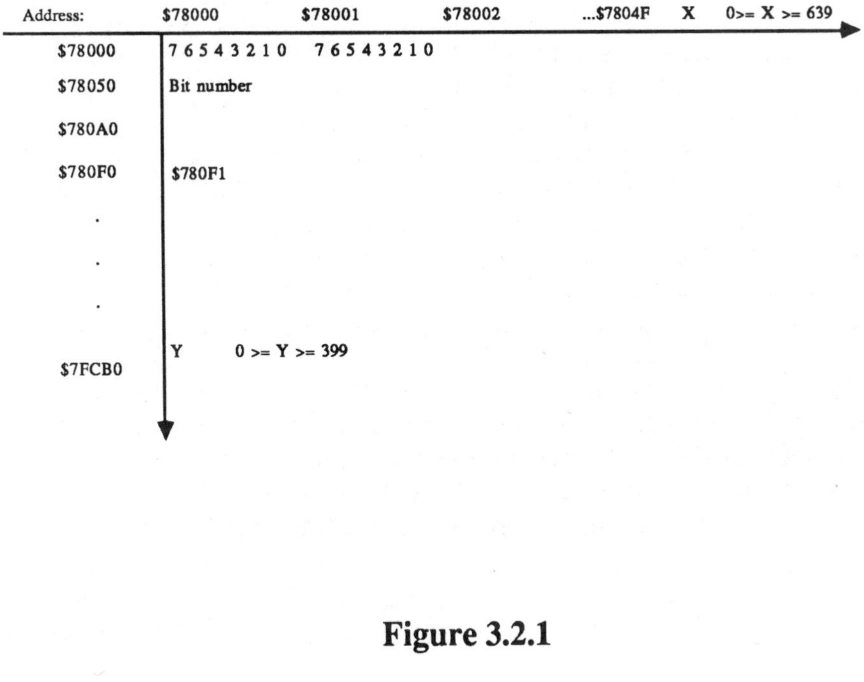

```
Address:      $78000      $78001      $78002      ...$7804F    X    0>= X >= 639

$78000    7 6 5 4 3 2 1 0    7 6 5 4 3 2 1 0

$78050    Bit number

$780A0

$780F0    $780F1


   .

   .

   .

          Y         0 >= Y >= 399
$7FCB0
```

Figure 3.2.1

The only routines required for screen manipulation are those for displaying a point and for drawing and erasing lines. A line of the video picture is formed from 80 bytes and the total picture is made up of 400 lines. The address of a picture point can be calculated as follows:

```
address = screen start + Y*80 + INT(X/8)
```

The bit number of the byte can be obtained with the following formula:

```
number = 7 - (X MOD 8)
```

The function INT truncates the positions after the decimal point of a real number, while the function MOD returns the remainder of the operand by the second. For example, 9 MOD 2 returns 1 as the result. Screen start is the starting address of the screen memory, which is $78000 on the 520 ST and 8F8000 on the 1040 ST

It may appear to be somewhat unusual to have the coordinate origin in the upper left corner, but it is easy to change to the lower left corner and this is accomplished by negating the Y values and adding 399. The X coordinates remain unchanged of course , since the zero point is already in the left corner of the display. The Y coordinate 370 in a normal left system becomes (-370+399) = 29 in the screen system. This conversion need be made only immediately before points are drawn. Some calculations are required to draw a single point. The speed advantage of tables for the calculation of the address of a point should also be considered here. This table holds the RAM address for every possible Y coordinate. This saves a multiplication for every calculation of the screen address. Since the plot-point routine is used very often for drawing lines, the speed advantage gained by using this table is correspondingly great.

3.2.1   Drawing lines

Since the size of a point on the screen is dependent on the resolution of the computer, it is not possible to represent a line in the mathematical sense. A line which connects two points P1 and P3, actually takes a more or less jagged path.

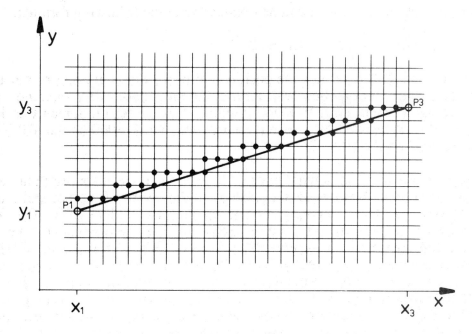

Figure 3.2.2

Starting from point P1, you have the problem of deciding which points must be set, in order to reach point P3. Note that it is possible to set the points only at the intersections of the raster lines. The line is formed when either the X coordinate is retained and a point drawn with an incremented Y coordinate or you can increment the X coordinate while the Y coordinate retains its value.

In mathematics, a line which connects two points is described through its slope m. m is a measure of the "steepness" of the line and the larger m becomes, the steeper the line becomes. With a positive m, the line rises from left to right, while with a negative m it slopes down from left to right. For a line parallel to the Y axis, the slope is infinite. The expression for the slope:

```
m = dy / dx
```

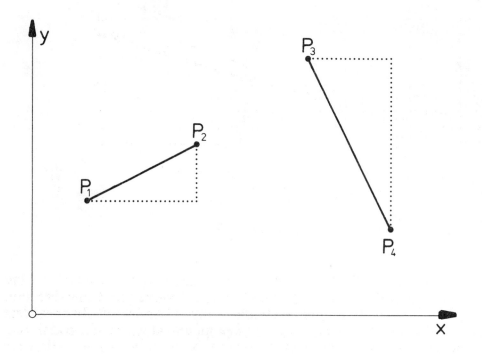

Figure 3.2.3

See Figure 3.2.4 for an explanation of the algorithm for drawing of lines.

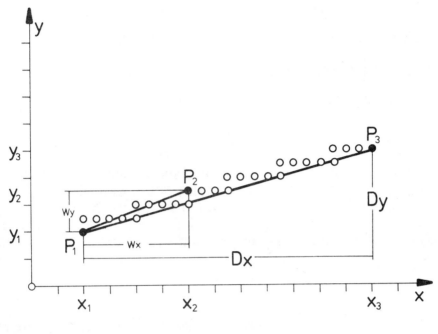

Figure 3.2.4

Let us assume that in drawing the line from P1 to P3 that we have already reached the point P2 already and now have to decide the direction in which to draw. In our example, the point P2 is "over" the ideal line from P1 to P3. Expressed mathematically, the slope of the connecting line from Point P1 to P2 $m1=(p2y-p1y)/(p2x-p1x) = wy/wx$ is greater than the rise of the line which connects the points P1 and P3 $m2=(p3y-p1y)/(p3x-p1x)=dy/dx$. As the illustration shows, the next step in drawing must be made in the X direction.

With the comparison of the two slopes, we have found a decision criterion for the direction of drawing: If the slope of the connecting line between the starting point of the drawing P1 and an intermediate point P2 is greater than the slope of the line between the beginning and end points (P1, P3), a drawing step should be made in the X direction . If the slope is smaller, the next point should be drawn in the Y direction. For the purpose of programming this criterion we shall define a decision variable D, which is assigned the difference between the desired and the actual slope.

$$D = (dy/dx) - (wy/wx)$$

If D is larger than zero ==> **Step in Y direction**

If D is smaller than zero ==> **Step in X direction**

After a small conversion we get:

$$D*dx*wx = (wx*dy) - (wy*dx)$$

Multiplications slow down calculations, so we should try to eliminate them from the calculation. The exact value of D is of no interest. It is only important to know how D changes with a step in the X or Y direction so that an eventual change in the sign of D can be recognized. For this reason it is also possible to replace the expression D*dx*dy with D again.

$$D = (wx*dy) - (wy*dx)$$

During a step in the X direction, wx is increased by one while we retain the old value of wx. For our D which we call new D or ND to distinguish it from D, the following results:

$$ND = (wx+1)*dy - wy*dx$$

$$ND = wx*dy + dy - wy*dx$$

The last expression is equal to old D + dy, where old D corresponds to the value of D before the step in the X direction. Analogous to this for a step in the Y direction:

$$ND = wx*dy - (wy+1)*dx$$

$$ND = wx*dy - wy*dx - dx$$

As you can see, D is reduced by dx with a step in the Y direction. For ND can be written:

Step in Y direction ND = D - dx
Step in X direction ND = D + dy

The multiplications have been replaced according to our desires by additions. To formulate the algorithm, we must still decide in what direction we will draw if D is zero. This can be decided at random and in our example ND=0 results in a step in the Y direction. Another special case which has not been mentioned is when dy is zero. In this case, steps can be made only in the X direction since the resulting line must be a parallel to the X axis. This case can only be determined with a test at the beginning of the routine.

Furthermore, we have only considered lines with a positive slope, that is, those where py3 is smaller than py1. To retain the decision method in this form, it is necessary to make negative dx and dy values positive through multiplication with -1, and to decrease the X and Y coordinates by one instead of increasing them for every step in the X or Y direction. The algorithm for drawing a line between the points P1[x1,y1] and P3[x3,y3] appears like this in a structogram:

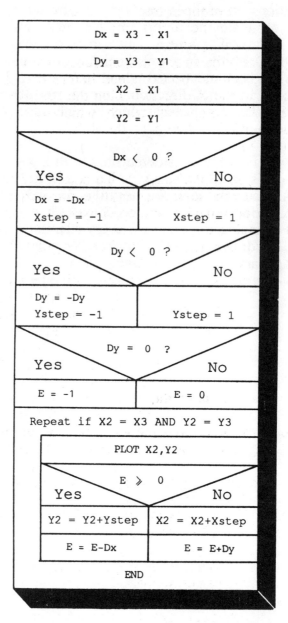

Figure 3.2.5: Structogram Draw line

3.3   Operating system functions

Since we will use only operating system functions for the 3-D graphics programming, some should be explained before they are used. One of these functions is the routine for switching the beginning address for the video controller. All computers which which can display animated graphics quickly and flicker free have the ability to work with two logical screen pages internally.

Fast drawing and erasing of objects on the screen and the rapid accesses to the screen RAM by the computer and the video controller, causes the monitor picture to be unstable and to flicker. If the hardware has the ability to tell the video controller where in RAM the screen memory starts, the strategy for the creation of flicker free graphic is very simple.

We define two logical screen pages. We will use the Atatri ST as a concrete example: in the Atari ST with 512K RAM the standard screen page is stored between $78000 to $7FFFF and it is possible to define a second screen page from $70000 to $77FFF. In the initial state, both screen pages are erased and the video controller shows the page starting at $78000. Now the first picture can be drawn in the RAM starting at address $70000. After drawing the picture, the video controller is informed at a suitable time of the new beginning address for the screen RAM ($70000). A suitable time for switching is the time period in which the electronic beam which draws the video picture returns, without being seen, from the lower right corner of the screen to the upper left corner.

This moment is even recognized by the operating system and the switching of the screen pages can be solved without any major programming effort. If the page starting at $70000 is being displayed by the video controller, the CPU can draw another picture, such as the object in another position, in the page starting at $78000 without disturbing the picture construction. After the new picture is completed, pages are switched again and you can erase the old picture in the storage area which is not being displayed. In general, the page which is being displayed is considered to be the physical page in which the drawing is taking place is the logical page. Only when both are identical do you see the progress of the drawing on the screen.

3.3.1 Starting a Program

To start a machine language program on the Atari ST you have to know what happens when a program icon is clicked with the mouse. The operating system loads the appropriate program and passes control to the program once it is loaded. After loading a program, the operating system declares the entire memory as occupied so that it is not possible to move data or program sections. To avoid this disadvantage, the called program must determine its actual memory requirements, declare this area as occupied, and leave the rest of the memory free. The Atari operating system simplifies this task by passing a pointer on the stack to the called program indicating the memory area occupied by the program and data.

The called program can calculate the memory actually required and declare the unused area as vacant to the operating system. **Note:** sufficient space must be reserved for the processor stack. From the Digital Research documentation, it is not clear how much stack space is required for the GEM functions, but the 4K bytes reserved for this purpose in the example should be sufficient for all purposes. To make it possible to use all GEM functions, it is recommended that the program call the functions `Application-Init` and then `Open-Virtual-Workstation` when it starts. After these two calls, GEM-DOS, the BIOS, Extended-BIOS and the AES and VDI functions are available to the program. An overview of these functions are available in the two Abacus Software books *Atari ST Internals* and the large *Atari ST GEM Programmer's Reference*.

All programs in this book were written using the assembler from Digital Research. For users of other home computers the assembler is probably new, and so I want to discuss it briefly. The assembler is completely disk oriented, i.e. all input and output comes from and goes to the diskette. First you create the source text of the program with an editor, store it on a diskette and call the assembler with name of the source text. The assembler processes the source text by creating several auxiliary files on the diskette. Finally it writes the desired object file on the diskette.

The object file which was created, recognizable by the extension .o, is not executable since it was assembled at the absolute address zero. To generate an executable program the absolute addresses must be replaced with relative addresses to make it possible to load the program into any memory area. For this purpose, you call the program RELMOD.PRG which then creates the desired run-time program file. In this you can write manner machine language programs whose length is limited only by the storage capacity of the computer and the floppy disk. It is impossible to combine two programs which are already object files with this method, however.

For this reason, one usually adds an intermediate step, as is also done with higher level languages, called linking. The linker permits several separately-assembled object files to be combined into one single file.

Large assembly language programs quickly become difficult to understand and it is recommended that they be divided into at least two modules. The first module initializes the program and contains all of the error-free and tested subroutines, while the second module contains the latest main program. This can reduce the assembly time considerably since the large basic module must be assembled only once and afterwards only linked to the main program. The use of the linker also permits the use of assembler directives which would otherwise not be possible. The assembler in conjunction with the linker can manage three separate program areas: text, data, bss. The text area contains the actual program, i.e. the program text, and the data area contains the initialized data. These are variables to which values were assigned already before the start of the program. In the bss area there is storage space reserved for the data which has not been initialized.

Each of the programs; assembler, linker and relocator require parameters, which are passed during the start. To assemble the basic module, first select `AS68.PRG` and then `INSTALL APPLICATION` from the `OPTIONS` menu as TOS-takes parameters. Then enter the following line into the dialog box which appears:

```
-p -l -u basic1.s > basic1.lst
```

where `basic1.s` is the name of the text file to be assembled. The `-p` and `> basic1.lst` statements create a listing to the disk of the assembly process which can later be printed for examination. The assembler creates a file with the name `basic1.o`. This object file contains the tested subroutines and will be linked to the current main program.

To assemble and link the main program, it is best to create a batch file, which contains the individual command sequences. The batch file could look like this:

```
as68 -l -u %2.s
wait.prg
link68 [u] %2.68k=%1.o,%2.o
relmod %2.68k %2.prg
rm %2.68k
rm %2.o
wait.prg
```

This batch file might be stored under the name `aslink.bat` on the diskette. The batch file is made very flexible through the use of two place holders, %1 and %2. To assemble the main program with the name `main1.s` and the subsequent linking with the basic module `basic1.o` You call the program `batch.ttp` and pass the command sequence in the dialog box:

```
aslink basic1 main1
```

After the assembly process the desired program file `main1.prg` is finally on the diskette. This creation of modules makes working with the disk drive more bearable and the coffee breaks during assembly shorter.

As a practical test of all this, we have here the first version of the `basic1.s` program and the first demo program. The basic program contains only the initialization of the program and the basic routines for screen manipulation such as screen erasing, and drawing of points and lines. Assembly is done with:

```
as68 -l -u basic1.s
```

The first main program demonstrates the speed of the computer by drawing random lines and demonstrates how to call the operating system. The steps for the creation of the ready-to-run program file `main1.prg`, without using a batch file are as follows:

1.   Assemble MAIN1.S with the AS68.PRG.

2.   Link the two object files with the
     Linker.
     link68 [u] main1.68k = basic1.o,main1.o

3.   Create a relocatable program with
     relmod main1.68k main1.prg

The file main1.prg can be started by clicking with the mouse after the
file Relmod, the two files main1.o and main1.68k, which are no
longer needed, are erased with the program RM.

The listing should be self-explanatory with all of its comments. It should
offer an easy introduction to graphics programming in machine language.
More detailed explanations of the routines used can be found with the
explanation of the link files grlink1.s in section 4.1. Starting with
Chapter 4 we will really start to program.

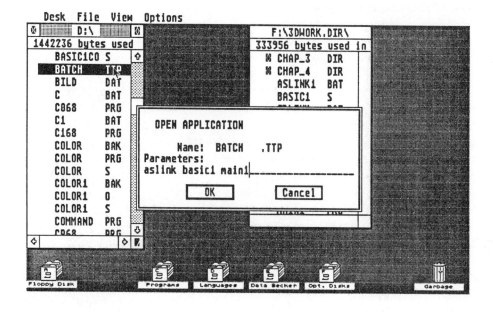

```
*************************************************************************
* Link file basicl.s, is linked with the main program whose entry    *
* routine must have the name main.                                    *
* U.B. 11.85                                                          *
*************************************************************************

        .globl   wait,waitl,drawl,ddrawl,inlinea
        .globl   grafhand
        .globl   grhandle
        .globl   global,contrl,intin,intout,ptsin,ptsout,addrin,addrout
        .globl   apinit,openwork,clwork,aes,vdi
        .globl   inkey
        .globl   mouse_on,mouse_off,printf

        .text



*************************************************************************
*  Entry to the program, initialization of all operating system      *
*  functions and creation of the Y-tables  (For computers with color *
*  monitors, replace "jsr start1"  with  "jsr start2".                *
*  Furthermore when using a color monitor, replace all               *
*  "jsr drawl" calls in the main program with "jsr ddrawl".           *
*                                                                     *
*************************************************************************



sstart:                 * initialize the program
    move.l   a7,a5      * Base page address is on the stack
    move.l   4(a5),a5   * base page address = program start - $100
    move.l   $c(a5),d0  * Program length
    add.l    $14(a5),d0 * Length of initialized data area
    add.l    $1c(a5),d0 * Length of data area not initialized
    add.l    #$1100,d0  * 4 K-Byte user stack=sufficient space
    move.l   a5,d1      * Starting address of the program
    add.l    d0,d1      * Plus number of reserved bytes = space required
    and.l    #-2,d1     * even address for stack
    move.l   d1,a7      * User stackpointer to last 4K- byte
    move.l   d0,-(sp)   * Length of reserved area
    move.l   a5,-(sp)   * Beginning address of reserved area
    move.w   d0,-(sp)   * Dummy-Word
    move.w   #$4a,-(sp) * GEM DOS function SETBLOCK
```

```
      trap      #1
      add.l     #12,sp      * old stack address restored again
      jsr       start1      * Create Y-table
      jsr       main        * Jump to main program. ( User-created )
      move.l    #0,-(a7)    * Terminate program running
      trap      #1          * Back to Gem-Desktop


****************************************************************
*   Call a AES-Routine, where the parameters are passed to     *
*   to the various arrays (contrl,etc.)                        *
****************************************************************


aes:      move.l    #aespb,d1          * call the AES routines
          move.w    #$c8,d0
          trap      #2
          rts


****************************************************************
*   Call a VDI-Routine                                         *
****************************************************************


vdi:      move.l    #vdipb,d1          * call the VDI routines
          move.w    #$73,d0
          trap      #2
          rts


****************************************************************
*   Announce the program                                       *
****************************************************************


apinit:   clr.l     d0                 * Announce the program as
          move.l    d0,ap1resv         * Application
          move.l    d0,ap2resv
          move.l    d0,ap3resv
          move.l    d0,ap4resv
          move.w    #10,opcode
          move.w    #0,sintin
          move.w    #1,sintout
          move.w    #0,saddrout
          move.w    #0,saddrin
          jsr       aes
          rts
```

```
*********************************************************************
* Check on screen handler and store for other functions       *
*********************************************************************

grafhand: move.w    #77,contrl          * Get the screen handler
          move.w    #0,contrl+2         * and store it in the global
          move.w    #5,contrl+4         * Variable grhandle
          move.w    #0,contrl+6
          move.w    #0,contrl+8
          jsr       aes
          move.w    intout,grhandle
          rts


*********************************************************************
* Open a Virtual Screen Work Station where all GEM drawing functions *
* will occur.                                                  *
*********************************************************************

openwork: move.w    #100,opcode         * open a workstation
          move.w    #1,d0
          move.w    #0,contrl+2
          move.w    #11,contrl+6
          move.w    grhandle,contrl+12  * screen handler
          move.w    d0,intin
          move.w    d0,intin+2
          move.w    d0,intin+4
          move.w    d0,intin+6
          move.w    d0,intin+8
          move.w    d0,intin+10
          move.w    d0,intin+12
          move.w    d0,intin+14
          move.w    d0,intin+16
          move.w    d0,intin+18
          move.w    #2,intin+20
          jsr       vdi
          rts
```

```
*************************************************************************
*   Clear the workstation                                              *
*************************************************************************

clwork:    move.w     #3,contrl         * Clear workstation
           move.w     #0,contrl+2       * clear the screen
           move.w     #1,contrl+6
           move.w     grhandle,contrl+12
           jsr        vdi
           rts


*************************************************************************
*   Turn on the mouse and its control.                                 *
*************************************************************************

mouse_on:  move.w     #122,contrl       * turn on the mouse and
           move.w     #0,contrl+2       * its control
           move.w     #1,contrl+6
           move.w     grhandle,contrl+12
           move.w     #0,intin
           jsr        vdi
           rts



*************************************************************************
*   Turn off the mouse and control.                                    *
*************************************************************************

mouse_off: move.w     #123,contrl       * turn off the mouse and
           move.w     #0,contrl+2       * its control
           move.w     #0,contrl+6
           move.w     grhandle,contrl+12
           jsr        vdi
           rts
```

```
*********************************************************************
*  Write a string on the screen                                    *
*********************************************************************

printf:   move.l    a0,-(a7)        * write the string, whose
          move.w    #9,-(a7)        * beginning address is in
          trap      #1              * register A0, on the screen.
          addq.l    #6,a7           * String must terminate with
          rts                       * zero.

wait1     dbra      d0,wait1        * Time loop, counts the d0-Register
          rts                       * down to -1

wait:     move.w    #1,-(a7)        * wait for a key stroke
          trap      #1              * GEM-DOS-Call
          addq.l    #2,a7
          rts


*********************************************************************
*    Sense keyboard status (does not wait for keypress) and return key *
*    code and also the scan code.                                  *
*********************************************************************

inkey:    move.w    #2,-(a7)    * Sense keyboard, does not wait for key
          move.w    #1,-(a7)    * activation and return an ASCII-code
          trap      #13         * of an activated key in the lower half
          addq.l    #4,a7       * of the long word of D0, and the scan code
          tst.w     d0          * in the upper half of the long word of
          bpl       endkey      * D0.
          move.w    #7,-(a7)
          trap      #1
          addq.l    #2,a7
endkey:   rts
```

```
*********************************************************************
* Draw-line-routine, draws directly into the screen storage and is   *
* used only for the high resolution mode (640*400 Points ). For color *
* monitor use ddrawl                                                 *
*********************************************************************

drawl:    move.l    d7,-(a7)        * Save register
          move.l    #ytab,a0        * Address of the Y-table
          clr.l     d4
          move.w    #1,a4           * X step = +1
          move.w    a4,a5           * Y step = +1
          move.w    a2,d6
          sub.w     d2,d6           * DX in d6 = X2 - X1
          bge       dxispos

          neg.w     d6              * If DX is negative, then
          move.w    #-1,a4          * make positive through negation
dxispos:  move.w    a3,d7
          sub.w     d3,d7           * DY in d7
          bgt       plotit          * If DY is larger than zero draw then
          beq       dyis_0          * first point
          neg.w     d7              * DY is negative, make positive
          move.w    #-1,a5          * Y-Step is then -1
          bra       plotit
dyis_0:   not.w     d4              * If DY = 0 then parallel to X-Axis

plotit:   tst.w     d2              * Test if drawing area was
          bmi       draw_it         * exceeded
          tst.w     d3
          bmi       draw_it
          cmp.w     #639,d2
          bhi       draw_it
          cmp.w     #399,d3
          bhi       draw_it
          move.w    d3,d0           * Y-value times two for access to
          lsl.w     #2,d0           * Plot table
          move.l    0(a0,d0.w),a1   * Screen address
          move.w    d2,d1           * X-value
          lsr.w     #3,d1           * INT (X/8)
          move.w    d2,d0           * X-value
          not.w     d0              * -X
```

97

```
**********************************
*  Here the point is drawn       *
**********************************
            bset    d0, 0(a1,d1.w)   * 7-(X MOD 8) with the bset-command

draw_it:    cmp.w   d2,a2            * End X reached?
            bne     notend           * no
            cmp.w   d3,a3            * End Y reached?
            beq     endit            * no
notend:     tst.w   d4               * D > 0 => Y step
            bge     ystep
xstep:      add.w   a4,d2            * else X step X=X+-1
            add.w   d7,d4            * ND = D + DY
            bra     plotit
ystep:      add.w   a5,d3            * Y=Y +- 1
            sub.w   d6,d4            * ND = D - DX
            bra     plotit
drawend:
endit:      movem.l (a7)+,d7         * restore register
            rts                      * Return to calling program


*******************************************************************
*  This Draw-line-routine is universal for all monitor types and  *
*  can be used with all resolutions.                              *
*******************************************************************

ddrawl:     move.l   d7,-(a7)
            move.l   #lineavar,a0
            move.w   d2,38(a0)       * X1
            move.w   d3,40(a0)       * Y1
            move.w   a2,42(a0)       * X2
            move.w   a3,44(a0)       * Y2
            .dc.w    $a003           * draw line
            move.l   (a7)+,d7
            rts
```

```
*****************************************************************
* Initialize the Line-A variables and store the address of the    *
* Variable block in lineavar.                                     *
*****************************************************************


inlinea:    .dc.w     $a000           * initialize the Line A variable.
            move.l    a0,lineavar
            move.w    #0,32(a0)
            move.w    #$ffff,34(a0)    * Sample of the line
            move.w    #0,36(a0)        * Writing mode
            move.w    #1,24(a0)        * drawing color
            rts



*****************************************************************
*  Creation of the Y table for the highest graphic mode (640*400)  *
*****************************************************************


start1:
            move.w    #2,-(a7)        * checks the screen address of the
            trap      #14             * System, recognizes which computer
            addq.l    #2,a7
            move.l    d0,physbase     * Display start minus 32 K-Byte
            move.l    #399,d1         * Number of lines minus one
            move.l    #ytab, a0       * Physical address

stloop1:    move.l    d0,(a0)+        * New address equals old address
            add.l     #80,d0          * plus 80
            dbra      d1,stloop1
            rts


*****************************************************************
*  Line-A initialization                                          *
*****************************************************************


start2:     jsr       inlinea              * Initialize line A
            rts
```

```
*********************************************************************
* Variables of the basic program                                   *
*********************************************************************


          .even
          .bss
lineavar: .ds.l    1               * Storage for address of Line-A variable
physbase: .ds.l    1               * Storage for screen address.

ytab:     .ds.l    400             * Storage for the Y table
contrl:                            * Arrays for AES and VDI functions
opcode:   .ds.w    1
sintin:   .ds.w    1
sintout:  .ds.w    1
saddrin:  .ds.w    1
saddrout: .ds.w    1
          .ds.w    6


global:
apversion: .ds.w   1
apcount:   .ds.w   1
apid:      .ds.w   1
apprivate: .ds.l   1
apptree:   .ds.l   1
ap1resv:   .ds.l   1
ap2resv:   .ds.l   1
ap3resv:   .ds.l   1
ap4resv:   .ds.l   1


intin:     .ds.w   128
ptsin:     .ds.w   256
intout:    .ds.w   128
ptsout:    .ds.w   128
addrin:    .ds.w   128
addrout:   .ds.w   128
grhandle:  .ds.w   1


           .data
vdipb:     .dc.l   contrl,intin,ptsin,intout,ptsout
aespb:     .dc.l   contrl,global,intin,intout,addrin,addrout


           .end
```

```
**********************************************************************
* Main program for link file basic1.o , runs only in connection with *
* this link file .     U.B. 11.85                                    *
* Draws random line in coordinate area 0-255. The value area         *
* is valid for both axis                                             *
**********************************************************************
           .globl    main
           .text



**********************************************************************
*  Entry point from the linkfile                                     *
**********************************************************************


main:      jsr       apinit       * Announce application
           jsr       grafhand     *
           jsr       openwork     * Open screen work station
           jsr       mouse_off    * Hide the Mouse
           jsr       clwork       * Clear Display
*          jsr       inlinea      * Color version only
loop1:     jsr       clwork
           move.l    #text1,a0    * Address of text after A0
           jsr       printf       * Write text
           move.l    loopc,d7

loop2:     jsr       random       * Generate random number
           and.w     border,d0    * bring to area 0-255
           move.w    d0,x0        * through masking out of the upper
           jsr       random       * 8 Bits of the lower word in D0
           and.w     border,d0
           move.w    d0,y0
           jsr       random
           and.w     border,d0

           move.w    d0,x1
           jsr       random
           and.w     border,d0
           move.w    d0,y1

           move.w    x0,d2        * transfer the two points to the
           move.w    x1,a2        * "right" registers
           move.w    y0,d3
```

```
              move.w    y1,a3
              jsr       drawl          * Draw line from X0,Y0 to X1,Y1 sketch
              dbra      d7,loop2       * Repeat loopc

              jsr       inkey          * Sense keyboard, do not wait for key
              swap      d0             * activation, scancode in D0
              cmp.w     #$44,d0        * compare with code in F10
              bne       loop1          * If not : loop again
              rts                      * otherwise terminate program


*******************************************************************
*  Call the operating system function for creation of a 4-byte integer*
*  random number, the number is returned to D0.                   *
*******************************************************************

random:       move.w    #17,-(a7)      * generate a 4-Byte Integer-
              trap      #14            * Random Number in D0. Use only
              addq.l    #2,a7          * the lower 2-Bytes
              rts

              .data
              .even
*******************************************************************
*                   Variables for the Main program               *
*                                                                 *
*******************************************************************


*******************************************************************
* Text for the printf function, 27 Y 34 96 positions the cursor   *
* Sequence is column, line, both with an offset of 32             *
*******************************************************************


text1:        .dc.b     27,'Y',40,42,' Random lines ',0

loopc:        .dc.l     60             * Number of lines

border:       .dc.w     $ff            * 255 as display limit, with the high-
*                                      * resolution B-W monitor the $ff
*                                      * can be replaced with $1ff = 511
```

```
*********************************************************************

              .bss
              .even

x0:           .ds.w     1          * Temporary storage for the two
y0:           .ds.w     1          * Points, the program runs with small
x1:           .ds.w     1          * changes even without the intermediate
y1:           .ds.w     1          * storage; what changes ?

              .end
```

Graphics using assembly-language routines

4.   Graphics using assembly-language routines

The programs presented in the following part of the book can be used with monochrome as well as color monitors, since the line drawing is performed by the operating system, or to be more accurate, by the LINE-A-routines. Of course it would be possible to convert the draw-line-algorithm from the first link file for the various picture formats, but this process has the disadvantage of requiring a subroutine for every picture format. The programs described here can be executed on all kinds of computer-monitor combinations. During program start, the main program recognizes what type of monitor is attached and what resolution is desired and on the basis of this information provides some variables with the required data. For example, the coordinate origin of the picture system is placed in the middle of the display. The larger memory capacity of the ST permits it to handle significantly larger quantities of data. Once the operating system of the smaller models is placed in ROM, the area released in RAM will be sufficient even for the largest applications. When calling the Metacombco Editor for input of the larger source files (grlink1, menu1, rotate1, paint1) you have to specify more memory space for listing to be entered along with the filename. To do this, enter grlink1.s 23000 in the dialog box that appears. This reserves about 80k for the source text. If you enter source text without comments the space reserved in the basic version of the editor should be sufficient.

4.1   Definition of a data structure for an object in space

The program modules presented here have the ability to represent on the screen any object in a user defined world in any position, as seen from various positions. The single disadvantage is the limitation of the valid value range to ±32000; this means that for the definition of the world a right angle three dimensional Cartesian coordinate system (right system) is available whose three coordinate axes (X-Y-Z) are labeled with values between +32000 and -32000. Whether these values are in meters, kilometers or the number of corrupt politicians in the Senate depends on the individual user and the application. For example, using the number of corrupt politicians is a questionable value, since it changes from moment to moment, and is far from constant.

Joking aside, a very simple object should suffice to describe the data structure. We will use simple house as in Figure 4.1.1.

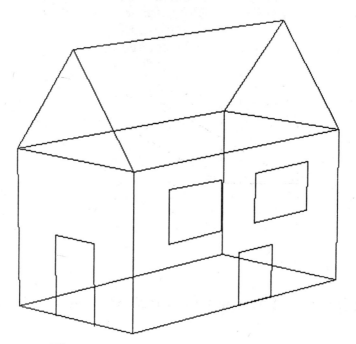

Figure 4.1.1: House as Wire Model

Every object in the coordinate system is described through a finite number of points and the lines which connect these points. To represent the object, these points in the world system must be specified by declaring of their coordinates. It has proved to be useful to define the object, in this case the house, in its own coordinate system and to transform it during the construction of the world coordinate system. To gain an advantage, the coordinate origin of the object system is located inside the house, if possible at a "rotationally neutral" point, i.e. during a rotation of the object around this point, the maximum changes of the individual points resulting from the rotation should be minimized. The object should not be distorted.

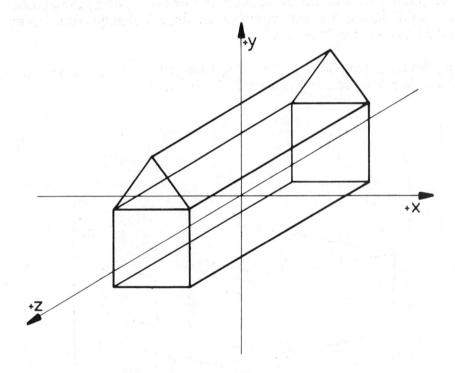

Figure 4.1.2: House with coordinate system included

The individual steps during the "construction" of the house therefore are:

1. Draw a total view of the object (on a piece of paper) and arbitrarily number of the individual points.

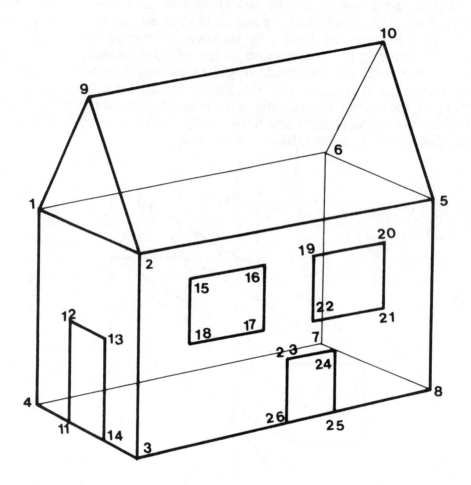

Figure 4.1.3: House with numbered points

2.   Draw the object in the various possible aspects with the current
      coordinate axis for accurate specification of the points.

Figure 4.1.4 - Figure 4.1.9: six views of the house

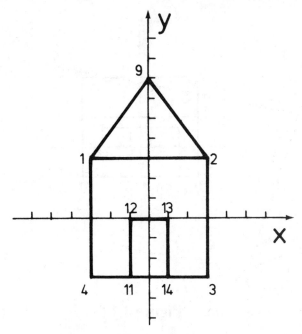

Figure 4.1.4

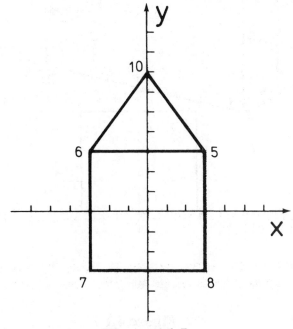

Figure 4.1.5

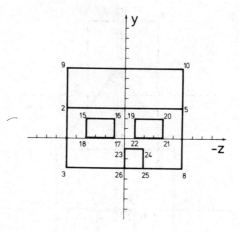

Figure 4.1.6

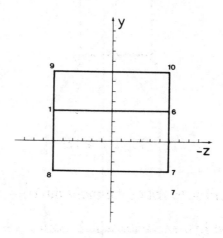

Figure 4.1.7

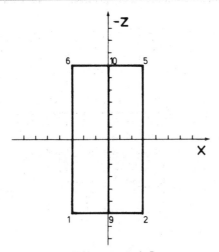

Figure 4.1.8

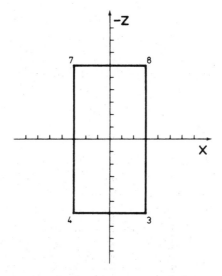

Figure 4.1.9

3. Set up a coordinate list of the individual points.

4. Create a line list, i.e. state which points are connected by lines.

5. Indicate the number of points and lines in the object.

Coordinate list of the house:

Point No.	X-coord.	Y-coord.	Z-coord.
1.	-30	30	60
2.	30	30	60
3.	30	-30	60
4.	-30	-30	60
5.	30	30	-60
6.	-30	30	-60
7.	-30	-30	-60
8.	30	-30	-60
9.	0	70	60
10.	0	70	-60
11.	-10	-30	60
12.	-10	0	60
13.	10	0	60
14.	10	-30	60
15.	30	20	40
16.	30	20	10
17.	30	0	10
18.	30	0	40
19.	30	20	-10
20.	30	20	-40
21.	30	0	-40
22.	30	0	-10
23.	30	-10	0
24.	30	-10	-20
25.	30	-30	-20
26.	30	-30	0

Total of 26 points.

Line list:

Line No.	from point	to point
1.	1	2
2.	2	3
3.	3	4
4.	4	1
5.	2	5
6.	5	8
7.	8	3
8.	8	7
9.	7	6
10.	6	5
11.	6	1
12.	7	4
13.	9	10
14.	1	9
15.	9	2
16.	5	10
17.	6	10
18.	11	12
19.	12	13
20.	13	14
21.	15	16
22.	16	17
23.	17	18
24.	18	15
25.	19	20
26.	20	21
27.	21	22
28.	22	19
29.	23	24
30.	24	25
31.	25	26
32.	26	23

Total of 32 lines.

Additional information on the object is required for the transformation of the house into the world coorinate system: the angles housxw, housyw, houszw, which describe a rotation of the house about one of the three axes in regard to the coordinate origin, and the location of the house in the world coordinate system. The location is the point to which the coordinate origin (rotationally neutral point) of the house system is displaced in the world system, housx0, housy0, housz0. In our first example program the coordinate origin of the house system is moved to the coordinate origin of the world system, housx0 etc. and therefore zero.

For further information, we need an observation point and a projection center, where both points naturally are described in world coordinates. In the simplest case the observation point is the coordinate origin point of the world system, and the projection center [prox,proy,proz] is located on the positive Z axis of the world system. The system of the observer (view system) is a right system in our programs and it is not necessary to transform to a left system, to multiply all Z values by -1. For our case this means that after transformation the view system a point with the coordinates [10,10,-300] is farther from the observer than a point with the coordinates [10,10,-200].

Furthermore, we need the normal vector (direction vector) of the projection plane. For simplification we assume that it is pointed from the projection center toward the coordinate origin of the world system and points toward the negative Z axis. The projection center lies on the Z axis and therefore has the coordinates [0,0,proz], since the normal vector of the projection plane points in the direction of the negative Z axis, the rotation of the observation direction vector to the negative Z axis is not necessary.

To help explain the coordinate systems and viewing points, we have here Figure 4.1.10 with the world system and the observation factors defined in it.

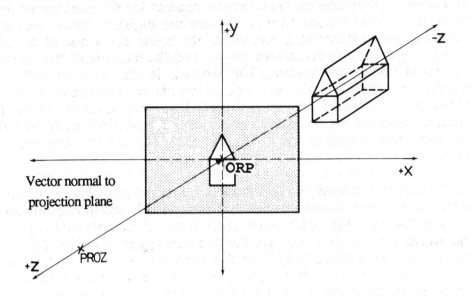

Figure 4.1.10

Summary:

To represent the house on the screen we need a total of four coordinate systems, where the various coordinate systems exist only in theory and all transformations occur in a single system. The defined points are stored in arrays in which the various coordinate systems are then reflected so they do not disappear after a transformation. The following coordinate systems are used:

1. The data system (housdatx, housdaty, housdatz), in which the house is defined at construction.

2. The world system (wrldx, wrldy, wrldz), in which, for example, a village is represented by several houses, where the houses are all created by transformation at various places in the world system from the one single house defined in the data system.

3. The view system (viewx, viewy, viewz), which is used for the description of the view transformation. The view transformation is the transformation into the observer system, which is described through the observation reference point and projection center as well as the vectors from projection center to the observation reference. The vector from the projection center to the observation reference point is therefore the normal vector of the projection plane.

4. The screen system has only two dimensions. The only transformation which occurs in this system is shifting the coordinate origin to any desired location with reversal of the Y axis. Something we also used in our example is the displacement to the screen center but other locations are also possible depending on the application.

After this simplified observation situation, now an example for the general view-transformation of a more complicated model. As a fictional example we will use a world system which represents an airplane standing on a runway. The observation point of the system should be in the middle of the cockpit window, which is therefore the projection plane, and the eye of the pilot should be the projection center. Let us also imagine a tanker truck and an airplane hangar at some distance from the airplane. Two types of transformations are possible.

1. A transformation of the object, which might mean that the tanker truck moves and approaches the airplane, for example. In this case the movement must occur in the world system and only the coordinates of the tanker truck need be recalculated in the world system.

2. A movement of the observer, in this example the airplane. Let's go back to the starting position and assume that the tanker truck remains in its original position. Now the airplane should move, and for simulation of this movement all objects in the world system, the tanker truck and the hangar, must be transformed. The entire world system would be rotated about the center of the cockpit window. For a left rotation of the airplane, everything must be rotated to the right. This connection can be easily verified: If you move your head to the left, the observed objects move to the right out of our field of view. When the airplane is moved without rotation the observer gets the impression of movement through the displacement of the coordinate origin of the world system before the projection.

3. A movement of the observer and the object, which means first a transformation of the truck in the world system and subsequent transformation of the total world system into the view system.

Only after completion of these various cases do we get to the perspective transformation, i.e the projection from space to the projection plane, or more precisely into the screen. This was an example of a more complex observation model.

You will probably ask why things have to be complicated by using an additional coordinate system, the view system, when we could do everything in the world system. This is true, but the addition of the view system improves the accuracy and provides for a better overview of the total system. Because of the rounding errors from the many transformations, our world of the tanker truck and the hangar, would according to the law of increasing entropy, degenerate to a chaotic mess after a few hundred transformations. The aspect of the better overview is at least as significant as the accuracy and I want to try to demonstrate this fact again .

As you will see, all transformations can be carried out with a single routine. Our application combines almost all of the rotations with matrix multiplication and performs displacements before and after these multiplications. The displacements are not included in the matrix multiplications and our point coordinates are therefore not extended coordinates but consist only of the three coordinates $[x,y,z]$ of the current point. The only routine used is the rotation around any selected point. As a reminder, during the rotation around any point, the coordinate origin must first be moved to this point, then rotated by the desired angle and finally the coordinate origin moved inverse to its original place by back transformation. For the sequence of our routine this means that the point about which rotation should occur is passed, also the rotation angles around the corresponding axes (xw,yw,zw). The rotation routine first calculates a multiplication matrix through multiplication of the rotation matrixes belonging to the various angles. Then all points belonging to the desired object $[x,y,z]$ are manipulated in the following sequence:

1. The point $[x,y,z]$ is moved to the rotation point. This is achieved through subtraction of the coordinates of the rotation point from the object coordinates. The result of this operation is the point $[x',y',z']$.

2. The point $[x',y',z']$ is multiplied by the previously calculated total rotation matrix.

    Result: $[x'',y'',z'']$.

3. The point $[x'',y'',z'']$ is transformed back to the "old" coordinate system by adding of the coordinates of the rotation point.

In this model the axes are not scaled. The size manipulation of the objects, i.e. their pictured size on the screen, is performed during the projection through movement of the projection plane. If different values are selected for the subtraction occurring at the beginning and the concluding addition, the movement of an observer in the world system is simulated. If the angles of the normal surface vector in relation to the world system are provided (in section 2.5 we calculated the angles through projection on the various surfaces) the position of the observer can be determined in space through one point and three angles.

Let us assume that a person is moving our world system, where the house discussed in the first example is located at the coordinate origin. The eye of this person, or actually the retina of the eye, is the projection plane. It is irrelevant that the projection center in the human eye is in front of the projection plane, since the reversed picture resulting from this is turned around by the brain. For the simulation of this moving observer the coordinate origin of the world system must be moved to the center of the retina, but we are limiting ourselves to a single eye. The coordinates of the eye in the world system must be known; furthermore the head of the observer can be moved through three different axis. You can easily determine the axis yourself. The rotation about the first axis in our coordinate system corresponds to the X axis, described by the observer nodding his head up and down. The Y axis rotation is shaking his head. The head rotates on the Z axis when the observer attempts to touch his ear to his shoulder. If the three rotaion angles are known, the coordinate origin will be rotated about this angle and the observed object lies in the coordinate system of the observer. It is not necessary to reverse the movement of the coordinate origin which is similar to the example of the airplane.

In principle, an unlimited number of displacements, rotations, and observer situations are possible: rotation of the house, rotation of the total system around one point, or any axis, and also the displacement with rotation into the observer system. To bring some order into this flood of rotations, our programming examples are limited to one fixed observer location point. This is no limitation on the observed effects on the screen however, i.e. in principle it is the same whether one assumes that an object rotated around a point, or the observer moved his head, provided the size relationships are suitably adjusted. Finally, the programmer must know the desired effect. There are many ways to achieve the same effects.

And now, the description of the transformations of our data structure for the first, fairly simple transformation program. The concrete object (house) is defined in a coordinate system (`housdatx, housdaty, housdatz`). During the initialization of the program, the subroutine `makewrld` moves the house to any desired location in the world system (`wrldx, wrldy, wrldz`), with possible rotation. In the first program it is moved to the point [0,0,0] without rotation.

All further operations concerning the house relate only to the world system. For example, the house can be rotated around any point of this world system, or only the position of the house can be changed by displacement. But now the initial scenario of our model changes through these transformations, so we store the data for the rotation of the world system in a new coordinate system (`viewx, viewy, viewz`), where the initial scene (in `wrldx, wrldy, wrldz`) is available at any time and can be reproduced at any time.

After each operation in this world system, the coordinates of the displaced house are stored in the view system. The object should also be displayed on the screen. To do this, it must be adapted to the perspective of the viewer situation. In our example, the projection center is at the coordinates [0,0,1500]--therefore on the positive z axis of the right handed coordinate system. Through the perspective transformation, the coordinates of the view storage are transformed into screen coordinates (screenx,screeny) whereby the desired location of the coordinate origin and the orientation of the Y axis are considered during the calculations. The screen coordinates are transferred with the aid of the line list of the drawing routine, which, through the built-in "Cohen-Sutherland clipper" draws only the desired screen area using the border points clipule and cliplri (clip upper left, clip lower right). To create some movement in this house, the rotation origin point or its rotation angle can be changed slightly after each drawing and the whole process can be programmed into a large loop for repeated execution.

In case you did not understand a few details, you can relax while typing in the following program listings. You should consider that the material discussed here corresponds to about a half a semester of lectures for upper-class computer science students and therefore requires intense consideration, even with the aid of the additional literature cited in the beginning.

Just as in the first small program (random lines) this program is also divided into a link file and main program. The new link file has the name grlink1.s and was enhanced with the sine and cosine routines, the clip algorithm, the screen switch routine, the matrix operations and the perspective transform routine. The main program house1.s contains the data of the house and the main loop in which the rotation angles of the house are changed in cycle and can be altered by the user. The steps for creating a ready-to-run program are the same as in the third chapter. You need only to replace basic1.s with grlink1.s and main1.s with house1.s in the command sequences. You should start typing in the first program since the following programs build on the first two files. That way you only have to type in the additional subroutines and data sections. The link file grlink1.s is the same for all following main programs and does not have to be changed.

```
************************************************************************
*   grlink1.s  Graphic Driver Version 4.0                           *
*   The main program must begin with the label " main ".            *
************************************************************************



************************************************************************
*     Global variables in the link files                            *
************************************************************************

        .globl    drawl,sin,sincos,physbase
        .globl    logbase
        .globl    sinx,siny,sinz,cosx,cosy,cosz,wait
        .globl    wait1,drawn1
        .globl    pers,grafhand
        .globl    nummark,xangle,yangle,zangle,numline,datx,daty,datz
        .globl    pointx,pointy
        .globl    pointz,xplot,yplot,x0,y0,z0,z1,linxy,sincos
        .globl    grhandle,global,contrl,intin,intout,ptsin,ptsout
        .globl    addrin,addrout
        .globl    apinit,openwork,clwork,aes,vdi
        .globl    rotate,dist,zobs
        .globl    matrix11,matrix12,matrix13
        .globl    matrix21,matrix22,matrix23
        .globl    matrix31,matrix32,matrix33
        .globl    xrotate,yrotate,zrotate,matinit,inkey
        .globl    mouse_on,mouse_off,printf
        .globl    clipxule,clipyule,clipxlri,clipylri
        .globl    filstyle,filindex,filform,filcolor,filmode,yrot
        .globl    lineavar,pageup,pagedown,plotpt
```

123

```
*******************************************************************
*    Program initialization and storage requirement  calculations  *
*******************************************************************


        .text


sstart:

        move.l    a7,a5        * Base page address on the stack
        move.l    4(a5),a5     * basepage address = program start - $100
        move.l    $c(a5),d0    * Program length
        add.l     $14(a5),d0   * Length of initialized data area
        add.l     $1c(a5),d0   * Data area not initialized
        add.l     #$1100,d0    * 4 K-byte user stack
        move.l    a5,d1        * Start address of the program
        add.l     d0,d1        * Plus number of occupied bytes = space requirement
        and.l     #-2,d1       * Even address for stack
        move.l    d1,a7        * User stack pointer to last 4K- byte
        move.l    d0,-(sp)     * Length of reserved area
        move.l    a5,-(sp)     * Beginning address of reserved area
        move.w    d0,-(sp)     * Dummy-word
        move.w    #$4a,-(sp)   * GEM DOS function SETBLOCK
        trap      #1
        add.l     #12,sp       * Restore old stack address
        jsr       start1       * Check on display address
        jsr       inlinea      * Initialize Line-A routines
        jsr       main         * Jump to main program (user-created)
        move.l    #0,-(a7)     * End current program
        trap      #1           * Back to Gem desktop


*******************************************************************
*  Pass upper screen page to video controller                     *
*  while drawing the other                                        *
*******************************************************************


pageup: move.w    #-1,-(a7)
        move.l    physbase,-(a7)   * Page displayed
        move.l    logbase,-(a7)    * Draw on this page
        move.w    #5,-(a7)
        trap      #14
        add.l     #12,a7
        rts
```

```
***********************************************************************
*  Display screen page at lower address, while all drawing          *
*  operations after the call go to the higher display               *
***********************************************************************

pagedown: move.w    #-1,-(a7)
          move.l    logbase,-(a7)   * display logical page
          move.l    physbase,-(a7)  * draw in the other one
          move.w    #5,-(a7)
          trap      #14
          add.l     #12,a7
          rts


***********************************************************************
*   This subroutine calls AES functions, the user must             *
*   save the Registers D0-D2 and A0-A2 before the aes call,        *
*   which are used by VDI and AES                                   *
***********************************************************************

aes:      move.l    #aespb,d1   * call the AES functions
          move.w    #$c8,d0
          trap      #2
          rts


***********************************************************************
*   call the VDI functions                                         *
***********************************************************************

vdi:      move.l    #vdipb,d1   * call the VDI functions
          move.w    #$73,d0
          trap      #2
          rts
```

```
**********************************************************************
*    initialize the Line-A functions, pass the address of          *
*    Line-A variable area in A0, which is then stored              *
*    in lineavar                                                   *
**********************************************************************


inlinea:  .dc.w     $a000
          move.l    a0,lineavar
          move.w    #0,32(a0)
          move.w    #$ffff,34(a0)
          move.w    #0,36(a0)
          move.w    #1,24(a0)
          rts




**********************************************************************
*    announces application                                         *
**********************************************************************


apinit:   clr.l     d0              * announces an application
          move.l    d0,ap1resv
          move.l    d0,ap2resv
          move.l    d0,ap3resv
          move.l    d0,ap4resv
          move.w    #10,opcode
          move.w    #0,sintin
          move.w    #1,sintout
          move.w    #0,saddrout
          move.w    #0,saddrin
          jsr       aes
          rts




**********************************************************************
*  Transfers desktop screen handler to caller                      *
**********************************************************************


grafhand: move.w    #77,contrl      * Transfer screen handler
          move.w    #0,contrl+2
          move.w    #5,contrl+4
          move.w    #0,contrl+6
          move.w    #0,contrl+8
```

126

```
            jsr        aes
            move.w     intout,grhandle
            rts



*********************************************************************
*    open a workstation                                            *
*********************************************************************

openwork:   move.w     #100,opcode          * opens a workstation
            move.w     #1,d0
            move.w     #0,contrl+2
            move.w     #11,contrl+6
            move.w     grhandle,contrl+12
            move.w     d0,intin
            move.w     d0,intin+2
            move.w     d0,intin+4
            move.w     d0,intin+6
            move.w     d0,intin+8
            move.w     d0,intin+10
            move.w     d0,intin+12
            move.w     d0,intin+14
            move.w     d0,intin+16
            move.w     d0,intin+18
            move.w     #2,intin+20
            jsr        vdi
            rts



*********************************************************************
*    Clear the screen                                              *
*********************************************************************

clwork:     move.w     #3,contrl            * clear screen VDI function
            move.w     #0,contrl+2
            move.w     #1,contrl+6
            move.w     grhandle,contrl+12
            jsr        vdi
            rts
```

```
**********************************************************************
*     Enable mouse                                                   *
**********************************************************************

mouse_on: move.w    #122,contrl        * enable mouse
          move.w    #0,contrl+2        * and control with
          move.w    #1,contrl+6        * operating system
          move.w    grhandle,contrl+12
          move.w    #0,intin
          jsr       vdi
          rts


**********************************************************************
*     Disable mouse                                                  *
**********************************************************************

mouse_off:  move.w    #123,contrl      * Disable mouse
            move.w    #0,contrl+2      * and control
            move.w    #0,contrl+6
            move.w    grhandle,contrl+12
            jsr       vdi
            rts



**********************************************************************
*     write string on screen                                        *
**********************************************************************

printf:   move.l    a0,-(a7)          * write a string
          move.w    #9,-(a7)          * whose starting
          trap      #1                * is in A0, on the
          addq.l    #6,a7             * screen. String
          rts                         * must end with a zero.


**********************************************************************
* Determine screen address                                          *
**********************************************************************

start1:
          move.w    #2,-(a7)          * Determine the screen
          trap      #14               * address of the system
          addq.l    #2,a7             * which computer ?
```

```
              move.l    d0,physbase   * screen start minus 32 K-byte
              sub.l     #$8000,d0
              move.l    d0,logbase    * equals logical display page
              rts


**********************************************************************
* Plot  routine  x-coordinate in d2, y-coordinate in d3            *
**********************************************************************

plotpt:   movem.l   d0-d2/a0-a2,-(a7)
              tst.w     d2            * X-value less than zero =>
              bmi       stop2
              tst.w     d3            * Y-value less zero
              bmi       stop2
              cmp.w     #639,d2       * X-value greater than 639?
              bhi       stop2         * Display limit
              cmp.w     #399,d3       * Y-value greater than 399?
              bhi       stop2
              move.w    d2,ptsin
              move.w    d3,ptsin+2
              move.w    #1,intin
              .dc.w     $a001
              movem.l   (a7)+,d0-d2/a0-a2
stop2:    rts



**********************************************************************
* draw-line routine with Cohen-Sutherland clipping. The points are *
* passed in d2, d3 (start point) and a2, a3 (end point)            *
**********************************************************************

drawl:    movem.l   d0-d7/a0-a6,-(a7)    * Save registers
              move.w    d2,d6               * Determine position
              move.w    d3,d7               * of start point and
              jsr       rel_pos             * store
              move.w    d1,code1
              move.w    a2,d6               * Position of second
              move.w    a3,d7               * point and store
              jsr       rel_pos
              move.w    d1,code2
              tst.w     d1                  * if points are not in
              bne       testw1              * drawing area continue
```

```
          tst.w     code1          * test. Otherwise test
          beq       drawit2        * first point. When visible,
*                                  * draw both points

testw1:   move.w    d1,d0          * If both points on the same
          and.w     code1,d0       * 'page' outside the viewing
          bne       drawend        * window, then do not draw,
          move.w    d2,a0          * else store starting points and
          move.w    d3,a1          * calculate intersecting points
          move.w    a2,a4
          move.w    a3,a5

          tst.w     code2          * is point 2 visible ?
          bne       testw2         * if not, find intersection point
          move.w    a2,rightx      * if yes, store
          move.w    a3,righty
          bra       testw3         * find left intersect point

testw2:   move.w    code1,p1code   * right intersect point
          move.w    code2,p2code
          jsr       fndpoint       * find intersect point
          tst.w     p1code         * if 'intersect point'not
          bne       drawend        * visible, then end

          move.w    d2,rightx      * if visible, then store
          move.w    d3,righty

testw3:   move.w    a4,d2          * and the left intersect point
          move.w    a5,d3          * with switched points
          move.w    a0,a2          * determine with the same routine
          move.w    a1,a3
          move.w    code2,p1code
          move.w    code1,p2code

          tst.w     p2code         * Point visible?
          bne       testw4         * if not, continue test
          move.w    a2,leftx       * if yes, store and
          move.w    a3,lefty       * connect both visible
          bra       drawit1        * points with a line
```

```
testw4:    jsr      fndpoint          * Find intersect point
           move.w   d2,leftx          * and store,
           move.w   d3,lefty

drawit1:   move.w   leftx,d2          * connect both points with
           move.w   lefty,d3          * a line
           clr.l    a2
           clr.l    a3
           move.w   rightx,a2
           move.w   righty,a3

drawit2:   move.l   lineavar,a0
           move.w   d2,38(a0)         * X1
           move.w   d3,40(a0)         * Y1
           move.w   a2,42(a0)         * X2
           move.w   a3,44(a0)         * Y2
           .dc.w    $a003             * Draw line
drawend:
endit:     movem.l  (a7)+,d0-d7/a0-a6 * Restore registers
           rts                        * Return to calling program



*********************************************************************
*   recognizes the position of a point passed in D6 and D7 relative  *
*   to the clip window defined in the variables clipoli and clipure  *
*********************************************************************


rel_pos:   clr.l    d1                * determines the position
           move.w   d7,d1             * of the point passed in
           sub.w    clipyule,d1       * d6 and d7 relative to
           lsl.l    #1,d1             * the drawing window
           move.w   d7,d1             * defined by clipure
           sub.w    clipylri,d1       * and clipoli
           neg.w    d1
           lsl.l    #1,d1
           move.w   d6,d1
           sub.w    clipxlri,d1
           neg.w    d1
           lsl.l    #1,d1
           move.w   d6,d1
           sub.w    clipxule,d1
           lsl.l    #1,d1
```

131

```
              swap       d1
              rts



        ******************************************************************
        *   Finds the intersect point, if present,                       *
        *   of the the connecting line from P1 to P2 with the clip window *
        *   the points are passed in D2, D3 and A2, A3 as in drawl        *
        ******************************************************************

fndpoint: move.w     d2,d4        * Find the center point of
          move.w     d3,d5        * the line P1 P2
          add.w      a2,d4        * (X1 + X2) / 2
          ext.l      d4

          lsr.l      #1,d4
          add.w      a3,d5        * (Y1 + Y2) / 2
          ext.l      d5           * = center point of line P1 P2

          lsr.l      #1,d5
          move.w     d4,d6        * Store center point coord.
          move.w     d5,d7        * Y middle
          jsr        rel_pos      * where is the intersect point ?

          move.w     p2code,d6 * Code of center pt. to D6
          and.w      d1,d6        * are the points on the same
          bne        fother       * page outside the screen

          cmp.w      d4,d2        * points coincide ?
          bne        findw1
          cmp.w      d5,d3
          beq        fendit       * if yes => stop

findw1:   cmp.w      d4,a2        * Do middle point and second
          bne        findw2       * point match ?
          cmp.w      d5,a3
          bne        findw2
          bra        fendit       * if yes = stop
```

```
findw2:    move.w    d4,d2      * else exchange middle and
           move.w    d5,d3      * first point and start again
           move.w    d1,p1code
           bra       fndpoint

fother:    cmp.w     d4,a2      * middle point and P2 match ?
           bne       fother1
           cmp.w     d5,a3
           beq       fendit     * if yes, then end
fother1:   cmp.w     d4,d2      * middle point and P1 match ?
           bne       fother2
           cmp.w     d5,d3
           beq       fendit     * if yes, then end

fother2:   tst.w     p1code     * is P1 in clip window
           beq       fother3
           move.w    d1,d7      * if not, and P1 and P2 lie
           and.w     p1code,d7  * both on one side of the
           bne       fexit      * Clip-window then none of line is visible
fother3:   move.w    d4,a2      * otherwise take middle point
           move.w    d5,a3      * as new P2 and start again
           move.w    d1,p2code  * until the intersect point
           bra       fndpoint   * is found

fexit:     move.w    #1,p1code  * Inform calling prog. of termination.

fendit:    rts                  * either in d2,d3 middle point, or
*                               * in p1code termination notice


*******************************************************************
* sine and cosine Function, angle is passed in D0 and           *
* the sine and cosine are returned in D1 and D2                 *
*******************************************************************


sincos:    tst.w     d0         * Angle negative, add 360 degrees
           bpl       noaddi
           add.w     #360,d0
noaddi:    move.l    #sintab,a1 * Beginning address of sine table
           move.l    d0,d2      * Angle in d0 and d2
           lsl.w     #1,d0      * Angle times two as index for access
           move.w    0(a1,d0.w),d1 * sine to d1
```

```
           cmp.w    #270,d2        * Calculate cosine through
           blt      plus9          * displacement of sine values
           sub.w    #270,d2        * by 90 degrees
           bra      sendsin
plus9:     add.w    #90,d2
sendsin:   lsl.w    #1,d2
           move.w   0(a1,d2.w),d2  * cosine to d2

           rts                     * and back to calling program


*********************************************************************
*    sine  function                                                 *
*    Angle is passed in d0 and the sine returned in d1              *
*********************************************************************

sin:       move.l   #sintab,a1
           tst.w    d0
           bpl      sin1
           add.w    #360,d0
sin1:      lsl.w    #1,d0
           move.w   0(a1,d0.w),d1
           rts



*********************************************************************
* Initialize the main diagnonal of the result matrix with          *
* ones which were multiplied by 2^14.  This subroutine must        *
* be called at least once before the call by rotate, or the        *
* result matrix will only consist of zeros.                        *
*********************************************************************

matinit:   move.w   #0,d1
           move.w   #16384,d2      * The initial value for
           move.w   d2,matrix11    * the main diagonal of
           move.w   d1,matrix12    * the result matrix
           move.w   d1,matrix13    * all other elements
           move.w   d1,matrix21    * at zero
           move.w   d2,matrix22
           move.w   d1,matrix23
           move.w   d1,matrix31
           move.w   d1,matrix32
```

```
        move.w    d2,matrix33
        rts



***********************************************************************
*  Multiplication of the rotation matrix by the rotation            *
*  matrix for rotation about the X-axis                             *
***********************************************************************


xrotate:    move.w    xangle,d0          * multiply matrix11-matrix33
            jsr       sincos             * with the rotation matrix for a
            move.w    d1,sinx            * rotation about the X-axis
            move.w    d2,cosx
            move.w    d1,d3
            move.w    d2,d4
            move.w    matrix11,rotx11    * The first column of the matrix
            move.w    matrix21,rotx21    * does not change with X rotation
            move.w    matrix31,rotx31
            muls      matrix12,d2
            muls      matrix13,d1
            sub.l     d1,d2
            lsl.l     #2,d2
            swap      d2
            move.w    d2,rotx12
            move.w    d3,d1
            move.w    d4,d2
            muls      matrix22,d2
            muls      matrix23,d1
            sub.l     d1,d2
            lsl.l     #2,d2
            swap      d2
            move.w    d2,rotx22
            move.w    d3,d1
            move.w    d4,d2
            muls      matrix32,d2
            muls      matrix33,d1
            sub.l     d1,d2
            lsl.l     #2,d2
            swap      d2
            move.w    d2,rotx32
            move.w    d3,d1
```

```
            move.w      d4,d2
            muls        matrix12,d1
            muls        matrix13,d2
            add.l       d1,d2
            lsl.l       #2,d2
            swap        d2
            move.w      d2,rotx13
            move.w      d3,d1
            move.w      d4,d2
            muls        matrix22,d1
            muls        matrix23,d2
            add.l       d1,d2
            lsl.l       #2,d2
            swap        d2
            move.w      d2,rotx23
            muls        matrix32,d3
            muls        matrix33,d4
            add.l       d3,d4
            lsl.l       #2,d4
            swap        d4
            move.w      d4,rotx33
            move.l      #rotx11,a1
            move.l      #matrix11,a2
            move.l      #9,d7           * Number of matrix elements
            subq.l      #1,d7

rotxlop1:   move.w      (a1)+,(a2)+     * Copy result matrix, which
            dbra        d7,rotxlop1     * is still in ROTXnn, to MATRIXnn
            rts

*********************************************************************
* multiply the general rotation matrix by the Y-axis               *
* rotation matrix. Results are stored in the general               *
* rotation matrix                                                  *
*********************************************************************

yrotate:    move.w      yangle,d0       * Angle around which rotation is made
            jsr         sincos
            move.w      d1,siny
            move.w      d2,cosy
            move.w      d1,d3           * Sine of Y-angle
            move.w      d2,d4           * Cosine of Y-angle
```

```
        muls      matrix11,d2
        muls      matrix13,d1
        add.l     d1,d2
        lsl.l     #2,d2
        swap      d2
        move.w    d2,rotx11
        move.w    d3,d1
        move.w    d4,d2
        muls      matrix21,d2
        muls      matrix23,d1
        add.l     d1,d2
        lsl.l     #2,d2
        swap      d2
        move.w    d2,rotx21
        move.w    d3,d1
        move.w    d4,d2
        muls      matrix31,d2
        muls      matrix33,d1
        add.l     d1,d2
        lsl.l     #2,d2
        swap      d2
        move.w    d2,rotx31
        neg.w     d3
        move.w    d3,d1          * -siny in the rotation matrix
        move.w    d4,d2
        move.w    matrix12,rotx12
        move.w    matrix22,rotx22   * The second column
        move.w    matrix32,rotx32   * of the starting
        muls      matrix11,d1       * matrix does not
        muls      matrix13,d2       * change
        add.l     d1,d2
        lsl.l     #2,d2
        swap      d2
        move.w    d2,rotx13
        move.w    d3,d1
        move.w    d4,d2
        muls      matrix21,d1
        muls      matrix23,d2
        add.l     d1,d2
        lsl.l     #2,d2
        swap      d2
        move.w    d2,rotx23
```

```
            muls        matrix31,d3
            muls        matrix33,d4
            add.l       d3,d4
            lsl.l       #2,d4
            swap        d4
            move.w      d4,rotx33
            move.l      #8,d7
            move.l      #rotx11,a1      * Address of result matrix
            move.l      #matrix11,a2    * Address of original matrix
yrotlop1:   move.w      (a1)+,(a2)+     * Copy result matrix
            dbra        d7,yrotlop1     * to the original matrix
            rts


*********************************************************************
* Z-axis - Rotation matrix multiplications                         *
*********************************************************************


zrotate:    move.w      zangle,d0
            jsr         sincos
            move.w      d1,sinz
            move.w      d2,cosz
            move.w      d1,d3
            move.w      d2,d4
            muls        matrix11,d2
            muls        matrix12,d1
            sub.l       d1,d2
            lsl.l       #2,d2
            swap        d2
            move.w      d2,rotx11
            move.w      d3,d1
            move.w      d4,d2
            muls        matrix21,d2
            muls        matrix22,d1
            sub.l       d1,d2
            lsl.l       #2,d2
            swap        d2
            move.w      d2,rotx21
            move.w      d3,d1
            move.w      d4,d2
            muls        matrix31,d2
            muls        matrix32,d1
            sub.l       d1,d2
```

```
        lsl.l      #2,d2
        swap       d2
        move.w     d2,rotx31
        move.w     d3,d1
        move.w     d4,d2
        muls       matrix11,d1
        muls       matrix12,d2
        add.l      d1,d2
        lsl.l      #2,d2
        swap       d2
        move.w     d2,rotx12
        move.w     d3,d1
        move.w     d4,d2
        muls       matrix21,d1
        muls       matrix22,d2
        add.l      d1,d2
        lsl.l      #2,d2
        swap       d2
        move.w     d2,rotx22
        muls       matrix31,d3
        muls       matrix32,d4
        add.l      d3,d4
        lsl.l      #2,d4
        swap       d4
        move.w     d4,rotx32
        move.w     matrix13,rotx13   * the third column
        move.w     matrix23,rotx23   * remains
        move.w     matrix33,rotx33   * unchanged
        move.l     #8,d7
        move.l     #rotx11,a1
        move.l     #matrix11,a2

zrotlop1: move.w   (a1)+,(a2)+       * copy to general
        dbra       d7,zrotlop1       * rotation matrix
        rts
```

```
*************************************************************************
* Multiply every point whose Array address is in datx etc.         *
* by previous translation of the coordinate source to              *
* point [offx,offy,offz], with the general rotation matrix.        *
* The coordinate source of the result coordinates is then          *
* moved to point [xoffs,yoffs,zoffs]                               *
*************************************************************************

rotate:     move.w      nummark,d0      * Number of points to be
            ext.l       d0              * transformed as counter
            subq.l      #1,d0
            move.l      datx,a1
            move.l      daty,a2
            move.l      datz,a3
            move.l      pointx,a4
            move.l      pointy,a5
            move.l      pointz,a6
rotate1:    move.w      (a1)+,d1        * X-coordinate
            add.w       offx,d1

            move.w      d1,d4
            move.w      (a2)+,d2        * Y-coordinate
            add.w       offy,d2         * Translation to point [offx,offy,offz]
            move.w      d2,d5
            move.w      (a3)+,d3        * Z-coordinate
            add.w       offz,d3

            move.w      d3,d6
            muls        matrix11,d1
            muls        matrix21,d2
            muls        matrix31,d3
            add.l       d1,d2
            add.l       d2,d3
            lsl.l       #2,d3
            swap        d3
            add.w       xoffs,d3

            move.w      d3,(a4)+        * rotated X-coordinate
            move.w      d4,d1
            move.w      d5,d2
            move.w      d6,d3
            muls        matrix12,d1
```

```
          muls       matrix22,d2
          muls       matrix32,d3
          add.l      d1,d2
          add.l      d2,d3
          lsl.l      #2,d3
          swap       d3
          add.w      yoffs,d3

          move.w     d3,(a5)+        * rotated Y-coordinate
          muls       matrix13,d4
          muls       matrix23,d5
          muls       matrix33,d6
          add.l      d4,d5
          add.l      d5,d6
          lsl.l      #2,d6
          swap       d6
          add.w      zoffs,d6

          move.w     d6,(a6)+        * rotated Z-coordinate
          dbra       d0,rotate1
          rts
```

```
****************************************************************
* Perspective, calculated from the transformed points in the arrays  *
* pointx, pointy and pointz the screen coordinates, which            *
* are then stored in the arrays xplot and yplot .                    *
****************************************************************
```

```
pers:     move.l     pointx,a1       * Beginning address of
          move.l     pointy,a2       * Point arrays
          move.l     pointz,a3
          move.l     xplot,a4        * xplot contains start address of the
          move.l     yplot,a5        * display coordinate array
          move.w     nummark,d0      * Number of points to be transformed
          ext.l      d0              * as counter
          subq.l     #1,d0

perlop:   move.w     (a3)+,d5        * z-coordinate of object
          move.w     d5,d6
          move.w     dist,d4         * Enlargement factor
          sub.w      d5,d4           * dist minus Z-coordinate of Obj.coord
```

```
            ext.l       d4
            lsl.l       #8,d4           * times 256 for value fitting
            move.w      zobs,d3         * Projection center Z-coordinates
            ext.l       d3

            sub.l       d6,d3           * minus Z-coordinate of object
            bne         pers1

            move.w      #0,d1           * Catch division by zero
            addq.l      #2,a1           * Not really required since
            addq.l      #2,a2           * computer catches this
            move.w      d1,(a4)+        * with an interrupt
            move.w      d1,(a5)+
            bra         perend1

pers1:      divs        d3,d4
            move.w      d4,d3
            move.w      (a1)+,d1        * X-coordinate of object
            move.w      d1,d2
            neg.w       d1
            muls        d1,d3           * multiplied by perspective factor
            lsr.l       #8,d3           * /256 save value range fitting

            add.w       d3,d2           * add to X-coordinate
            add.w       x0,d2           * add screen offset (center point)
            move.w      d2,(a4)+        * Display X-coordinate
            move.w      (a2)+,d1        * Y-coordinates of object
            move.w      d1,d2
            neg.w       d1
            muls        d1,d4
            lsr.l       #8,d4           * /256

            add.w       d4,d2
            neg.w       d2              * Display offset, mirror of Y-axis
            add.w       y0,d2           * Source at [X0,Y0]
            move.w      d2,(a5)+        * Display Y-coordinate
perend1:    dbra        d0,perlop       * All points transformed ?
            rts                         * If yes, return
```

```
***********************************************************************
* Draw number of lines from array from lines in linxy          *
***********************************************************************


drawnl: move.l   xplot,a4        * Display X-coordinate
        move.l   yplot,a5        *      "    Y-coordinate
        move.w   numline,d0      * Number of lines
        ext.l    d0
        subq.l   #1,d0           * as counter
        move.l   linxy,a6        * Address of line array

drlop:  move.l   (a6)+,d1        * first line ,(P1,P2)
        subq.w   #1,d1           * fit to list structure
        lsl.w    #1,d1           * times list element length (2)
        move.w   0(a4,d1.w),d2   * X-coordinate of second point
        move.w   0(a5,d1.w),d3   * Y-coordinate of second point
        swap     d1              * same procedure for first point
        subq.w   #1,d1
        lsl.w    #1,d1
        move.w   0(a4,d1.w),a2   * X-coordinate of  first point
        move.w   0(a5,d1.w),a3   * Y-coordinate of first point
        jsr      drawl           * draw line from P2 to P2
        dbra     d0,drlop        * All lines drawn ?
        rts



***********************************************************************
*  simple counting loop                                            *
***********************************************************************


wait1     dbra      d0,wait1      * delay loop, counts d0 register
          rts                     * down to -1

***********************************************************************
*   wait for key press, for Test and Error detection              *
***********************************************************************


wait:     move.w    #1,-(a7)      * wait for key activation
          trap      #1            * GEM DOS call
          addq.l    #2,a7
          rts
```

```
*********************************************************************
*   Key sensing, ASCII code returned in lower byte word of D0      *
*   Scan code in upper sord lower byte of D0                       *
*   Returns zero if no input                                       *
*********************************************************************


inkey:    move.w    #2,-(a7)        * Key sensing, does not
          move.w    #1,-(a7)        * wait for a key
          trap      #13             * press
          addq.l    #4,a7
          tst.w     d0
          bpl       endkey
          move.w    #7,-(a7)
          trap      #1
          addq.l    #2,a7
endkey:   rts



*********************************************************************
*********************************************************************
** The six following subroutines are only required              **
** for the second main program and do not have to be            **
** entered for linking to the first main program                **
*********************************************************************
*********************************************************************


filstyle: move.w    #23,contrl          * VDI function, set
          move.w    #0,contrl+2         * fill style passed
          move.w    #1,contrl+6         * in D0
          move.w    grhandle,contrl+12
          move.w    d0,intin
          jsr       vdi
          rts


filindex: movem.l   d0-d2/a0-a2,-(a7)   * set fill pattern

          move.w    #24,contrl          * also passed in D0

          move.w    #0,contrl+2
          move.w    #1,contrl+6
          move.w    grhandle,contrl+12
          move.w    d0,intin
```

```
          jsr       vdi
          movem.l   (a7)+,d0-d2/a0-a2
          rts


filcolor: move.w    #25,contrl        * set fill color to
          move.w    #0,contrl+2
          move.w    #1,contrl+6
          move.w    grhandle,contrl+12
          move.w    #1,intin          * one
          jsr       vdi
          rts


filmode:  move.w    #32,contrl        * set write mode
          move.w    #0,contrl+2
          move.w    #1,contrl+6
          move.w    grhandle,contrl+12 * passed in D0
          move.w    d0,intin
          jsr       vdi
          rts


filform:  move.w    #104,contrl       * switch on border
          move.w    #0,contrl+2       * around area
          move.w    #1,contrl+6
          move.w    grhandle,contrl+12
          move.w    #1,intin
          jsr       vdi
          rts



***********************************************************************
* Rotation of a number of points (nummark) in array datx etc. around*
* angle yangle around Y-axis to array pointx = address of array      *
***********************************************************************


yrot:  move.w    yangle,d0      * rotate the definition line
       jsr       sincos         * of a rotation body nummark
       move.w    d1,siny        * times about the Y-axis
       move.w    d2,cosy        * Rotation is done without
       move.l    datx,a1        * matrix multiplication,
       move.l    daty,a2        * but directly, from arrays datx
       move.l    datz,a3        * in which the address of the definition
       move.l    pointx,a4      * line was stored into the array
```

```
            move.l      pointy,a5     * whose address is stored
            move.l      pointz,a6     * in pointx etc.
            move.w      nummark,d0
            ext.l       d0            * the rotation is about
            subq.l      #1,d0         * angle -y, i.e. from direction
ylop:       move.w      (a1)+,d1      * positive Y-axis
            move.w      d1,d3         * counterclockwise
            move.w      (a3)+,d2
            move.w      d2,d4         * z' = x*siny + z*cosy
            muls        cosy,d2
            lsl.l       #2, d2        * retract area extension
            swap        d2            * sine values
            muls        siny,d1
            lsl.l       #2,d1
            swap        d1
            add.w       d1,d2
            move.w      d2,(a6)+      * store z'
            muls        siny,d4       * calculate x'
            lsl.l       #2,d4         * x' = x*cosy - z*siny
            swap        d4
            neg.w       d4
            muls        cosy,d3
            lsl.l       #2,d3
            swap        d3
            add.w       d3,d4

            move.w      d4,(a4)+      * store x'
            move.w      (a2)+,(a5)+   * y' = y, since rotation is
            dbra        d0,ylop       * around Y-axis
            rts


***********************************************************************
* Variables for the basic program                                    *
***********************************************************************

            .even
            .data       * Sine table starts here

sintab: .dc.w           0,286,572,857,1143,1428,1713,1997,2280
        .dc.w           2563,2845,3126,3406,3686,3964,4240,4516
        .dc.w           4790,5063,5334,5604,5872,6138,6402,6664
```

```
.dc.w    6924,7182,7438,7692,7943,8192,8438,8682
.dc.w    8923,9162,9397,9630,9860,10087,10311,10531
.dc.w    10749,10963,11174,11381,11585,11786,11982,12176
.dc.w    12365,12551,12733,12911,13085,13255,13421,13583
.dc.w    13741,13894,14044,14189,14330,14466,14598,14726
.dc.w    14849,14962,15082,15191,15296,15396,15491,15582
.dc.w    15668,15749,15826,15897,15964,16026,16083,16135
.dc.w    16182,16225,16262,16294,16322,16344,16362,16374
.dc.w    16382,16384

.dc.w    16382,16374,16362,16344,16322,16294,16262,16225
.dc.w    16182
.dc.w    16135,16083,16026,15964,15897,15826,15749,15668
.dc.w    15582,15491,15396,15296,15191,15082,14962,14849
.dc.w    14726,14598,14466,14330,14189,14044,13894,13741
.dc.w    13583,13421,13255,13085,12911,12733,12551,12365
.dc.w    12176,11982,11786,11585,11381,11174,10963,10749
.dc.w    10531,10311,10087,9860,9630,9397,9162,8923
.dc.w    8682,8438,8192,7943,7692,7438,7182,6924
.dc.w    6664,6402,6138,5872,5604,5334,5063,4790
.dc.w    4516,4240,3964,3686,3406,3126,2845,2563
.dc.w    2280,1997,1713,1428,1143,857,572,286,0

.dc.w    -286,-572,-857,-1143,-1428,-1713,-1997,-2280
.dc.w    -2563,-2845,-3126,-3406,-3686,-3964,-4240,-4516
.dc.w    -4790,-5063,-5334,-5604,-5872,-6138,-6402,-6664
.dc.w    -6924,-7182,-7438,-7692,-7943,-8192,-8438,-8682
.dc.w    -8923,-9162,-9397,-9630,-9860,-10087,-10311,-10531
.dc.w    -10749,-10963,-11174,-11381,-11585,-11786,-11982
.dc.w    -12176
.dc.w    -12365,-12551,-12733,-12911,-13085,-13255,-13421
.dc.w    -13583
.dc.w    -13741,-13894,-14044,-14189,-14330,-14466,-14598
.dc.w    -14726
.dc.w    -14849,-14962,-15082,-15191,-15296,-15396,-15491
.dc.w    -15582
.dc.w    -15668,-15749,-15826,-15897,-15964,-16026,-16083
.dc.w    -16135
.dc.w    -16182,-16225,-16262,-16294,-16322,-16344,-16362
.dc.w    -16374,-16382,-16384
```

```
        .dc.w    -16382,-16374,-16362,-16344,-16322,-16294,-16262
        .dc.w    -16225,-16182
        .dc.w    -16135,-16083,-16026,-15964,-15897,-15826,-15749
        .dc.w    -15668
        .dc.w    -15582,-15491,-15396,-15296,-15191,-15082,-14962
        .dc.w    -14849
        .dc.w    -14726,-14598,-14466,-14330,-14189,-14044,-13894
        .dc.w    -13741
        .dc.w    -13583,-13421,-13255,-13085,-12911,-12733,-12551
        .dc.w    -12365
        .dc.w    -12176,-11982,-11786,-11585,-11381,-11174,-10963
        .dc.w    -10749
        .dc.w    -10531,-10311,-10087,-9860,-9630,-9397,-9162,-8923
        .dc.w    -8682,-8438,-8192,-7943,-7692,-7438,-7182,-6924
        .dc.w    -6664,-6402,-6138,-5872,-5604,-5334,-5063,-4790
        .dc.w    -4516,-4240,-3964,-3686,-3406,-3126,-2845,-2563
        .dc.w    -2280,-1997,-1713,-1428,-1143,-857,-572,-286,0


        .even
        .bss

x0:     .ds.w    1        * Position of the coordinate origin on
y0:     .ds.w    1        * the screen
z0:     .ds.w    1
z1:     .ds.w    1

linxy   .ds.l    1        * This is the address of the line array

nummark: .ds.w   1         * Number of points
numline: .ds.w   1         * Number of lines

pointx: .ds.l    1        * Variables of point arrays for world,
pointy: .ds.l    1        * view, and screen coordinates
pointz: .ds.l    1

xplot   .ds.l    1
yplot   .ds.l    1

datx:   .ds.l    1
daty:   .ds.l    1
datz:   .ds.l    1
```

```
sinx:      .ds.w    1        * Temporary storage for sine and
sinz:      .ds.w    1        * cosine values
siny:      .ds.w    1

cosx:      .ds.w    1
cosz:      .ds.w    1
cosy:      .ds.w    1

var1:      .ds.w    1        * general variables
var2:      .ds.w    1
var3:      .ds.w    1

xangle:    .ds.w    1        * Variables for passing angles
yangle:    .ds.w    1        * to the rotation subroutine
zangle:    .ds.w    1

physbase:  .ds.l    1        * Address of first screen page
logbase:   .ds.l    1        * Address of second screen page


contrl:                      * Arrays for AES and VDI functions
opcode:    .ds.w    1        * for passing parameters
sintin:    .ds.w    1
sintout:   .ds.w    1
saddrin:   .ds.w    1
saddrout:  .ds.w    1
           .ds.w    6

global:
apversion: .ds.w    1
apcount:   .ds.w    1
apid:      .ds.w    1
apprivate: .ds.l    1
apptree:   .ds.l    1
ap1resv:   .ds.l    1
ap2resv:   .ds.l    1
ap3resv:   .ds.l    1
ap4resv:   .ds.l    1

intin:     .ds.w    128
ptsin:     .ds.w    256
intout:    .ds.w    128
```

```
ptsout:      .ds.w    128
addrin:      .ds.w    128
addrout:     .ds.w    128
grhandle:    .ds.w    1

lineavar:    .ds.l    1            * Starting address of Line-A var

             .data
vdipb:       .dc.l    contrl,intin,ptsin,intout,ptsout
aespb:       .dc.l    contrl,global,intin,intout,addrin,addrout

leftx:       .dc.w    0
lefty:       .dc.w    0
rightx:      .dc.w    0
righty:      .dc.w    0

p1code:      .dc.w    0
p2code:      .dc.w    0
code1:       .dc.w    0
code2:       .dc.w    0
mid_code:    .dc.w    0

clipxule:    .dc.w    0            * Clip window variables
clipyule:    .dc.w    0
clipxlri:    .dc.w    639
clipylri:    .dc.w    399

dist:        .dc.w    0
zobs:        .dc.w    1500

rotx11:      .dc.w    16384        * Space here for the result matrix of
rotx12:      .dc.w    0            * matrix multiplication
rotx13:      .dc.w    0
rotx21:      .dc.w    0
rotx22:      .dc.w    16384
rotx23:      .dc.w    0
rotx31:      .dc.w    0
rotx32:      .dc.w    0
rotx33:      .dc.w    16384

             .bss
```

```
matrix11:   .ds.w    1       * Space here for the general
matrix12:   .ds.w    1       * rotation matrix
matrix13:   .ds.w    1
matrix21:   .ds.w    1
matrix22:   .ds.w    1
matrix23:   .ds.w    1
matrix31:   .ds.w    1
matrix32:   .ds.w    1
matrix33:   .ds.w    1

            .end
```

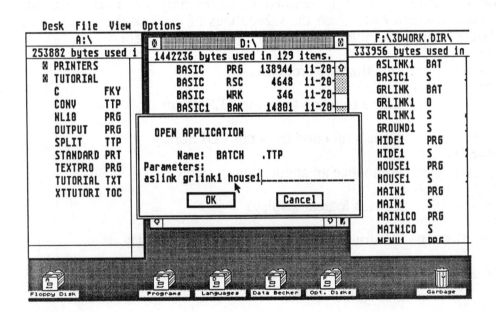

4.1.1   Explanation of the subroutines used

`grlink1.s`

The transfer of addresses of all data, coordinates, number of corners and lines is not made directly, but through global variables. This increases flexibility and makes it possible to use just one rotation routine. For example, the perspective transformation routine (pers) transforms the data whose beginning addresses are passed in the variables `pointx`, `pointy`, `pointz` and the number of which is passed in the variable `nummark`, in an array, whose starting address is also passed (`xplot,yplot`). Because of this it does not matter where data is stored in memory and the amount is irrelevant. For example, the transformation can be carried out for all defined points or only for a few. The brief overview which follows on the subroutines of the link file `grlink1.s` should be supplemented with the comments in the program.

`sstart:`   Initialize the program.

`aes:`   Call a function from the AES library.

`vdi:`   Calls a function from the VDI library.

`apinit:`   Announce an application.

`openwork:`   Open a logical display.

`grafhand:`   Returns the number of this logical display.

`mouse_on:`   Enables the mouse and its controller through the operating system.

`mouse_off:` Switches off mouse and controller.

`sincos:`   Returns the sine (D1) and cosine value (D2) of an angle (-360,+360) passed in D0.

`start1:`   Asks for the display address of the system and recognizes what screen resolution is being used; this serves to determine the two screen pages.

clwork: VDI-Function, clears the current logical display.

plotpt: Plots a point, X-coordinate in D2, Y-coordinate in D3.

drawl: Draws a line from X1, Y1 to X2, Y2 taking the Clip window specified by the variables clipule, cliplre into account using the line-A routine.

rel_pos: Recognizes the area in which the point passed in D6 (X-coord.) and D7 (Y-coord.) lies relative to the clip window. The result is returned in D1 (4-bit code).

end point: Finds, if present, an intersection point of the line with the border of the clip window.

matinit: Initializes the main diagonal of the rotation matrix (matrix11-matrix33) with 16384 which corresponds to a sine value of one.

xrotate: Multiplies the rotation matrix by the matrix for one rotation about the X-axis.

yrotate: Multiplies matrix with the matrix for rotation about the Y-axis.

zrotate: Same for Z-axis.

rotate: This is the general rotation routine. Here every point from the point array (passed in pointx etc.) is rotated around the angles xw, yw, zw, and then is moved to point [xoffs, yoffs, zoffs] after a preliminary displacement of the coordinate origin to point [offx, offy, offz],

pers: Calculates the perspective screen coordinates and stores them at addresses passed in xplot, yplot.

symbol: Connects the points in the screen coordinate array with lines. The address of the line array is in linxy, and the number of lines in numlin.

pagedown: Turns on the logical screen page. After the call drawing is done on the other page.

page up: Turns on the physical (higher) display page. Subsequent drawing is done on the logical page (toggle).

wait1:   A timer loop which only counts the D0-register down to -1.

wait: Waits for a key press and then returns.

inkey: Senses the keyboard without waiting. The ASCII and key codes are returned in register D0.

printf: Writes a string on the display which must be terminated with a zero. The address is passed in A0.

yrot: This routine, and the five following routines are not used by the first main program. It rotates a number of points around the Y-axis directly and without use of matrix multiplication.

filstyle: The VDI function sets the fill style which is passed in D0 (0=no fill, 1=fill with color, 2=fill with dots, 3=shade, 4=user-defined fill pattern).

filindex: Sets the various fill patterns according to style

filcolor: Determines the fill color (for monochrome display only black or white, 1=black).

filmode: Sets the write mode, 1 = replace.

filform: Subsequent filled surfaces will be surrounded with a border after calling this routine.

```
************************************************************************
*  house1.s        14.1.1986                                          *
*  Display a wire-model house Uwe Braun 1985  Version 1.1             *
*                                                                      *
************************************************************************

            .globl    main,xoffs,yoffs,zoffs,offx,offy,offz
            .globl    viewx,viewy,viewz
            .globl    wlinxy,setrotdp,inp_chan,pointrot
            .text


main:
            jsr       apinit        * Announce program
            jsr       grafhand      * Get screen handler
            jsr       openwork      * Announce screen
            jsr       mouse_off     * Turn off mouse
            jsr       getreso       * which monitor is connected ?
            jsr       setcocli      * Set clip window

            jsr       makewrld      * Create the world system
            jsr       worldset      * Pass the world parameters

            jsr       setrotdp      * initialize obs. ref. point
            jsr       clwork        * erase both screen pages
            jsr       pagedown      * Display logical screen page
            jsr       clwork
            jsr       inp_chan      * Input and change parameters

mainlop1:
            jsr       pointrot      * rotate around obs. ref. point
            jsr       pers          * perspective transformation
            jsr       drawn1        * Draw lines in linxy array
            jsr       pageup        * Display physical screen page

            jsr       inp_chan      * Input new parameters
            jsr       clwork        * erase logical screen page
            jsr       pointrot      * Rotate around Rot. ref. point
            jsr       pers          * Transform. of new points
            jsr       drawn1        * draw in logical page, then
            jsr       pagedown      * display this logical page
            jsr       inp_chan      * Input and change parameters
```

```
            jsr      clwork        * erase physical page
            jmp      mainlop1      * to main loop

mainend:    move.l   physbase,logbase

            jsr      pageup        * switch to normal display page
            rts                    * back to linkfile, and end


***********************************************************************
* Remove all accumulated characters in the keyboard buffer          *
***********************************************************************

clearbuf:   move.w   #$b,-(a7)     * Gemdos funct. Character in buffer?
            trap     #1
            addq.l   #2,a7
            tst.w    d0            * If yes, get character
            beq      clearend      * If no, terminate
            move.w   #1,-(a7)      * Gemdos funct.CONIN
            trap     #1            * repeat until all characters are
            addq.l   #2,a7         * removed from the buffer
            bra      clearbuf

clearend:   rts


***********************************************************************
* Change observation parameters with keyboard sensing              *
* Angle increments, location of the projection plane, etc.         *
***********************************************************************

inp_chan:   jsr      inkey         * Read keyboard, code in D0
            cmp.b    #'D',d0       * shift D = print
            bne      inpwait
            jsr      scrdmp        * make hardcopy

inpwait:    swap     d0            * test D0, if
            cmp.b    #$4d,d0       * Cursor-right
            bne      inp1
            addq.w   #1,ywplus     * if yes, add one to Y-angle
            bra      inpend1       * increment and continue

inp1:       cmp.b    #$4b,d0       * Cursor-left, if yes, then
            bne      inp2          * subtract one from Y-angle
```

```
           subq.w      #1,ywplus      * increment
           bra         inpend1

inp2:      cmp.b       #$50,d0        * Cursor-down, if yes
           bne         inp3
           addq.w      #1,xwplus      * then add one to X-angle increment
           bra         inpend1

inp3:      cmp.b       #$48,d0        * Cursor-up
           bne         inp3a
           subq.w      #1,xwplus      * subtract one
           bra         inpend1

inp3a:     cmp.b       #$61,d0        * Undo key
           bne         inp3b
           subq.w      #1,zwplus
           bra         inpend1

inp3b:     cmp.b       #$62,d0        * Help key
           bne         inp4
           addq.w      #1,zwplus
           bra         inpend1

inp4:      cmp.b       #$4e,d0        * plus key on numerical keypad
           bne         inp5           * if yes, subtract 25 from location
           sub.w       #25,dist       * Projection plane (Z-coordinate)
           bra         inpend1
inp5:      cmp.b       #$4a,d0        * minus key on the numerical keypad
           bne         inp6           *
           add.w       #25,dist       * if yes, add 25
           bra         inpend1

inp6:      cmp.b       #$66,d0        * astersisk key on numerical keypad
           bne         inp7           * if yes, subtract 15 from rotation
           sub.w       #15,rotdpz     * point Z-coordinate
           bra         inpend1        * Make changes

inp7:      cmp.b       #$65,d0        * Division key on num.keypad
           bne         inp10
           add.w       #15,rotdpz     * add 15
           bra         inpend1
```

```
inp10:     cmp.b      #$44,d0        * F10 activated ?
           bne        inpend1
           addq.l     #4,a7          * if yes, jump to
           bra        mainend        * program end


inpend1:   move.w     hyangle,d1     * Rotation angle about Y-axis
           add.w      ywplus,d1      * add increment
           cmp.w      #360,d1        * if larger than 360, then
           bge        inpend2        * subtract 360
           cmp.w      #-360,d1       * is smaller than 360, then
           ble        inpend3        * add 360
           bra        inpend4
inpend2:   sub.w      #360,d1
           bra        inpend4
inpend3:   add.w      #360,d1


inpend4:   move.w     d1,hyangle


           move.w     hxangle,d1     * proceed in the same manner
           add.w      xwplus,d1      * with the rotation angle about
           cmp.w      #360,d1        * the X-axis
           bge        inpend5
           cmp.w      #-360,d1
           ble        inpend6
           bra        inpend7
inpend5:   sub.w      #360,d1
           bra        inpend7
inpend6:   add.w      #360,d1


inpend7:   move.w     d1,hxangle     * store angle


           move.w     hzangle,d1
           add.w      zwplus,d1
           cmp.w      #360,d1
           bge        inpend8
           cmp.w      #-360,d1
           ble        inpend9
           bra        inpend10
inpend8:   sub.w      #360,d1
           bra        inpend10
inpend9:   add.w      #360,d1
```

```
inpend10: move.w     d1,hzangle
          rts



*******************************************************************
* Initialize the rotation reference point to [0,0,0]          *
*******************************************************************

setrotdp: move.w     #0,d1            * set the start-rotation-
          move.w     d1,rotdpx        * datum-point
          move.w     d1,rotdpy
          move.w     d1,rotdpz
          move.w     #0,hyangle       * Start-rotation angle
          move.w     #0,hzangle
          move.w     #0,hxangle
          rts



*******************************************************************
* Rotation around one point, the rotation reference point      *
*******************************************************************

pointrot: move.w     hxangle,xangle * rotate the world around the angle
          move.w     hyangle,yangle * hxangle, hyangle, hzangle about the
          move.w     hzangle,zangle
          move.w     rotdpx,d0        * rotation reference point
          move.w     rotdpy,d1
          move.w     rotdpz,d2
          move.w     d0,xoffs         * add for back transformation.
          move.w     d1,yoffs
          move.w     d2,zoffs
          neg.w      d0
          neg.w      d1
          neg.w      d2
          move.w     d0,offx          * subtract for transformation.
          move.w     d1,offy
          move.w     d2,offz
          jsr        matinit          * Matrix initialization
          jsr        zrotate          * first rotate around Z-axis
          jsr        yrotate          * rotate 'matrix' around Y-axis
          jsr        xrotate          * then rotate around X-axis
          jsr        rotate           * Multiply points with the matrix.
          rts
```

```
********************************************************************
* Creation of the world system from the object data              *
********************************************************************


makewrld: move.l    #housdatx,a1 * create the world system by
          move.l    #housdaty,a2
          move.l    #housdatz,a3
          move.l    #worldx,a4
          move.l    #worldy,a5
          move.l    #worldz,a6
          move.w    hnummark,d0
          ext.l     d0
          subq.l    #1,d0
makewl1:  move.w    (a1)+,(a4)+  * copying the house data into the
          move.w    (a2)+,(a5)+  * world data
          move.w    (a3)+,(a6)+
          dbra      d0,makewl1
          move.w    hnumline,d0
          ext.l     d0
          subq.l    #1,d0
          move.l    #houslin,a1
          move.l    #wlinxy,a2
makewl2:  move.l    (a1)+,(a2)+
          dbra      d0,makewl2
          rts


********************************************************************
* Pass the world parameters to the link file variables           *
********************************************************************


worldset: move.l    #worldx,datx * Pass variables for
          move.l    #worldy,daty * the rotation routine
          move.l    #worldz,datz
          move.l    #viewx,pointx
          move.l    #viewy,pointy
          move.l    #viewz,pointz
          move.l    #wlinxy,linxy
          move.w    picturex,x0
          move.w    picturey,y0
          move.w    proz,zobs
          move.w    r1z1,dist
          move.l    #screenx,xplot
```

160

```
           move.l      #screeny,yplot
           move.w      hnumline,numline
           move.w      hnummark,nummark
           rts


*********************************************************************
* sense current display resolution and set coordinate origin of the *
* screen system to the center of the screen                         *
*********************************************************************

getreso:   move.w      #4,-(a7)
           trap        #14
           addq.l      #2,a7
           cmp.w       #2,d0
           bne         getr1
           move.w      #320,picturex      * for monochrome monitor
           move.w      #200,picturey
           bra         getrend
getr1:     cmp.w       #1,d0
           bne         getr2
           move.w      #320,picturex      * medium resolution (640*200)
           move.w      #100,picturey
           bra         getrend
getr2:     move.w      #160,picturex      * low resolultion (320*200)
           move.w      #100,picturey
getrend:   rts



*********************************************************************
* Hardcopy of the display after activating Shift d on keyboard      *
*********************************************************************

scrdmp:    move.w      #20,-(a7)
           trap        #14
           addq.l      #2,a7
           jsr         clearbuf      * prevent another hardcopy
           rts
```

```
*********************************************************************
* Sets the limit of the display window for the draw-line algorithm *
* built into the Cohen-Sutherland clip algorithm                   *
* The limits are freely selectable by the user, making the draw-   *
* line algorithm very flexible.                                    *
*********************************************************************

setcocli: move.w    #0,clipxule   * Clip    left  X-Coord.
          move.w    #0,clipyule   *  "            Y-Coord
          move.w    picturex,d1
          lsl.w     #1,d1         * times two
          subq.w    #1,d1         * minus one equal
          move.w    d1,clipxlri   * 639 for monochrom
          move.w    picturey,d1
          lsl.w     #1,d1         * times two minus one equal
          subq.w    #1,d1         * 399 for monochrom
          move.w    d1,clipylri   * Clip    right  Y-Coord
          rts

          .even



*********************************************************************
* Here begins the variable area for the program module             *
*                                                                  *
*********************************************************************
*********************************************************************


*********************************************************************
*                                                                  *
*          Definition of the house                                 *
*                                                                  *
*********************************************************************


          .data

housdatx: .dc.w     -30,30,30,-30,30,-30,-30,30,0,0,-10,-10,10,10
          .dc.w     30,30,30,30,30,30,30,30,30,30,30,30

housdaty: .dc.w     30,30,-30,-30,30,30,-30,-30,70,70,-30,0,0,-30
          .dc.w     20,20,0,0,20,20,0,0
          .dc.w     -10,-10,-30,-30
```

```
housdatz:  .dc.w    60,60,60,60,-60,-60,-60,-60,60,-60,60,60,60,60
           .dc.w    40,10,10,40,-10,-40,-40,-10
           .dc.w    0,-20,-20,0

houslin:   .dc.w    1,2,2,3,3,4,4,1,2,5,5,8,8,3,8,7,7,6,6,5,6,1,7,4
           .dc.w    9,10,1,9,9,2,5,10,6,10,11,12,12,13,13,14
           .dc.w    15,16,16,17,17,18,18,15,19,20,20,21,21,22,22,19
           .dc.w    23,24,24,25,25,26,26,23

hnummark:  .dc.w    26       * Number of corner points of the house
hnumline:  .dc.w    32       * Number of lines of the house

hxangle:   .dc.w    0        * Rotation angle of the house around X-axis
hyangle:   .dc.w    0        *          "          "        " Y-axis
hzangle:   .dc.w    0        *          "          "        " Z-axis

xwplus:    .dc.w    0        * Angle increment around the X-axis
ywplus:    .dc.w    0        * Angle increment around the Y-axis
zwplus:    .dc.w    0        * Angle increment around the Z-axis

picturex:  .dc.w    320      * Definition of zero point of display
picturey:  .dc.w    200      * here it is in the display center
rotdpx:    .dc.w    0        * Rotation datum point
rotdpy:    .dc.w    0
rotdpz:    .dc.w    0


r1z1:      .dc.w    0
normz:     .dc.w    1500



           .bss

plusrot:   .ds.l    1
first:     .ds.l    1
second:    .ds.w    1
delta1:    .ds.w    1

           .data
```

```
flag:       .dc.b     1
            .even

            .bss

diffz:      .ds.w     1

dx:         .ds.w     1
dy:         .ds.w     1
dz:         .ds.w     1

worldx:     .ds.w     1600      * World coordinate array
worldy:     .ds.w     1600
worldz:     .ds.w     1600

viewx:      .ds.w     1600      * View coordinate array
viewy:      .ds.w     1600
viewz:      .ds.w     1600

screenx:    .ds.w     1600      * Display coordinate array
screeny:    .ds.w     1600

wlinxy:     .ds.l     3200      * Line array

            .data

prox:       .dc.w     0         * Coordinates of the Projection-
proy:       .dc.w     0         * center, on the positive
proz:       .dc.w     1500      * Z-axis

            .data

offx:       .dc.w     0         * Transformation during Rotation
offy:       .dc.w     0         * to point [offx,offy,offz]
offz:       .dc.w     0
xoffs:      .dc.w     0         * Back transformation to Point
yoffs:      .dc.w     0         * [xoff,yoffs,zoffs]
zoffs:      .dc.w     0
            .bss
loopc:      .ds.l     1
            .end
```

4.1.2   Description of the Subroutines of the first Main program:

main:
: This is the entry point to the program module. The program announces itself and initializes the AES and VDI functions and senses the current screen resolution. The window size and the screen are determined from the resolution. The program section between the labels mainop1: and mainend: is the main loop, which is repeated until the F10 key is pressed.

makewrld:
: Creates a world in the world coordinate system by simple copying of the house data into the world system. These are the coordinates of the house (housdatx, housdaty, housdatz) in the world coordinate system (wrldx, wrldy, wrldz), the lines of the house in houslin in the world line storage area (wlinxy), the number of corner points the house (hnummark) in the total-number variable of the world system (nummark) and finally the number of house lines (hnumline) in numline. This subroutine need only be called once unless you want to add objects to the world system which we will do in a later program.

wrldset:
: After creating the world system the array addresses (wrldx etc.) must be passed to the global variables of the rotation subroutine (datx etc.). Furthermore the coordinate origin of the display is determined in the Variables X0 and Y0, and the presets for the perspective parameters (zobs, dist).

setrotdp:
: Initializes the rotation reference point to [0,0,0] and the rotation angles to 0 degrees.

`pointrot:`   This subroutines provides the rotation routine with the current data and then performs the rotation around the point [`rotdpx`, `rotdp`, `rotdpz`] of all three axes with a call to the proper routines of the link file. in the sequence Z-axis, Y-axis, X-axis. A change in the sequence also changes the results.

`inp_chan:`   Input and change the parameters, rotation angle, rotation reference point and position of the projection plane.

`getreso:`   Checks the current display resolution and from this determines the data for the screen center and the clip window, which in this case is the whole visible display.

`scrdmp:`   Hardcopy routine, is called form `inp_chan` by pressing shift 'D' and replaces the key combination Alternate/Help, which the operating system uses to make a hardcopy of the screen. Since in this program the displayed page is never the same as the page in which the drawing occurs, a hardcopy through Alternate/Help would not correspond to the displayed picture ·but would print the picture under construction or the just-erased display. The trick is to call the `scrdmp` routine before the displayed page is erased.

`setcocli:`   Set the clip-window for the Cohen-Sutherland clip algorithm on the whole display, 0,0 to 639,399 hi-res, 639,199 med-res, or 319,199 lo-res.

`clearbuf:`   Remove characters that may be in the keyboard buffer. Is used only by the hardcopy routine, since several hardcopies could otherwise be made in succession (Key repeat).

4.1.3   General comments on the program

The specific explanations of the variables can be found in the remarks in the program listing. In each iteration of the main loop the program adds an angle increment (xwplus, ywplus, zwplus) to the rotation angle (hxangle, hyangle, hzangle) of the house. The input routine changes the angle increments which causes the house to rotate faster on the screen, though this is really an optical illusion. The end points of the house have to travel a longer distance between each drawing operation, which causes this effect. The cursor keys, the <Help> and <Undo> keys control the rotation, the '+' and '-'keys change the display size by moving the projection plane, and the '/' and '*' keys move the rotation reference point on the Z-axis. Pressing of the shift and 'D' keys at the same time produces hardcopy if a printer is attached.

The best thing to do is to try out the various changes possible, preferably by changing the constants in the listing. You can, for example move the rotation reference point on the X and Y axis, or the variable proz, which changes the position of the projection center. The closer you move the projection center in the direction of the house, the greater the perspective distortion. You should also define an object yourself, and you should start with a simple object, like a pyramid. You only have to enter the points of the pyramid (in a pyramid with a quadratic base there are five) in place of the house coordinates in the arrays (housdatx etc.). Furthermore, the number of points (5) must be entered in houslin in hnummark, the number of lines (8) in hnumline and then the information regarding which points are connected by lines. You only have to change the storage area and you can represent any defined object with the same program.

Here I want to provide some additional information about the storage space required. The arrays (wrldx etc., viewx, screenx, wlinxy) are already dimensioned quite generously for future expansion. You can define objects with 1600 corners and connect these corners with 3200 lines. About 40 KByte of storage space is needed for this array dimensioning. Even though 1600 corners appear to be sufficient at first glance, we shall reach this number in the next chapter without too much effort. But first of all stop for a while and play around with this program. You can also add a window on the other side of the house by simply entering the new coordinates.

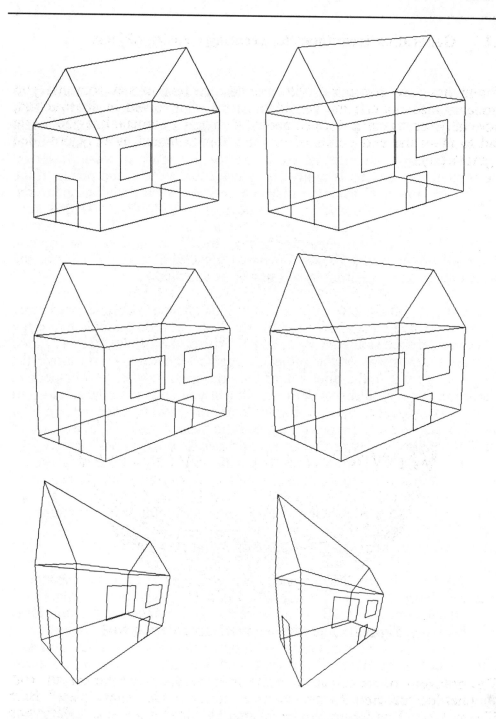

Figure 4.1.11: House with various projection centers

4.2   Generation techniques for creating rotating objects

If you have experimented with the construction of new objects, you probably also noticed the considerable effort involved in construction, especially for regularly-formed bodies with many corners. Imagine if you had to input the end points of the ball approximated by polygons (See figure 4.2.1).

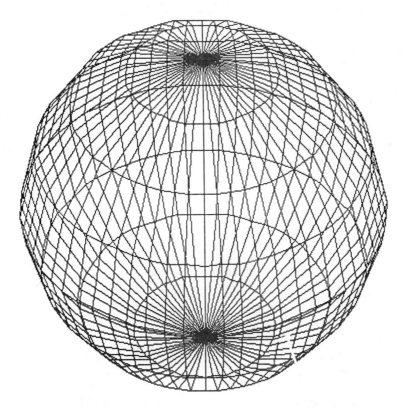

Figure 4.2.1: Hardcopy of the rotation ball

The drudgery of input can be performed by the computer for all axis-symmetrical objects. As an example, consider the "chess piece" from Figure 4.2.2. This figure can be created by rotating a line (the definition line) around any axis, in this case the Y-axis. The programmer must define the one line and indicate how many times it should be rotated. You can follow the construction of the figure easily on the following hardcopies. The rotation number must be a division of 360 for programming reasons or a portion of the figure will be missing. From two to four to three hundred sixty rotations are available. More than 180 just produces a heap of points on the display (the screen resolution is too low). Now the space requirement will become obvious. If you rotate the 12 points 360 times it results in 4,332 points not to mention the 8,291 lines created by the rotation. The number of points is calculated as follows: `nummark:=numpt*(rotations+1)`. The lines include the connecting lines of the points in the rotating definition line as well as the horizontal connecting lines of the points in the rotation line.

The routines for the creation of the rotation body are contained in the listing of the file `rotate1.s`. The rotation body is described by a line, i.e. a number of points (`r1numpt`), whose coordinates are in `r1xdat`, `r1ydat`, `r1zdat` and the number of rotations about the Y-axis which this line should perform. The different bodies are created by varying the number of rotations. The maximum number of rotations in our case is 120, which is predetermined by the dimensioning of the array to 1600 etc. and of course could be changed. The number of points of the rotation body is contained in the variable `r1numpt`. The link file remains the same as in the first program. You only have to assemble the first file and link it to the link file: `aslink grlink1 rotate1`.

```
 Desk  File  View  Options
┌────────────────┬──────────────────────────────┬────────────────────┐
│     A:\        │ ▨▒▒▒▒▒▒▒▒▒▒ D:\ ▒▒▒▒▒▒▒▒▒▒ ▨ │   F:\3DWORK.DIR\    │
│253882 bytes used i│1442236 bytes used in 129 items.│333956 bytes used in│
│▨ PRINTERS      │ BASIC    PRG  138944  11-26⇧ │ HOUSE1    PRG      │
│▨ TUTORIAL      │ BASIC    RSC    4648  11-26  │ HOUSE1    S        │
│  C        FKY  │ BASIC    WRK     346  11-26  │ MAIN1     PRG      │
│  CONV     TTP  │ BASIC1   BAK   14801  11-26  │ MAIN1     S        │
│  NL10     PRG  │                              │ MAIN1CO   PRG      │
│  OUTPUT   PRG  │ ┌──────────────────────────┐ │ MAIN1CO   S        │
│  SPLIT    TTP  │ │  OPEN APPLICATION        │ │ MENU1     PRG      │
│  STANDARD PRT  │ │                          │ │ MENU1     S        │
│  TEXTPRO  PRG  │ │    Name:  BATCH   .TTP   │ │ MULTI1    PRG      │
│  TUTORIAL TXT  │ │  Parameters:             │ │ MULTI1    S        │
│  XTTUTORI TOC  │ │  aslink grlink1 rotate1__ │ │ PAINT1    PRG      │
│                │ │                          │ │ PAINT1    S        │
│                │ │    ┌────┐      ┌──────┐  │ │ ROTATE1   PRG      │
│                │ │    │ OK │      │Cancel│  │ │ ROTATE1   S        │
│                │ │    └────┘   ▶  └──────┘  │ │                   │
│                │ └──────────────────────────┘ │                   │
```

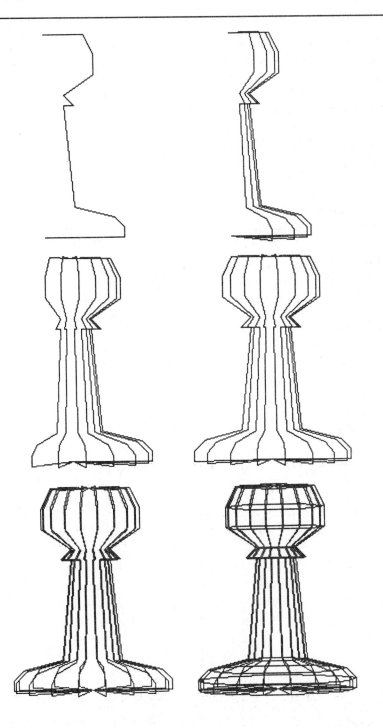

Figure 4.2.2: Hardcopy of the rotation body construction

```
*****************************************************************
*  rotate1.s          16.1.1986                                 *
*  Creation of rotation bodies Uwe Braun 1985  Version 2.0      *
*                                                               *
*****************************************************************
        .text
        .globl    main,xoffs,yoffs,zoffs,offx,offy,offz
        .globl    viewx,viewy,viewz
        .globl    wlinxy,mouse_off,setrotdp,inp_chan,pointrot

main:
        jsr       apinit        * Announce program
        jsr       grafhand      * Get screen handle
        jsr       openwork      * Display
        jsr       mouse_off     * Turn off mouse
        jsr       getreso       * Which monitor is connected ?
        jsr       setcocli      * Set clip window

        jsr       makerot1

        jsr       makewrld      * Create world system
        jsr       wrld2set      * Pass world parameters

        jsr       setrotdp      * initialize observation ref. point
        jsr       clwork
        jsr       pagedown      * Display logical screen page
        jsr       clwork
        jsr       inp_chan      * Input and change parameters

mainlop1:
        jsr       pointrot      * rotate around observation ref. point
        jsr       pers          * Perspective transformation
        jsr       drawn1
        jsr       pageup        * Display physical page
        jsr       inp_chan      * Input new parameters
        jsr       clwork        * Erase logical page
        jsr       pointrot      * Rotate around rotation ref. point
        jsr       pers          * Transform, new points
        jsr       drawn1

        jsr       pagedown      * Display this logical page
        jsr       inp_chan      * Input and change
```

```
          jsr       clwork        * clear physical page
          jmp       mainlop1      * to main loop

mainend:  move.l    physbase,logbase

          jsr       pageup        * switch to normal display page
          rts                     * back to link file, and end




**********************************************************
* remove all characters from the keyboard buffer        *
**********************************************************

clearbuf: move.w    #$b,-(a7)     * Gemdos funct. char in buffer?
          trap      #1
          addq.l    #2,a7
          tst.w     d0            * if yes, get character
          beq       clearend      * if no, terminate
          move.w    #1,-(a7)      * Gemdos funct. CONIN
          trap      #1            * repeat until all characters
          addq.l    #2,a7         * are removed from the buffer
          bra       clearbuf

clearend: rts




**********************************************************
*   Create the rotation body r1                         *
**********************************************************

makerot1: jsr       r1set         * Create the rotation body
          jsr       rotstart      * first the coordinates,
          jsr       rotlin        * then the lines
          rts
```

```
*********************************************************************
*    Input and change observation parameters                      *
*    the angles hxangle,hyangle,hzangle, are rotation angles of    *
*    world system                                                  *
*********************************************************************

inp_chan: jsr        inkey        * Sense keyboard, code in
          cmp.b      #'D',d0
          bne        inpwait
          jsr        scrdmp       * make hardcopy

inpwait:  swap       d0           * test D0 if
          cmp.b      #$4d,d0      * Cursor-right
          bne        inp1
          addq.w     #1,ywplus    * if yes, add one to Y-angle increment
          bra        inpend1      * and continue

inp1:     cmp.b      #$4b,d0      * Cursor-left, if yes
          bne        inp2         * subtract one from Y-angle
          subq.w     #1,ywplus    * increment
          bra        inpend1

inp2:     cmp.b      #$50,d0      * Cursor-down, if yes
          bne        inp3
          addq.w     #1,xwplus    * add one to X-angle increment
          bra        inpend1

inp3:     cmp.b      #$48,d0      * Cursor-up
          bne        inp3a
          subq.w     #1,xwplus    * subtract one
          bra        inpend1

inp3a:    cmp.b      #$61,d0      * Undo-key
          bne        inp3b
          subq.w     #1,zwplus    * lower Z-increment
          bra        inpend1

inp3b:    cmp.b      #$62,d0      * Help-key
          bne        inp4
          addq.w     #1,zwplus    * add to Z-increment
          bra        inpend1
```

```
inp4:      cmp.b      #$4e,d0      * plus key on keypad
           bne        inp5         * if yes, subtract 25 from
           sub.w      #25,dist     * position of projection
           bra        inpend1      * plane (Z-coordinate)
inp5:      cmp.b      #$4a,d0      * minus key on keypad
           bne        inp6         *
           add.w      #25,dist     * if yes, add 25
           bra        inpend1

inp6:      cmp.b      #$66,d0      * times-key on the keypad
           bne        inp7         * if yes, then subtract 15
           sub.w      #15,rotdpz   * from the rotation ref. point Z-coord.
           bra        inpend1      * make changes

inp7:      cmp.b      #$65,d0      * division-key on keypad
           bne        inp10
           add.w      #15,rotdpz   * add 15
           bra        inpend1

inp10:     cmp.b      #$44,d0      * F10 activated ?
           bne        inpend1
           addq.l     #4,a7        * if yes, jump to
           bra        mainend      * Program end

inpend1:   move.w     hyangle,d1   * rotation angle, Y-axis
           add.w      ywplus,d1    * add increment
           cmp.w      #360,d1      * if larger than 360, then subtract 360
           bge        inpend2
           cmp.w      #-360,d1     * if smaller than 360,
           ble        inpend3      * add 360
           bra        inpend4
inpend2:   sub.w      #360,d1
           bra        inpend4
inpend3:   add.w      #360,d1

inpend4:   move.w     d1,hyangle

           move.w     hxangle,d1   * proceeed in the same
           add.w      xwplus,d1    * manner with rotation
           cmp.w      #360,d1      * angle, X-axis
           bge        inpend5
           cmp.w      #-360,d1
```

```
          ble         inpend6
          bra         inpend7
inpend5:  sub.w       #360,d1
          bra         inpend7
inpend6:  add.w       #360,d1
inpend7:  move.w      d1,hxangle     *
          move.w      hzangle,d1
          add.w       zwplus,d1
          cmp.w       #360,d1
          bge         inpend8
          cmp.w       #-360,d1
          ble         inpend9
          bra         inpend10
inpend8:  sub.w       #360,d1
          bra         inpend10
inpend9:  add.w       #360,d1

inpend10: move.w      d1,hzangle
          rts


***********************************************************************
* Initialize the rotation reference point to [0,0,0]                 *
***********************************************************************

setrotdp: move.w      #0,d1          * set the start-rotation
          move.w      d1,rotdpx      * reference point
          move.w      d1,rotdpy
          move.w      d1,rotdpz
          move.w      #0,hyangle     * Start rotation angle
          move.w      #0,hzangle
          move.w      #0,hxangle
          rts


***********************************************************************
* Rotation of the total world system around the rotation            *
* reference point                                                    *
***********************************************************************

pointrot: move.w      hxangle,xangle * rotate the world around
          move.w      hyangle,yangle
          move.w      hzangle,zangle
          move.w      rotdpx,d0      * the rotation reference point
```

```
          move.w    rotdpy,d1
          move.w    rotdpz,d2
          move.w    d0,xoffs      * add for inverse transformation
          move.w    d1,yoffs
          move.w    d2,zoffs
          neg.w     d0
          neg.w     d1
          neg.w     d2
          move.w    d0,offx       * subtract for transformation
          move.w    d1,offy
          move.w    d2,offz
          jsr       matinit       * matrix initialization
          jsr       zrotate       * rotate around Z-axis first
          jsr       yrotate       * rotate 'matrix' around Y-axis
          jsr       xrotate       * then rotate around X-axis
          jsr       rotate        * multiply points with the
          rts                     * matrix. The Z-axis is not taken into
*                                 * account
makewrld: move.l    #r1datx,a1    * create the world system
          move.l    #r1daty,a2    * by copying data of rotation body
          move.l    #r1datz,a3    * into world system
          move.l    #worldx,a4
          move.l    #worldy,a5
          move.l    #worldz,a6
          move.w    r1nummark,d0  * number of corners repeated
          ext.l     d0
          subq.l    #1,d0
makewl1:  move.w    (a1)+,(a4)+   * Copy coordinates
          move.w    (a2)+,(a5)+   * Y-coords.
          move.w    (a3)+,(a6)+   * Z-coords.
          dbra      d0,makewl1

          move.w    r1numline,d0  * Copy the line arrays
          ext.l     d0            * of the rotation body
          subq.l    #1,d0         * into the world system
          move.l    #r1lin,a1     * Number of lines as counter
          move.l    #wlinxy,a2
makewl2:  move.l    (a1)+,(a2)+   * copy lines
          dbra      d0,makewl2
          rts
```

```
***********************************************************************
*    Pass world parameters to variables of link files             *
***********************************************************************

worldset: move.l      #worldx,datx      * Passing house variables
          move.l      #worldy,daty      * for the rotation routine
          move.l      #worldz,datz      * and the global subroutine
          move.l      #viewx,pointx     * of the link module
          move.l      #viewy,pointy
          move.l      #viewz,pointz
          move.l      #wlinxy,linxy
          move.w      picturex,x0
          move.w      picturey,y0
          move.w      proz,temp         * Projection center Z-coordinate
          move.w      r1z1,dist         * Location of projection plane on
          move.l      #screenx,xplot    * the Z-axis
          move.l      #screeny,yplot
          move.w      hnumline,numline  * Number of house lines
          move.w      hnummark,nummark  * Number of house corners
          rts



***********************************************************************
*    Creation of rotation body in the array, the address of which  *
*    is passed in the variables rotdatx, rotdaty, rotdatz          *
***********************************************************************

r1set:
          move.l      #r1xdat,rotxdat   * Transmit
          move.l      #r1ydat,rotydat   * parameters of this
          move.l      #r1zdat,rotzdat   * rotation body to
          move.l      #r1datx,rotdatx   * the routine for
          move.l      #r1daty,rotdaty   * creation of the
          move.l      #r1datz,rotdatz   * rotation body
          move.l      rotdatx,datx
          move.l      rotdaty,daty
          move.l      rotdatz,datz
          move.w      r1numro,numro     * Number of desired
          move.w      r1numpt,numpt     * rotations. Number
          move.l      #r1lin,linxy      * of points in def.line.
          rts                           * Address of line array
```

```
rotstart:  move.w     numpt,d0          * Rotate def line
           lsl.w      #1,d0             * numro+1 about Y-axis
           ext.l      d0
           move.l     d0,plusrot
           move.w     numpt,nummark
           move.l     rotdatx,pointx    * Pass data array
           move.l     rotdaty,pointy    * to subroutine yrot
           move.l     rotdatz,pointz
           move.w     #0,yangle
           move.w     #360,d0           * 360 / numro = angle increment
           divs       numro,d0          * per rotation
           move.w     d0,plusagle
           move.w     numro,d0          * numro +1 times
           ext.l      d0

rloop1:    move.l     d0,loopc          * as loop counter
           move.l     rotxdat,datx      * for passing to yrot
           move.l     rotydat,daty
           move.l     rotzdat,datz
           jsr        yrot              * rotate
           move.l     pointx,d1         * add offset to
           add.l      plusrot,d1        * address
           move.l     d1,pointx
           move.l     pointy,d1
           add.l      plusrot,d1
           move.l     d1,pointy
           move.l     pointz,d1
           add.l      plusrot,d1
           move.l     d1,pointz
           move.w     yangle,d7         * Add angle increment
           add.w      plusagle,d7       * to rotation angle
           move.w     d7,yangle         * and rotate line
           move.l     loopc,d0          * again until all
           dbra       d0,rloop1         * end points are generated.

           move.w     r1numro,numro     * store for following
           move.w     r1numpt,numpt     * routines for line generation
           rts
```

```
rotlin:                                     * Create the line array of the
            move.w      #1,d7               * rotation body
            move.w      numro,d4            * Number of rotations repeated
            ext.l       d4
            subq.l      #1,d4
            move.w      numpt,d1
            subq.w      #1,d1
            lsl.w       #2,d1
            ext.l       d1
            move.l      d1,plusrot


rotlop1:    move.w      numpt,d5            * Number of points -
            ext.l       d5                  * repeat once
            subq.l      #2,d5
            move.l      linxy,a1            * Lines created stored
            move.w      d7,d6               * here
rotlop2:    move.w      d6,(a1)+            * The first line goes from
            addq.w      #1,d6               * point one to point two
            move.w      d6,(a1)+            * (1,2) then (2,3) etc.
            dbra        d5,rotlop2

            move.l      linxy,d1            * generate cross connections
            add.l       plusrot,d1          * of individual lines
            move.l      d1,linxy
            move.w      numpt,d0
            add.w       d0,d7
            dbra        d4,rotlop1

            move.w      numpt,d7
            move.w      d7,delta1
            lsl.w       #2,d7
            ext.l       d7
            move.l      d7,plusrot
            move.w      #1,d6
            move.w      numpt,d0
            ext.l       d0
            subq.l      #1,d0

rotlop3:    move.w      numro,d1
            ext.l       d1
            subq.l      #1,d1
            move.w      d6,d5
```

```
rotlop4:   move.w     d5,(a1)+
           add.w      delta1,d5
           move.w     d5,(a1)+
           dbra       d1,rotlop4

           add.w      #1,d6
           dbra       d0,rotlop3
           move.w     numro,d1
           add.w      #1,d1

           muls       nummark,d1

           move.w     d1,r1nummark    * Store total number of
           move.w     numpt,d1        * corners created
           muls       numro,d1
           move.w     numpt,d2
           subq.w     #1,d2
           muls       numro,d2
           add.w      d1,d2
           move.w     d2,r1numline    * Total of lines created
           rts


*********************************************************************
*  Pass parameters of the world system to variables                *
*  of the link file for the rotation body                          *
*********************************************************************

wrld2set: move.l     #worldx,datx    * Pass parameter of
          move.l     #worldy,daty    * rotation body to the
          move.l     #worldz,datz    * subroutines in the link
          move.l     #viewx,pointx   * module
          move.l     #viewy,pointy
          move.l     #viewz,pointz
          move.l     #wlinxy,linxy
          move.w     picturex,x0
          move.w     picturey,y0
          move.w     proz,temp
          move.w     r1z1,dist
          move.l     #screenx,xplot
          move.l     #screeny,yplot
```

```
            move.w    r1numline,numline * Number of lines
            move.w    r1nummark,nummark * Number of corners
            rts



************************************************************************
*   Sense current display resolution and set the coordinate          *
*   origin of the screen system to the screen center                 *
************************************************************************

getreso:    move.w    #4,-(a7)
            trap      #14
            addq.l    #2,a7
            cmp.w     #2,d0
            bne       getr1
            move.w    #320,picturex     * monochrome monitor
            move.w    #200,picturey
            bra       getrend
getr1:      cmp.w     #1,d0
            bne       getr2
            move.w    #320,picturex     * medium resolution (640*200)
            move.w    #100,picturey
            bra       getrend
getr2:      move.w    #160,picturex     * low resolution (320*200)
            move.w    #100,picturey
getrend:    rts




************************************************************************
*   Hardcopy after inp_chan call                                     *
************************************************************************

scrdmp:     move.w    #20,-(a7)
            trap      #14
            addq.l    #2,a7
            jsr       clearbuf
            rts
```

```
********************************************************************
* Set the limit of the window for the Cohen-Sutherland    *
* clip algorithm built into the draw-line algorithm       *
* The user can choose the limits freely, which makes the  *
* draw-line algorithm very flexible.                      *
********************************************************************

setcocli: move.w    #0,clipxule
          move.w    #0,clipyule
          move.w    picturex,d1
          lsl.w     #1,d1           * times two
          subq.w    #1,d1           * minus one equals
          move.w    d1,clipxlri     * 639 for monochrom
          move.w    picturey,d1
          lsl.w     #1,d1           * times two minus one
          subq.w    #1,d1           * equals 399 for monochrom
          move.w    d1,clipylri
          rts


          .even


********************************************************************
********************************************************************
*    Begin variable area for Program module                *
*                                                          *
********************************************************************


********************************************************************
* Data area for the rotation body                         *
********************************************************************
          .bss                    * Space for the variables

numro:    .ds.w    1
numpt:    .ds.w    1

worldfla: .ds.l    1

rotxdat:  .ds.l    1
rotydat:  .ds.l    1
rotzdat:  .ds.l    1
```

```
rotdatx:  .ds.l     1
rotdaty:  .ds.l     1
rotdatz:  .ds.l     1

r1numline: .ds.w    1
r1nummark: .ds.w    1
r1numfla:  .ds.w    1

plusagle: .ds.w     1

r1datx:   .ds.w    1540
r1daty:   .ds.w    1540
r1datz:   .ds.w    1540

r1lin:    .ds.l    3200          * for every line 4-Bytes

          .data


***********************************************************************
* These are the coordinates of the definition line which             *
* generates the rotation body through rotation about                 *
* the Y-axis. By changing coordinates the body to be                 *
* created can be changed. Of course, the number of points in         *
* r1numpt must be adapted to the new situation. By changing          *
* r1numro the current body can be changed as well.                   *
* Storage reserved here is enough for a maximum 120 rotations        *
* of 12 points. This means that for a user-defined                   *
* rotation line, the product of the number of points and            *
* number of desired rotations plus one, cannot be greater           *
* than 1500.                                                         *
***********************************************************************


r1xdat:   .dc.w 0,40,50,50,20,30,20,30,70,80,80,0

r1ydat:   .dc.w 100,100,80,60,40,30,30,-70,-80,-90,-100,-100

r1zdat:   .dc.w 0,0,0,0,0,0,0,0,0,0,0,0

r1numpt:  .dc.w     12
r1numro:  .dc.w     8      * Number of rotations for creation
```

```
*************************************************************************
*                                                                       *
*                                                                       *
*          Definition of the house                                      *
*                                                                       *
*************************************************************************


          .data

housdatx: .dc.w     -30,30,30,-30,30,-30,-30,30,0,0,-10,-10,10,10
          .dc.w     30,30,30,30,30,30,30,30,30,30,30,30

housdaty: .dc.w     30,30,-30,-30,30,30,-30,-30,70,70,-30,0,0,-30
          .dc.w     20,20,0,0,20,20,0,0
          .dc.w     -10,-10,-30,-30

housdatz: .dc.w     60,60,60,60,-60,-60,-60,-60,60,-60,60,60,60,60
          .dc.w     40,10,10,40,-10,-40,-40,-10
          .dc.w     0,-20,-20,0

houslin:  .dc.w     1,2,2,3,3,4,4,1,2,5,5,8,8,3,8,7,7,6,6,5,6,1,7,4
          .dc.w     9,10,1,9,9,2,5,10,6,10,11,12,12,13,13,14
          .dc.w     15,16,16,17,17,18,18,15,19,20,20,21,21,22,22,19
          .dc.w     23,24,24,25,25,26,26,23

hnummark: .dc.w     26       * Number of corners in the house
hnumline: .dc.w     32       * Number of lines in the house

hxangle:  .dc.w     0        * Rotation angle of house about X-axis
hyangle:  .dc.w     0        *          "         "        "    Y-axis
hzangle:  .dc.w     0        *          "         "        "    Z-axis

xwplus:   .dc.w     0        * Angle increment around X-axis
ywplus:   .dc.w     0        * Angle increment around Y-axis
zwplus:   .dc.w     0        * Angle increment around Z-axis

picturex: .dc.w     0 * Definition of zero point of the screen
picturey: .dc.w     0 * provided with values from subroutine getreso
```

```
rotdpx:    .dc.w      0
rotdpy:    .dc.w      0
rotdpz:    .dc.w      0


r1z1:      .dc.w      0
normz:     .dc.w      1500



           .bss

plusrot:   .ds.l      1
first:     .ds.w      1
second:    .ds.w      1
delta1:    .ds.w      1

           .data

flag:      .dc.b      1
           .even

           .bss

diffz:     .ds.w      1

dx:        .ds.w      1
dy:        .ds.w      1
dz:        .ds.w      1

worldx:    .ds.w      1600     * World coordinate array
worldy:    .ds.w      1600
worldz:    .ds.w      1600

viewx:     .ds.w      1600     * View coordinate array
viewy:     .ds.w      1600
viewz:     .ds.w      1600

screenx:   .ds.w      1600     * Screen coordinate array
screeny:   .ds.w      1600
```

```
wlinxy:    .ds.l      3200      * Line array
           .data
prox:      .dc.w      0         * Coordinates for projection-
proy:      .dc.w      0         * center here on the positive
proz:      .dc.w      1500      * Z-axis


           .data

offx:      .dc.w      0         * Transformation for rotation
offy:      .dc.w      0         * to point [offx,offy,offz]
offz:      .dc.w      0

xoffs:     .dc.w      0         * Inverse transformation for point
yoffs:     .dc.w      0         * [xoff,yoffs,zoffs]
zoffs:     .dc.w      0


           .bss

loopc:     .ds.l      1
           .end
```

4.2.1 New subroutines in this program:

r1set: Supplies the rotation body creation routine with the parameters of the specific rotation body, i.e. with the address of its definition line, with the number of the points forming this line and the desired number of rotations.

makerot1:   Creates the rotation body `rot1` in the array `r1datx`, `r1daty`, `r1datz`, and the lines (`r1lin`) and passes the total number of points and lines created.

rotstart: Creates the points of the rotation body and is called by `makerot1` as is:

rotlin: Creates the lines of the rotation body.

wrld2set: Passes the parameters of the world system and the rotation body to the link file variables. The variables for storing of the rotation angle `hxangle` remain the same, nothing in `inp_chan` needs to be changed.

In contrast to the first program where the house was already explicitly provided, the object to be represented must first be created. This is the task of the subroutine `makerot1`, which generates the rotation body in the array `r1datx`, `r1daty`, `r1datz`. This array corresponds to the house array `housdatx`, `housdaty`, `housdatz`. The rotation body is transferred to the world system and its position parameters in the main loop are modified in a loop. You should experiment freely with this program and change the definition line for the rotation body and the number of rotations. The only limitation is in the maximum number of points and lines where the total number of lines r1numline is calculated as follows:

r1nummark: Total number of corners in the rotation body

r1numline: Total number of lines in the rotation body

r1numpt: Number of points in the definition line

r1numro: Number of desired rotations of the definition line

r1numline:= ((r1numpt   -   1)   *   (r1numro)   +
            (r1numpt * r1numro))

r1nummark:= (r1numpt * (r1numro + 1))

The number of points can not exceed 1600 and the number of lines
cannot be greater than 3200.

The expression (r1numro+1) results from the programming trick, of
rotating the definition line one time more than necessary. The definition
line, which is the first line in the array, is created a second time at the end
of the array. This simplifies the construction of the line array. And now
you can try the various rotation lines such as the following:

Definition of a Ball:

```
* * * * * * * * * * * * * * * * * * * * * * * * * * * * * * * * * * * * * * * * * * * * *
*    Definition line and parameter of the ball    *
*    from Fig. 4.2.1                               *
* * * * * * * * * * * * * * * * * * * * * * * * * * * * * * * * * * * * * * * * * * * * *
r1xdat:    .dc.w 0,40,70,90,100,90,70,40,0
r1ydat:    .dc.w 100,90,70,40,0,-40,-70,-90,-100
r1zdat:    .dc.w 0,0,0,0,0,0,0,0,0
r1numpt:   .dc.w      9
r1numro:   .dc.w      60     * Number of rotations
for creation
```

You need only exchange the corresponding lines in the listing for these.

The operation parameters of the program are the same as in house1:

cursor left and right:
Change the Y-rotation angle increment

cursor up and down:
Change the X-rotation angle increment

undo and   help:
Change the Z-rotation angle increment

+ and - on the keypad:
Move the projection plane on the Z-axis (increase or decrease the size of object).

* and / on the keypad:
Move the rotation reference point on the Z-axis

Shift 'D':
Hardcopy on the printer

4.3   Hidden line algorithm for convex bodies

If you are familiar with real time 3-D graphics on other computers, you were probably surprised by the speed of the display of the wire frame drawings on the Atari ST. On the other hand some game freaks may remark that "I've seen the fastest 3-D games on my 8-bit C-64 and these wire models just don't compare." For game programming, the main emphasis is on the desired effect. Therefore the active figures for these 3-D-Games are mostly space ships and landscapes which are pre-calculated and their point coordinates are already stored in the computer. For the display which follows on the screen, the object is simply drawn, which naturally can be done quickly, even with 8-bit computers. A disadvantage of this method is the enormous storage requirement, since every possible position of the object must be available in memory, meaning that this procedure cannot be used with complex bodies. In this case only the rotation matrices for the rotation around three axes are calculated ahead of time and stored in a table. Even with this method the limits of the storage are reached quickly. An extreme example: If you want to calculate the rotation matrices of all possible values for subsequent rotation about three axes, with an angle increment of one degree previously calculated, the result will be more than 46 million possibilities (variations of three rotations around 360 possible angles). If this method is used, the degree of freedom of the objects must be limited to one or two possible axes, and/or the gradations of the angle values must be raised so that the table is calculated, for example, only in ten degree steps, or only rotations from zero to to ninety degrees are permitted. Another common method consists of defining the objects as picture shapes, quasi-sprites, in various positions and to switch back and forth between the various shapes and to move the whole shape over the display. Of course the last procedure is the fastest since nothing has to be calculated and the only operation is moving data into the screen memory.

Now back to the Atari ST, which, because of its enormous computing power, can not only calculate the wire frame drawing in real time, but as you will see also offers the ability to display simple convex bodies in real time without the hidden lines. The method used corresponds to the surface method used in chapter 2.7. To use this method you must specify every surface of the object precisely. For the example of our house, we need two new variables. First the number of surfaces of the house (hnumpla=13), and second the storage space for the description of these surfaces (houspla). Every surface is described by the number of lines pertaining to it, followed by the lines themselves. The description: 4,1,2,2,3,3,4,4,1 would mean:

Four lines belong to this surface and appear as follows:

Line #. connects Point #   with Point #

1	1	2
2	2	3
3	3	4
4	4	1

To return to the example of our house, it will be necessary to describe all of the surfaces of this house in the same manner. For this reason we draw the various views of the house and number the surfaces in any desired sequence as in Figures 4.3.1 to 4.3.6. In these illustrations the desired result is already achieved, i.e. the hidden lines are already removed to prevent confusion.

Figure 4.3.1 - 4.3.6: Hardcopy of House Views

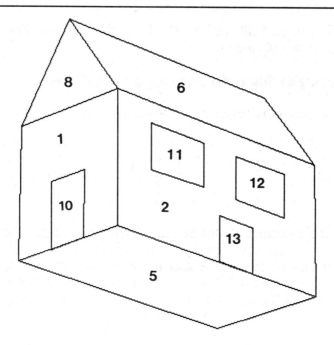

Figure 4.3.1

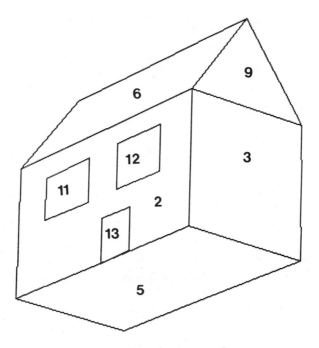

Figure 4.3.2

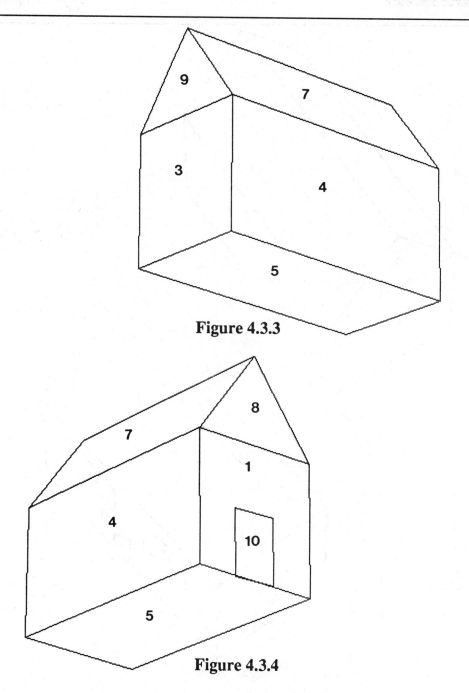

Figure 4.3.3

Figure 4.3.4

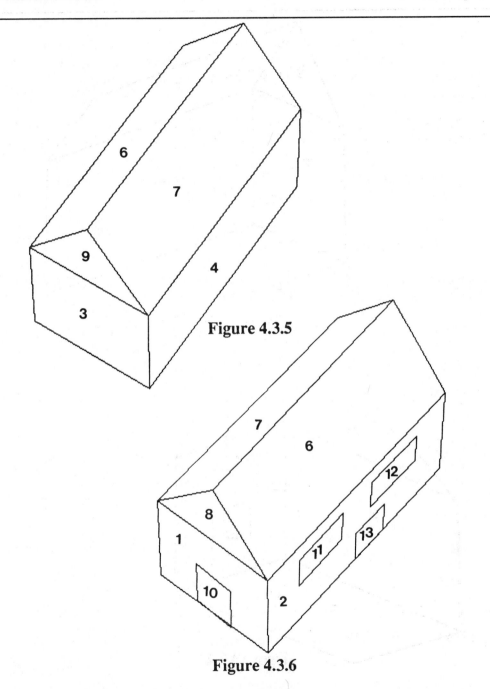

Figure 4.3.5

Figure 4.3.6

To assign connecting lines to every surface, view the object from the outside as in the illustration and start with the assignment at any desired point. To make it possible for the algorithm to recognize the hidden surfaces, the sequence of the line points (the direction of the individual lines) is not arbitrary but must be done in the clockwise direction. This is the procedure:

1. Number the surfaces.

2. Create a surface array containing the number of lines (counted clockwise) of each surface as well as the lines of each surface, as viewed from the outside.

3. When all surfaces have been taken care of the number of surfaces are stored in a variable (numpla).

Here is the surface list for the thirteen surfaces of the house from Figure 4.3.1. You can get the point indices from Figure 4.1.3.

Surface #	Number Lines	Lines from Point # to Point #			
1	4	1, 2	2, 3	3, 4	4, 1
2	4	2, 5	5, 8	8, 3	3, 2
3	4	5, 6	6, 7	7, 8	8, 5
4	4	7, 6	6, 1	1, 4	4, 7
5	4	4, 3	3, 8	8, 7	7, 4
6	4	2, 9	9,10	10, 5	5, 2
7	4	10, 9	9, 1	1, 6	6,10
8	3	1, 9	9, 2	2, 1	
9	3	5,10	10, 6	6, 5	
10	4	11,12	12,13	13,14	14,11
11	4	15,16	16,17	17,18	18,15
12	4	9,20	20,21	21,22	22,19
13	4	23,24	24,25	25,26	26,23

Number of surfaces: 13

With this method of surface definition you can describe up to 32,000 lines which can be the connecting lines for 16,000 different points, though only if you have enough memory, of course. The actual main program hide1.s corresponds to the first main program house1.s. Two subroutines have been added: hideit: and surfdraw: and two other changes were made in the main loop. The subroutine hideit determines which surfaces are visible from the projection center with the help of the information in the surface arrray (wplane). The information on the visible surfaces, which correspond to the normal surfaces in the structure, first the number of lines followed by individual lines, is entered into a second array (vplane) and the total number of visible surfaces is stored in the surface counter surfcnt. All visible surfaces are subsequently drawn on the display by the subroutine surfdraw: whereby many lines are drawn twice since the subroutine surfdraw: takes the lines to be drawn directly from the surface array (vplane). Figure 4.3.1 and the connecting lines of points 2 and 3 show a concrete illustration. This connecting line belongs to the visible surface 1 and the visible surface 2. Naturally all the lines in the surface array (vplane) could be sorted before drawing and double lines removed. My experience shows that the time saved in drawing is lost in the additional sorting and testing, at least for less complicated bodies. Furthermore, the surface information is lost by the separation of the lines, which is needed in the following program sections. Again to run this program you must first compile and link it to grlink1.s using the batch.ttp file and entering: aslink grlink1 hide1

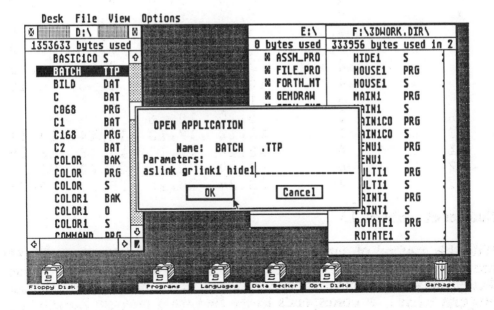

```
*********************************************************************
*  hide1.s   19.1.86  Version 3.0                                  *
*  House with hidden-line algorithm                                *
*                                                                  *
*********************************************************************
            .globl    main,xoffs,yoffs,zoffs,offx,offy,offz
            .globl    viewx,viewy,viewz
            .globl    wlinxy,mouse_off,setrotdp,inp_chan,pointrot
            .text

main:
            jsr       apinit      * Announce program
            jsr       grafhand    * Get screen handler
            jsr       openwork    * Display
            jsr       mouse_off   * Turn off mouse
            jsr       getreso     * what resolution ?
            jsr       setcocli    * Prepare clip window

            move.l    #houspla,worldpla * Address of surface array

            jsr       makewrld    * Create world system
            jsr       wrldset     * Pass world parameters

            jsr       setrotdp    * initialize observer ref. point
            jsr       clwork
            jsr       pagedown    * Display logical page
            jsr       clwork
            jsr       inp_chan    * Input and change parameters

mainlop1:
            jsr       pointrot    * rotate about observer ref. point
            jsr       pers        * Perspective transformation
            jsr       hideit
            jsr       surfdraw

            jsr       pageup      * Display physical page
            jsr       inp_chan    * Input new parameters
            jsr       clwork
            jsr       pointrot    * Rotate around rotation ref. point
            jsr       pers        * Transform new points
            jsr       hideit
            jsr       surfdraw
```

```
            jsr       pagedown      * Display this logical page
            jsr       inp_chan      * Input and change parameters
            jsr       clwork        * erase physical page
            jmp       mainlop1      * to main loop

mainend:    move.l    physbase,logbase

            jsr       pageup        * switch to normal display page
            rts                     * back to link file, and end


********************************************************************
*   Input and change parameters such as angle increments and      *
*   Z-coordinate of the projection plane                          *
********************************************************************


inp_chan: jsr       inkey         * Sense keyboard, keyboard code in
          cmp.b     #'D',d0
          bne       inpwait
          jsr       scrdmp        * Make harcopy

inpwait:  swap      d0            * Test D0 for
          cmp.b     #$4d,d0       * Cursor-right
          bne       inp1
          addq.w    #1,ywplus     * if yes, then add one to
          bra       inpend1       * Y-angle increment and continue

inp1:     cmp.b     #$4b,d0       * Cursor-left, if yes
          bne       inp2          * then subtract one from
          subq.w    #1,ywplus     * Y-angle increment
          bra       inpend1

inp2:     cmp.b     #$50,d0       * Cursor-down, if yes
          bne       inp3
          addq.w    #1,xwplus     * then add one to X-angle increment
          bra       inpend1

inp3:     cmp.b     #$48,d0       * Cursor-up
          bne       inp3a
          subq.w    #1,xwplus     * subtract one
          bra       inpend1
```

```
inp3a:      cmp.b       #$61,d0       * Undo key
            bne         inp3b
            subq.w      #1,zwplus
            bra         inpend1


inp3b:      cmp.b       #$62,d0       * Help key
            bne         inp4
            addq.w      #1,zwplus
            bra         inpend1


inp4:       cmp.b       #$4e,d0       * + key on keypad
            bne         inp5          * if yes then subtract 25 from
            sub.w       #25,dist      * location of projection plane
            bra         inpend1       * (Z-coordinate)
inp5:       cmp.b       #$4a,d0       * - key on keypad
            bne         inp6          *
            add.w       #25,dist      * if yes then add 25
            bra         inpend1


inp6:       cmp.b       #$66,d0       * * key on keypad
            bne         inp7          * if yes, subtract 15 from the
            sub.w       #15,rotdpz    * rotation point Z-coordinate
            bra         inpend1       * Make change


inp7:       cmp.b       #$65,d0       * / key of keypad
            bne         inp10
            add.w       #15,rotdpz    * Add 15
            bra         inpend1


inp10:      cmp.b       #$44,d0       * F10 pressed ?
            bne         inpend1
            addq.l      #4,a7         * if yes, jump to
            bra         mainend       * program end

inpend1:    move.w      hyangle,d1    * Rotation angle about Y-axis
            add.w       ywplus,d1     * add increment
            cmp.w       #360,d1       * if larger than 360, subtract 360
            bge         inpend2
            cmp.w       #-360,d1      * if smaller than 360
            ble         inpend3       * add 360
            bra         inpend4
```

```
inpend2:    sub.w      #360,d1
            bra        inpend4
inpend3:    add.w      #360,d1


inpend4:    move.w     d1,hyangle


            move.w     hxangle,d1      * Treat
            add.w      xwplus,d1       * rotation angle about X-axis
            cmp.w      #360,d1         * in the same manner
            bge        inpend5
            cmp.w      #-360,d1
            ble        inpend6
            bra        inpend7
inpend5:    sub.w      #360,d1
            bra        inpend7
inpend6:    add.w      #360,d1


inpend7:    move.w     d1,hxangle         *


            move.w     hzangle,d1
            add.w      zwplus,d1
            cmp.w      #360,d1
            bge        inpend8
            cmp.w      #-360,d1
            ble        inpend9
            bra        inpend10
inpend8:    sub.w      #360,d1
            bra        inpend10
inpend9:    add.w      #360,d1


inpend10:   move.w     d1,hzangle
            rts


*****************************************************************
*    Initialize the rotation reference point to [0,0,0] and the      *
*    rotation angle also to 0,0,0                                     *
*****************************************************************


setrotdp:   move.w     #0,d1         * set the start rotation-
            move.w     d1,rotdpx     * datum point
            move.w     d1,rotdpy
            move.w     d1,rotdpz
```

```
            move.w      #0,hyangle      * Start rotation angle
            move.w      #0,hzangle
            move.w      #0,hxangle
            rts


*****************************************************************
* Rotate the total world system around one point, the rotation  *
* reference point                                               *
*****************************************************************

pointrot:   move.w      hxangle,xangle  * rotate the world around the
            move.w      hyangle,yangle
            move.w      hzangle,zangle
            move.w      rotdpx,d0       * rotation reference point
            move.w      rotdpy,d1
            move.w      rotdpz,d2
            move.w      d0,xoffs        * add for inverse transformation
            move.w      d1,yoffs
            move.w      d2,zoffs
            neg.w       d0
            neg.w       d1
            neg.w       d2
            move.w      d0,offx         * subtract for transformation
            move.w      d1,offy
            move.w      d2,offz
            jsr         matinit         * Matrix initialization
            jsr         zrotate         * first rotate about Z-axis
            jsr         yrotate         * rotate 'matrix' about Y-axis
            jsr         xrotate         * then about X-axis
            jsr         rotate          * Multiply points with matrix
            rts


*****************************************************************
*  Generate world system from object data. All points, lines,   *
*  and surfaces are transferred to the world system             *
*****************************************************************

makewrld:   move.l      #housdatx,a1    * Generate world system by
            move.l      #housdaty,a2
            move.l      #housdatz,a3
            move.l      #wrldx,a4
            move.l      #wrldy,a5
```

```
              move.l     #wrldz,a6
              move.w     hnummark,d0
              ext.l      d0
              subq.l     #1,d0
makewl1:      move.w     (a1)+,(a4)+      * Copying point coordinates
              move.w     (a2)+,(a5)+      * to world system
              move.w     (a3)+,(a6)+
              dbra       d0,makewl1
              move.w     hnumline,d0      * Number of house lines
              ext.l      d0
              subq.l     #1,d0
              move.l     #houslin,a1
              move.l     #wlinxy,a2
makewl2:      move.l     (a1)+,(a2)+      * Copy all lines into
              dbra       d0,makewl2       * world system

              move.l     worldpla,a0
              move.l     #wplane,a1
              move.w     hnumsurf,d0       * Number of surfaces on house
              ext.l      d0
              subq.l     #1,d0

makewl3:      move.w     (a0)+,d1         * Copy all surface
              move.w     d1,(a1)+         * definitions into the
              ext.l      d1               * world system
              subq.l     #1,d1

makewl4:      move.l     (a0)+,(a1)+      * Copy every line of this
              dbra       d1,makewl4       * surface into the world array
              dbra       d0,makewl3       * until all surfaces are processed
              rts


***********************************************************************
*    Passing the world parameters to the link file variables       *
***********************************************************************

wrldset:      move.l     #wrldx,datx      * Pass variables for
              move.l     #wrldy,daty      * the rotation routine
              move.l     #wrldz,datz
              move.l     #viewx,pointx
```

```
            move.l      #viewy,pointy
            move.l      #viewz,pointz
            move.l      #wlinxy,linxy
            move.w      picturex,x0
            move.w      picturey,y0
            move.w      proz,zobs
            move.w      r1z1,dist
            move.l      #screenx,xplot
            move.l      #screeny,yplot
            move.w      hnumline,numline
            move.w      hnummark,nummark
            move.w      hnumsurf,numsurf
            rts


*******************************************************************
* remove all characters from the keyboard buffer                  *
*******************************************************************

clearbuf: move.w      #$b,-(a7)
            trap        #1
            addq.l      #2,a7
            tst.w       d0
            beq         clearnd
            move.w      #1,-(a7)
            trap        #1
            addq.l      #2,a7
            bra         clearbuf


clearnd:  rts




***********************************************************************
*    Sense display resolution and set coordinate origin of screen    *
*    to screen center                                                *
***********************************************************************

getreso:  move.w      #4,-(a7)           * Sense screen resolution
            trap        #14
            addq.l      #2,a7
            cmp.w       #2,d0
            bne         getr1
            move.w      #320,picturex    * Monochrome monitor
```

```
        move.w    #200,picturey
        bra       getrend
getr1:  cmp.w     #1,d0
        bne       getr2
        move.w    #320,picturex    * medium resolution (640*200)
        move.w    #100,picturey
        bra       getrend
getr2:  move.w    #160,picturex    * low resolution (320*200)
        move.w    #100,picturey
getrend: rts


****************************************************************
*    Hardcopy routine, called by inp_chan                     *
****************************************************************

scrdmp: move.w    #20,-(a7)
        trap      #14
        addq.l    #2,a7
        jsr       clearbuf
        rts


****************************************************************
* Sets the limits of the display window for the Cohen-Sutherland *
* clip algorithm built into the draw-line algorithm.          *
* The limits can be freely selected by the user, which makes the *
* draw-line algorithm very flexible.                          *
****************************************************************

setcocli: move.w  #0,clipxule
          move.w  #0,clipyule
          move.w  picturex,d1
          lsl.w   #1,d1         * times two
          subq.w  #1,d1         * minus one equal
          move.w  d1,clipxlri   * 639 for monochrome
          move.w  picturey,d1
          lsl.w   #1,d1         * times two minus one equal
          subq.w  #1,d1         * 399 for monochrome
          move.w  d1,clipylri
          rts
```

```
******************************************************************
*   Recognition of hidden surfaces and entry of these into the    *
*   vplane array, the surface information is in the surface array  *
*   wplane, as well as in view system, viewx, viewy, viewz,        *
*   also the total number of surfaces must be passed in numsurf    *
******************************************************************

hideit:
        move.w    numsurf,d0    * Number of surfaces as counter
        ext.l     d0
        subq.l    #1,d0
        move.l    #viewx,a1     * Store point coordinates here
        move.l    #viewy,a2
        move.l    #viewz,a3
        move.l    #wplane,a0    * Information for every surface
        move.l    #vplane,a5    * here.
        move.w    #0,surfcount  * counts the known visible surfaces.

visible: move.w   (a0),d1       * start with first surface, number
        ext.l     d1            * of points of this surface in D1.
        move.w    2(a0),d2      * Offset of first point of this surf.
        move.w    4(a0),d3      * Offset of second point
        move.w    8(a0),d4      * Offset of third point
        subq.w    #1,d2         * for access to point arrays subtract
        subq.w    #1,d3         * one from current point offset
        subq.w    #1,d4         * multiply by two
        lsl.w     #1,d2
        lsl.w     #1,d3
        lsl.w     #1,d4         * and finally access current point
        move.w    (a1,d3.w),d6  * coordinates
        cmp.w     (a1,d4.w),d6  * comparison recognizes two points
        bne       doit1         * with same coordinates which can
        move.w    (a2,d3.w),d6  * result during construction of
        cmp.w     (a2,d4.w),d6  * rotation bodies. During recognition
        bne       doit1         * of two points in which all point
        move.w    (a3,d4.w),d6  * coordinates match (x,y,z) the
        cmp.w     (a3,d3.w),d6  * program selects a third point for
        bne       doit1         * determination of the two vectors
        move.w    12(a0),d4
        subq.w    #1,d4
        lsl.w     #1,d4
```

```
doit1:
          move.w    (a1,d3.w),d5      * Here the two vectors, which lie
          move.w    d5,kx             * in the surface plane, are
          sub.w     (a1,d2.w),d5      * determined by subtracting the
          move.w    d5,px             * coordinates of two points
          move.w    (a2,d3.w),d5      * from this surface.
          move.w    d5,ky             * The direction coordinates of the
          sub.w     (a2,d2.w),d5      * vectors are stored in the
          move.w    d5,py             * variables qx,qy,qz and px,py,pz
          move.w    (a3,d3.w),d5
          move.w    d5,kz
          sub.w     (a3,d2.w),d5
          move.w    d5,pz

          move.w    (a1,d4.w),d5      * Calculate vector Q
          sub.w     (a1,d2.w),d5
          move.w    (a2,d4.w),d6
          sub.w     (a2,d2.w),d6
          move.w    (a3,d4.w),d7
          sub.w     (a3,d2.w),d7
          move.w    d5,d1             * qx
          move.w    d6,d2             * qy
          move.w    d7,d3             * qz

          muls      py,d3             * Calculate the cross product
          muls      pz,d2             * of the vertical vector for the
          sub.w     d2,d3             * current surface.
          move.w    d3,rx
          muls      pz,d1
          muls      px,d7
          sub.w     d7,d1             * The direction coordinates of the
          move.w    d1,ry             * vertical vector are stored
          muls      px,d6             * zobsorarily in rx,ry,rz
          muls      py,d5
          sub.w     d5,d6
          move.w    d6,rz

          move.w    prox,d1           * The projection center
          sub.w     kx,d1             * is used as the comparison
          move.w    proy,d2           * point for the visibility
          sub.w     ky,d2             * of a surface.
          move.w    proz,d3           * One can also use the
```

```
           sub.w     kz,d3           * observation ref. point
           muls      rx,d1           * as the comparison point. Now comes
           muls      ry,d2           * the comparison of vector R with
           muls      rz,d3           * the vector from a point on the
           add.l     d1,d2           * surface to the projection center
           add.l     d2,d3           * for creating the scalar product
           bmi       dosight         * of the two vectors.

* If the scalar product is negative, the surface is visible

           move.w    (a0),d1         * Number of lines of the surface
           ext.l     d1
           lsl.l     #2,d1           * Number of lines times 4 = space for
           addq.l    #2,d1           * lines plus 2 bytes for the number of

           add.l     d1,a0           * lines added to surface array, for
sight1:    dbra      d0,visible      * access to next surface. When all
           bra       hideend         * surfaces completed then end.

dosight:   move.w    (a0),d1         * Number of lines for this surface,
           ext.l     d1              * gives the number of words to be
           lsl.l     #1,d1           * transmitted when multiplied by 2.

sight3:    move.w    (a0)+,(a5)+     * pass the number of lines and the
           dbra      d1,sight3       * the individual lines

           addq.w    #1,surfcount    * the number of surfaces plus one
           bra       sight1          * and process the next

hideend:   rts


*****************************************************************
*   Draw visible surfaces passed in vplane                     *
*****************************************************************

surfdraw:                           * Draws a number of surfaces (passed
           move.l    xplot,a4        * in surfcount) whose description
           move.l    yplot,a5

           move.l    #vplane,a6      * is in the array at address
           move.w    surfcount,d0    * vplane, and was entered by routine
```

```
           ext.l     d0           * hideit
           subq.l    #1,d0        * if no surface is entered in the
           bmi       surfend      * array, then end.
surflop1:  move.w    (a6)+,d1     * Number of lines in this surface as
           ext.l     d1           * counter of lines to be drawn.
           subq.l    #1,d1

surflop2:  move.l    (a6)+,d5     * First line of this surface
           subq.w    #1,d5        * Access screen array which contains
           lsl.w     #1,d5        * screen coordinates of the points.
           move.w    0(a4,d5.w),d2
           move.w    0(a5,d5.w),d3  * extract points from routine and
           swap      d5           * pass.
           subq.w    #1,d5
           lsl.w     #1,d5
           move.w    0(a4,d5.w),a2  * second point of line
           move.w    0(a5,d5.w),a3
           jsr       drawl        * Draw line until all lines of this
           dbra      d1,surflop2  * surface have been drawn and repeat
           dbra      d0,surflop1  * until all surfaces are drawn.
surfend:   rts                    * Return.



*******************************************************************
*******************************************************************
*   Here begins the variable area of the program module          *
*                                                                 *
*******************************************************************


*******************************************************************
*                                                                 *
*        Definition of the house                                 *
*                                                                 *
*******************************************************************

           .data

housdatx: .dc.w      -30,30,30,-30,30,-30,-30,30,0,0,-10,-10,10,10
          .dc.w      30,30,30,30,30,30,30,30,30,30,30,30
```

```
housdaty: .dc.w     30,30,-30,-30,30,30,-30,-30,70,70,-30,0,0,-30
          .dc.w     20,20,0,0,20,20,0,0
          .dc.w     -10,-10,-30,-30

housdatz: .dc.w     60,60,60,60,-60,-60,-60,-60,60,-60,60,60,60,60
          .dc.w     40,10,10,40,-10,-40,-40,-10
          .dc.w     0,-20,-20,0

houslin:  .dc.w     1,2,2,3,3,4,4,1,2,5,5,8,8,3,8,7,7,6,6,5,6,1,7,4
          .dc.w     9,10,1,9,9,2,5,10,6,10,11,12,12,13,13,14
          .dc.w     15,16,16,17,17,18,18,15,19,20,20,21,21,22,22,19
          .dc.w     23,24,24,25,25,26,26,23


*********************************************************************
* here are the definitions of the surfaces belonging to the house    *
*********************************************************************

houspla:  .dc.w     4,1,2,2,3,3,4,4,1,4,2,5,5,8,8,3,3,2
          .dc.w     4,5,6,6,7,7,8,8,5,4,7,6,6,1,1,4,4,7
          .dc.w     4,4,3,3,8,8,7,7,4,4,2,9,9,10,10,5,5,2
          .dc.w     4,10,9,9,1,1,6,6,10,3,1,9,9,2,2,1
          .dc.w     3,5,10,10,6,6,5,4,11,12,12,13,13,14,14,11
          .dc.w     4,15,16,16,17,17,18,18,15,4,19,20,20,21,21,22,22,19
          .dc.w     4,23,24,24,25,25,26,26,23

hnummark: .dc.w     26       * Number of corner points of the house
hnumline: .dc.w     32       * Number of lines of the house
hnumsurf: .dc.w     13       * Number of surfaces of the house

hxangle:  .dc.w     0        * Rotation angle of house about X-axis
hyangle:  .dc.w     0        *         "         "        " Y-axis
hzangle:  .dc.w     0        *         "         "        " Z-axis

xwplus:   .dc.w     0        * Angle increment about X-axis
ywplus:   .dc.w     0        * Angle increment about Y-axis
zwplus:   .dc.w     0        * Angle increment about Z-axis

picturex: .dc.w     0        * Definition of zero point of display
picturey: .dc.w     0        * entered by getreso
```

```
rotdpx:     .dc.w      0
rotdpy:     .dc.w      0
rotdpz:     .dc.w      0


r1z1:       .dc.w      0
normz:      .dc.w      1500


            .bss

plusrot:    .ds.l      1
first:      .ds.w      1
second:     .ds.w      1
delta1:     .ds.w      1


worldpla:   .ds.l      1          * Address of surface array

            .data

plag:       .dc.b      1
            .even

            .bss

diffz:      .ds.w      1

dx:         .ds.w      1
dy:         .ds.w      1
dz:         .ds.w      1

wrldx:      .ds.w      1600       * World coordinate array
wrldy:      .ds.w      1600
wrldz:      .ds.w      1600

viewx:      .ds.w      1600       * View coordinate array
viewy:      .ds.w      1600
viewz:      .ds.w      1600

screenx:    .ds.w      1600       * Display coordinate array
screeny:    .ds.w      1600
```

```
wlinxy:     .ds.l    3200    * Line array



wplane:     .ds.l    6600    * Surface array

vplane:     .ds.l    6600    * Surface array of visible surfaces

surfcount:  .ds.w    1

numsurf:    .ds.w    1

zcount:     .ds.l    1       * Sum of all Z-coordinates
zpla:       .ds.w    1       * Individual Z-coordinates of surface

sx:         .ds.w    1
sy:         .ds.w    1
sz:         .ds.w    1

px:         .ds.w    1
py:         .ds.w    1
pz:         .ds.w    1

rx:         .ds.w    1
ry:         .ds.w    1
rz:         .ds.w    1

qx:         .ds.w    1
qy:         .ds.w    1
qz:         .ds.w    1

kx:         .ds.w    1
ky:         .ds.w    1
kz:         .ds.w    1

            .data

prox:       .dc.w    0       * Coordinates of the projection center
proy:       .dc.w    0       * on the positive Z-axis
proz:       .dc.w    1500
```

```
              .data

offx:         .dc.w     0      * Transformation during rotation
offy:         .dc.w     0      * to point [offx,offy,offz]
offz:         .dc.w     0

xoffs:        .dc.w     0      * Inverse transformation to point
yoffs:        .dc.w     0      * [xoff,yoffs,zoffs]
zoffs:        .dc.w     0


              .bss

loopc         .ds.l     1
              .end
```

4.3.1   Explanation of the newly-added subroutines

hideit: In contrast to the explanation in the mathematical part, the
view system used by the program is a right system; this
saves the multiplication of the Z-values by -1. The
subroutine hideit forms two vectors within the surface
from the first three points of every surface. These are the
vectors from point one to point two as well as the vector
from point one to point three. These two vectors
correspond to the vectors P[px,py,pz] and
Q[qx,qy,qz] from chapter 2.7. Furthermore, a third
vector R[rx,ry,rz] is generated through the formation
of the cross product of the vectors P and Q. According to
the definition, the cross product is perpendicular to the
vectors P and Q and, in this sequence forms a right-hand
system with them [p,q,r]. Finally, a vector is created
from a point on the surface to the projection center
(S[sx,sy,sz]), and its direction is compared with the
direction of the vector R by creation of the scalar products
of the vectors S and R. All the surfaces which are in front
of the projection center are visible.

Scalar product= sx*rx+sy*ry+sz*rz =
|s|*|r|*cos(Alpha)

Alpha is the angle suspended between the vectors R and S.
If the result of the scalar product is negative, this means an
angle larger than 90 degrees and smaller than 270 degrees
between the two vectors, which point in different
directions (See also Figure 2.7.1), and so this surface is
visible, according to the surface definition (clockwise
direction) and right system used.

surfdraw: Here the visible surfaces are displayed by drawing the
lines of the array vplane. The whole job was done
already by hideit.

The operation parameters of the program are the same as in house1.s,
The rotation point on the Z-axis can be moved with the * and / keys on
the keypad, the projection plane can be moved with the - and + keys on
the keypad, and the angle increments of the rotation angle around the X

and Y-axis can be changed with the cursor keys and the Help and Undo keys. Of course you can also change all the parameters within the program (projection center, rotation reference point to X and Y-axis, etc.).

4.3.1.1   Errors with non-convex bodies

If the rotation creation routine is added to the main program and the chess figure is created with `hideit:` and `pladraw` without hidden lines: you can see the problem. With concave bodies such as this chess figure there is the possibility that one of the surfaces recognized by the `hideit:` algorithm as visible can be hidden by another visible surface during viewing. In this case the `hideit:` algorithm fails and the problem must be solved with another algorithm.

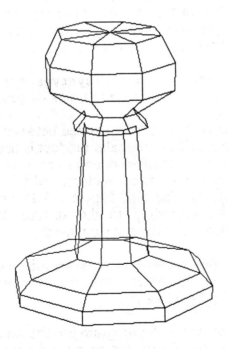

Figure 4.3.7

4.4   The painter algorithm

Recall the problem we're trying to solve: Surfaces which are seen from an observation point have their surface normal vector pointed in another direction from a vector from any point on the surface to the projection center, are hidden by other surfaces which according to this criterium are also visible. If you start from the observation point (projection center) on the positive Z-axis, the middle Z-coordinate of a surface is a possible description of it and its position in the world system. The middle Z-coordinate is obtained by defining the arithmetic center of the corner point coordinates belonging to the surface, i.e. summation of all surface corner point Z-coordinates and division by the number of corner points belonging to the surface. The relationship can be made clear with the simple example with three different surfaces in Figure 4.4.1.

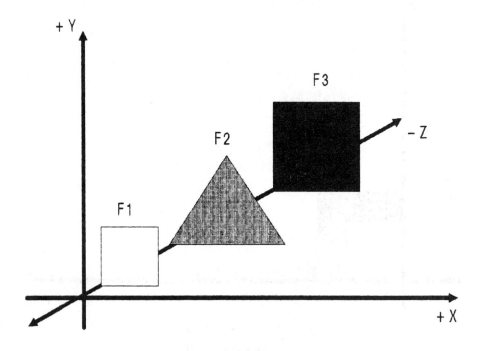

Figure 4.4.1

216

Viewing the defined world system from one point on the positive Z axis, we can say: the surface with the largest middle Z-coordinate is visible in its entire size and is not hidden by any other surface. Note that all observed surfaces are on the negative Z-axis (-200 > -400). This completely visible surface covers parts of surfaces with a smaller middle Z coordinate. Surfaces 2 and 3 are covered by surface 1 and surface 3 is again covered by surface 2. The surfaces are sorted by their Z-coordinates and they are drawn starting with the smallest middle z-coordinate, surface 3, and then the surfaces with the larger Z coordinates, and we have found a possible solution to the problem by covering hidden surfaces with other surfaces. You must consider that it is not enough just to draw every surface. The individual surfaces must be filled with "color" or a pattern so that the surfaces drawn first are really covered. Figure 4.4.2 shows one possible result.

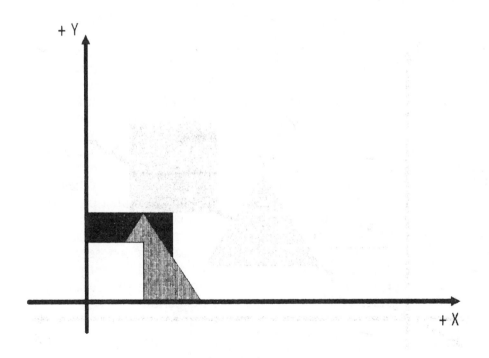

Figure 4.4.2

If we think about our rotation body from chapter 4.2, this means first of all that when the rotation body is created its surfaces must also be created, second a middle Z coordinate must be calculated and stored some place for every surface. Another problem is sorting the surfaces. If one wanted to sort every defined form with its lines, it would require an enormous movement of data in storage. To avoid this, a new storage area is created in which the Z-coordinates together with the beginning address of the surface it pertains to are stored. The individual surfaces are stored in a simple linear list. The beginning address of every surface is the storage address at which the number of lines for this surface is stored. Through storage of this address, it is possible to access every single surface directly, which previously was not possible because of the number of lines belonging to each surface.

To better handle the two pieces of information, (Z-coordinates of the surface and address of the surface) we select a long word as data size for both, i.e. in the newly constructed array (`surfaddr`) there are four successive bytes for the Z-coordinate and four bytes for the address of the surface. Each description of a surface "occupies" eight bytes of storage space. This array contains the visible surfaces represented by their middle Z-coordinates and their beginning addresses in the new addition to the subroutine `hideit:` (`sight2`). In this special case of the rotation body whose surfaces all consist of four lines, the division by the line number (4) for calculation of the middle Z-coordinate can be performed by shifting right by two bit positions. If you want to include surfaces with more or less than four lines in the paint routine, you must alter the `hideit`-routine and divide by the number of surfaces. After the adaptation of the subroutine `hideit:` all visible surfaces are in the two arrays, in `vplane:` and in `surfaddr:`. The number of surfaces, like in the first version of `hideit:`, goes in the variable `placount:`. Fortunately, we do not have to write the shading function since the operating system offers a function for filling display areas with a shading pattern (Filled Area). This function fills a polygon whose points are passed in the `ptsin` array, with one of a total of 36 different predefined, and one user-defined shading pattern. Before calling this function with the opcode 9, we set up the different shading parameters which is done using the subroutines `filmode`, `filform`, `filcolor`, `filstyle` and `filindex` which are contained in the link file (`grlink1`).

The shading routine is called by the subroutine `paintit`, which first sorts all surfaces contained in `surfaddr:` according to ascending Z-coordinates. Next you must pass the individual surfaces, i.e. their end point coordinates, to the function "Filled Area". This begins with the surface which has the smallest middle Z-coordinate. The function "Filled

Area" can, in connection with the function "Set Clipping Rectangle", Opcode 129, fill surfaces limited to a display window. It is necessary to call the function "Set Clipping Rectangle" when the display window is the total screen area, bordered by the coordinates 0,0 and 639,399 (for BW monitors). if this is not done, "Filled Area" may draw parts of the polygon sticking beyond the display frame on the neighboring display page (wrapping). You could fill all surfaces with the same pattern, which could also be white. You can assign a shading pattern for every surface corresponding to its Z-coordinates. We will limit ourselves to only six of the 36 possible fill patterns. This is done purely for optical reasons since shaded surfaces, and even completely filled color surfaces, can have a negative effect on the picture. You can influence this choice or omit it entirely. Simply set the desired pattern on entry to the subroutine. With a color monitor, a various fill colors can be used instead of a shading pattern. The choice of colors is completely up to you. The visual effect of these three-dimensional graphics can best be appreciated with a high-resolution monitor. Doubling the resolution in both directions increases the quality of the picture four times.

If you have a color monitor, you can choose between filling with color or patterns. If you want to try filling with color you must call the function `filstyle` with the value one in the `D0` register when entering the `paintit` routine. The subroutine `filcolor:` makes it possible to use different colors. Owners of monochrome monitors don't have to change anything in the program. To run this program call the batch file batch.ttp then enter: `aslink grlink1 paint1`

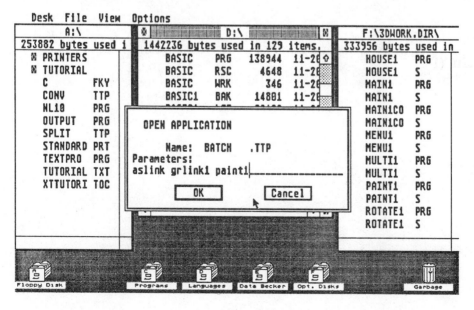

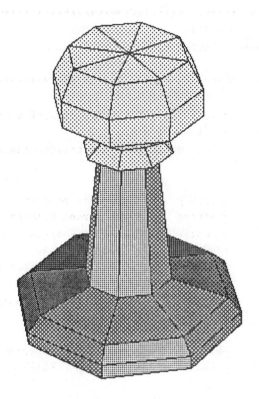

Figure 4.4.3

Here is the listing of the fourth main program for the link file
grlink1.s. It is called paint1.s. The operating parameters again
correspond to the previous program.

```
*********************************************************************
*  paint1.s        9.2.1986                                        *
*  Display a shaded rotation body                                  *
*                                                                  *
*********************************************************************
          .text
          .globl    main,xoffs,yoffs,zoffs,offx,offy,offz
          .globl    viewx,viewy,viewz
          .globl    wlinxy,mouse_off,setrotdp,inp_chan,pointrot

main:
          jsr       apinit      * Announce program
          jsr       grafhand    * Get screen handler
          jsr       openwork    * open workstation
          jsr       mouse_off   * Turn off mouse
          jsr       getreso     * Display resolution ?
          jsr       setcocli    * Set clip window
          jsr       makerot1    * Create rotation body


          jsr       makewrld    * Create world system
          jsr       wrld2set    * Pass world parameters

          jsr       setrotdp    * initialize observation ref. point
          jsr       clwork
          jsr       pagedown    * Display logical page
          jsr       clwork
          jsr       inp_chan

mainlop1:
          jsr       pointrot    * rotate around observ. ref. point
          jsr       pers        * Perspective transformation
          jsr       hideit      * hide hidden surfaces
          jsr       paintit     * sort and shade

          jsr       pageup      * Display physical page
          jsr       inp_chan    * Input new parameters
          jsr       clwork      * clear screen page not displayed
          jsr       pointrot    * Rotate around rot. ref. point
          jsr       pers        * Transform new points
          jsr       hideit      * hide
          jsr       paintit     * sort and shade
```

```
            jsr       pagedown     * Display this logical page
            jsr       inp_chan     * Input and change parameters
            jsr       clwork       * erase physical page
            jmp       mainlop1     * to main loop

mainend:  move.l    physbase,logbase

            jsr       pageup       * Switch to normal screen page
            rts                    * back to link file and end




*********************************************************************
*    Creation of rotation body by passing parameters             *
*    and calling rotation routine                                *
*********************************************************************

makerot1: jsr       r1set        * Set parameters of rot. body
            jsr       rotstart     * and create rot. body
            rts




*********************************************************************
*   Input and change parameters with the keyboard                *
*********************************************************************

inp_chan: jsr       inkey        * Read keyboard, code in
            cmp.b     #'D',d0
            bne       inpwait
            jsr       scrdmp       * Make hardcopy

inpwait:  swap      d0           * Test D0 for
            cmp.b     #$4d,d0      * Cursor-right
            bne       inp1
            addq.w    #1,ywplus    * if yes, add one to
            bra       inpend1      * Y-angle increment and continue

inp1:     cmp.b     #$4b,d0      * Cursor-left, if yes
            bne       inp2         * subtract one from
            subq.w    #1,ywplus    * Y-angle increment
            bra       inpend1
```

```
inp2:       cmp.b       #$50,d0         * Cursor-down, if yes
            bne         inp3
            addq.w      #1,xwplus       * add one to X-angle
            bra         inpend1         * increment


inp3:       cmp.b       #$48,d0         * Cursor-up
            bne         inp3a
            subq.w      #1,xwplus       * subtract one
            bra         inpend1


inp3a:      cmp.b       #$61,d0         * Undo key
            bne         inp3b
            subq.w      #1,zwplus       * decrease Z-increment
            bra         inpend1


inp3b:      cmp.b       #$62,d0         * Help key
            bne         inp4
            addq.w      #1,zwplus       * increase Z-increment
            bra         inpend1


inp4:       cmp.b       #$4e,d0         * + key on keypad
            bne         inp5            * if yes, subtract 25 from
            sub.w       #25,dist        * location of projection
            bra         inpend1         * plane (Z-coordinate)
inp5:       cmp.b       #$4a,d0         * minus key on keypad
            bne         inp6            *
            add.w       #25,dist        * if yes, add 25
            bra         inpend1


inp6:       cmp.b       #$66,d0         * * key on keypad
            bne         inp7            * if yes, subtract 15 from
            sub.w       #15,rotdpz      * rotation point Z-coordinate
            bra         inpend1         * Make change


inp7:       cmp.b       #$65,d0         * / key on keypad
            bne         inp10
            add.w       #15,rotdpz      * add 15
            bra         inpend1
```

```
inp10:     cmp.b      #$44,d0      * F10 pressed ?
           bne        inpend1
           addq.l     #4,a7        * if yes, then jump to
           bra        mainend      * program end

inpend1:   move.w     hyangle,d1   * Rotat.angle about Y-axis
           add.w      ywplus,d1    * add increment
           cmp.w      #360,d1      * if larger than 360, then
           bge        inpend2      * subtract 360
           cmp.w      #-360,d1     * if smaller than 360, then
           ble        inpend3      * add 360
           bra        inpend4
inpend2:   sub.w      #360,d1
           bra        inpend4
inpend3:   add.w      #360,d1


inpend4:   move.w     d1,hyangle

           move.w     hxangle,d1   * do the same for
           add.w      xwplus,d1    * the rotation angle
           cmp.w      #360,d1      * about X-axis
           bge        inpend5
           cmp.w      #-360,d1
           ble        inpend6
           bra        inpend7
inpend5:   sub.w      #360,d1
           bra        inpend7
inpend6:   add.w      #360,d1


inpend7:   move.w     d1,hxangle      *

           move.w     hzangle,d1
           add.w      zwplus,d1
           cmp.w      #360,d1
           bge        inpend8
           cmp.w      #-360,d1
           ble        inpend9
           bra        inpend10
inpend8:   sub.w      #360,d1
           bra        inpend10
inpend9:   add.w      #360,d1
```

```
inpend10: move.w      d1,hzangle
          rts


******************************************************************
*    Initialize the rotation reference point to [0,0,0]        *
******************************************************************


setrotdp: move.w      #0,d1        * set the Initial rotation
          move.w      d1,rotdpx    * ref. point
          move.w      d1,rotdpy
          move.w      d1,rotdpz
          move.w      #0,hyangle   * initial rotation angle
          move.w      #0,hzangle
          move.w      #0,hxangle
          rts


******************************************************************
*    Rotation around the rotation reference point about all    *
*    three axes                                                *
******************************************************************


pointrot: move.w      hxangle,xangle * rotate the world around
          move.w      hyangle,yangle
          move.w      hzangle,zangle
          move.w      rotdpx,d0      * rotation reference point
          move.w      rotdpy,d1
          move.w      rotdpz,d2
          move.w      d0,xoffs       * add for inverse transform
          move.w      d1,yoffs
          move.w      d2,zoffs
          neg.w       d0
          neg.w       d1
          neg.w       d2
          move.w      d0,offx        * subtract for transform
          move.w      d1,offy
          move.w      d2,offz
          jsr         matinit        * initialize matrix
          jsr         zrotate        * rotate first about Z-axis
          jsr         yrotate        * rotate 'matrix' about Y-axis
          jsr         xrotate        * then rotate about X-axis
          jsr         rotate         * Multiply points with matrix.
          rts
```

```
*******************************************************************
* Create world system by copying the object data into world system   *
*******************************************************************

makewrld: move.l     #r1datx,a1    * Create world system by
          move.l     #r1daty,a2
          move.l     #r1datz,a3
          move.l     #wrldx,a4
          move.l     #wrldy,a5
          move.l     #wrldz,a6
          move.w     r1nummark,d0
          ext.l      d0
          subq.l     #1,d0
makewl1:  move.w     (a1)+,(a4)+    * copying point coordinates
          move.w     (a2)+,(a5)+    * into the world system
          move.w     (a3)+,(a6)+
          dbra       d0,makewl1
          move.w     r1numline,d0
          ext.l      d0
          subq.l     #1,d0
          move.l     #r1lin,a1
          move.l     #wlinxy,a2
makewl2:  move.l     (a1)+,(a2)+    * Copy lines into world
          dbra       d0,makewl2    * system

          move.l     worldpla,a0
          move.l     #wplane,a1
          move.w     r1numsurf,d0
          ext.l      d0
          subq.l     #1,d0

makewl3:  move.w     (a0)+,d1       * Copy surfaces into
          move.w     d1,(a1)+       * world system
          ext.l      d1
          subq.l     #1,d1

makewl4:  move.l     (a0)+,(a1)+    * Copy every line of
          dbra       d1,makewl4    * this surface into

          dbra       d0,makewl3    * world array until all
          rts                      * surfaces are completed
```

```
********************************************************************
*  Pass the world parameters to the variables in the              *
*  link files                                                     *
********************************************************************

wrldset:   move.l      #wrldx,datx    * Pass the variables
           move.l      #wrldy,daty    * for the rotation
           move.l      #wrldz,datz    * routine
           move.l      #viewx,pointx
           move.l      #viewy,pointy
           move.l      #viewz,pointz
           move.l      #wlinxy,linxy
           move.w      picturex,x0
           move.w      picturey,y0
           move.w      proz,zobs
           move.w      r1z1,dist
           move.l      #screenx,xplot
           move.l      #screeny,yplot
           move.w      hnumline,numline
           move.w      hnummark,nummark
           move.w      hnumsurf,numsurf
           rts


********************************************************************
* Remove all characters from keyboard buffer                      *
********************************************************************

clearbuf: move.w       #$b,-(a7)
          trap         #1
          addq.l       #2,a7
          tst.w        d0
          beq          clearnd
          move.w       #1,-(a7)
          trap         #1
          addq.l       #2,a7
          bra          clearbuf

clearnd:  rts
```

```
***************************************************************
*    Sense display resolution and set coordinate             *
*    origin to screen center                                 *
***************************************************************

getreso:   move.w     #4,-(a7)          * Sense display resolution
           trap       #14
           addq.l     #2,a7
           cmp.w      #2,d0
           bne        getr1
           move.w     #320,picturex    * Monochrome monitor
           move.w     #200,picturey
           bra        getrend
getr1:     cmp.w      #1,d0
           bne        getr2
           move.w     #320,picturex    * medium resolution (640*200)
           move.w     #100,picturey
           bra        getrend
getr2:     move.w     #160,picturex    * low resolution (320*200)
           move.w     #100,picturey
getrend:   rts



***************************************************************
*    Hardcopy of screen, called by inp_chan                  *
*                                                            *
***************************************************************

scrdmp:    move.w     #20,-(a7)
           trap       #14
           addq.l     #2,a7
           jsr        clearbuf
           rts
```

```
*****************************************************************
* Sets the limits of the display window for the              *
* Cohen-Sutherland clipping algorithm built into the         *
* draw-line algorithm                                        *
* The limits can be freely selected by the user which makes  *
* the draw-line algorithm very flexible.                     *
*****************************************************************
setcocli: move.w    #0,clipxule
          move.w    #0,clipyule
          move.w    picturex,d1
          lsl.w     #1,d1          * times two
          subq.w    #1,d1          * minus one equals
          move.w    d1,clipxlri    * 639 for monochrom
          move.w    picturey,d1
          lsl.w     #1,d1          * times two minus one
          subq.w    #1,d1          * equals 399 for monochrome
          move.w    d1,clipylri
          rts


*****************************************************************
*    Pass visible surfaces into vplane array and             *
*    into pladress array for subsequent sorting              *
*    of surfaces                                             *
*****************************************************************

hideit:
          move.w    numsurf,d0     * Number of surfaces as
          ext.l     d0             * counter
          subq.l    #1,d0
          move.l    #viewx,a1      * The point
          move.l    #viewy,a2      * coordinates are stored here
          move.l    #viewz,a3
          move.l    #wplane,a0     * Here is the information
          move.l    #vplane,a5     * for every surface
          move.w    #0,surfcount   * Counts the known visible surfaces.

          move.l    #pladress,a6   * Address of surface storage

visible:  move.w    (a0),d1        * Start with first surface
          ext.l     d1             * Number of points on this surface in D1
          move.w    2(a0),d2       * Offset of first point of this surface
```

```
        move.w    4(a0),d3        * Offset of second point
        move.w    8(a0),d4        * Offset of third point
        subq.w    #1,d2           * For access to point array
        subq.w    #1,d3           * subtract one from current
        subq.w    #1,d4           * point offset.
        lsl.w     #1,d2           * Multiply by two
        lsl.w     #1,d3
        lsl.w     #1,d4           * and access current
        move.w    (a1,d3.w),d6    * point coordinates
        cmp.w     (a1,d4.w),d6    * Comparison recognizes two points
        bne       doit1           * with the same coordinates
*                                 * created through
        move.w    (a2,d3.w),d6    * construction of
        cmp.w     (a2,d4.w),d6    * rotation bodies. When
        bne       doit1           * two points are found
        move.w    (a3,d4.w),d6    * where all point coordinates (x,y,z)
        cmp.w     (a3,d3.w),d6    * match, the program selects the
        bne       doit1           * third point to find
        move.w    12(a0),d4       * both vectors
        subq.w    #1,d4
        lsl.w     #1,d4

doit1:
        move.w    (a1,d3.w),d5    * the two vectors which
        move.w    d5,kx           * lie in the surface plane
        sub.w     (a1,d2.w),d5    * are found by subtracting the
        move.w    d5,px           * coordinates of two points
        move.w    (a2,d3.w),d5    * in this surface
        move.w    d5,ky           * the direction coord. of the
        sub.w     (a2,d2.w),d5    * vectors is stored in
        move.w    d5,py           * variables qx,qy,qz and
        move.w    (a3,d3.w),d5    * px,py,pz
        move.w    d5,kz
        sub.w     (a3,d2.w),d5
        move.w    d5,pz

        move.w    (a1,d4.w),d5    * Calculate vector Q
        sub.w     (a1,d2.w),d5
        move.w    (a2,d4.w),d6
        sub.w     (a2,d2.w),d6
        move.w    (a3,d4.w),d7
        sub.w     (a3,d2.w),d7
```

```
        move.w    d5,d1          * qx
        move.w    d6,d2          * qy
        move.w    d7,d3          * qz

        muls      py,d3          * Compute cross product
        muls      pz,d2          * of the vector perpendicular
        sub.w     d2,d3          * to the current surface
        move.w    d3,rx
        muls      pz,d1
        muls      px,d7
        sub.w     d7,d1          * The direction coordinates of
        move.w    d1,ry          * the vector perpendicular to
        muls      px,d6          * the surface are stored
        muls      py,d5          * in rx,ry,rz
        sub.w     d5,d6
        move.w    d6,rz

        move.w    prox,d1        * The projection center serves as
        sub.w     kx,d1          * comparison point for the visibility
        move.w    proy,d2        * of a surface which seems
        sub.w     ky,d2          * adquate for the viewing
        move.w    proz,d3        * situation. The observation
        sub.w     kz,d3          * ref. point can also
        muls      rx,d1          * be used as the comparison point.
        muls      ry,d2          * Compare vector R and
        muls      rz,d3          * the vector from one
        add.l     d1,d2          * point of the surface to
        add.l     d2,d3          * the projection center by forming
        bmi       dosight        * the scalar product of the two vectors

* If the scalar product is negative, surface is visible

        move.w    (a0),d1        * Number of lines in surface
        ext.l     d1
        lsl.l     #2,d1          * Number of lines times 4 = space for lines
        addq.l    #2,d1          * plus 2 bytes for number of lines

        add.l     d1,a0          * add to surface array for
sight1: dbra      d0,visible     * access to next surface
        bra       hideend        * All surfaces processed ? End
```

```
dosight:   move.w    (a0),d1    * Number of lines for this surface
           ext.l     d1         * multiplied by two results in


********************************************************************
** Changes from the program rot1.s                              **
**                                                              **
********************************************************************

           move.l    d1,d2
           lsl.l     #1,d1      * Number of words to be passed
           move.l    a0,a4
           addq.l    #2,a4      * Access to first line of the surface
           move.w    #0,zsurf   * Clear addition storage

sight2:    move.l    (a4)+,d6   * first line of surface
           swap      d6         * first point in lower half of D0
           subq.w    #1,d6      * fit index
           lsl.w     #1,d6      * fit operand size (2-Byte)

           move.w    (a3,d6.w),d6   * Z-coordinate of this point
           add.w     d6,zsurf       * add all Z-coordinates
           dbra      d2,sight2      * until all lines are computed

           move.w    zsurf,d6   * Divide sum of all Z-coordinates
*                               * for this
           ext.l     d6         * surface by the number of lines
           lsr.l     #2,d6      * Surfaces created by rotation
           ext.l     d6         * always have four lines.
           move.l    d6,(a6)+   * Store middle Z-Coordinate
           move.l    a0,(a6)+   * followed by address of surface

sight3:    move.w    (a0)+,(a5)+  * pass number of lines

           dbra      d1,sight3      * and individual lines
           addq.w    #1,surfcount   * increase number of surfaces by one
           bra       sight1         * and work on next surface
hideend:   rts
```

```
********************************************************************
*  Create rotation body by passing parameters,                   *
*  rotating the definition line, and creating the line and       *
*  surface arrays                                                 *
********************************************************************


r1set:
          move.l    #r1xdat,rotxdat    * Pass the
          move.l    #r1ydat,rotydat    * parameters for
          move.l    #r1zdat,rotzdat    * rotation body to
          move.l    #r1datx,rotdatx    * routine for
          move.l    #r1daty,rotdaty    * creating the
          move.l    #r1datz,rotdatz    * rotation body
          move.l    rotdatx,datx       * array addresses of
          move.l    rotdaty,daty       * the points
          move.l    rotdatz,datz
          move.w    r1numro,numro      * Number of desired rotations
          move.w    r1numpt,numpt      * Number of points to be rotated
          move.l    #r1lin,linxy       * Address of line array
          move.l    #r1plane,worldpla  * Address of surface array
          rts

rotstart: move.w    numpt,d0           * Rotation of def line
          lsl.w     #1,d0              * numro+1 times about Y-axis
          ext.l     d0
          move.l    d0,plusrot         * Storage for one line
          move.w    numpt,nummark      * Number of points
          move.l    rotdatx,pointx     * rotated
          move.l    rotdaty,pointy
          move.l    rotdatz,pointz
          move.w    #0,yangle
          move.w    #360,d0            * 360 / numro = angle increment
          divs      numro,d0           * per rotation
          move.w    d0,plusagle        * store
          move.w    numro,d0           * numro +1 times
          ext.l     d0

rloop1:   move.l    d0,loopc           * as loop counter
          move.l    rotxdat,datx
          move.l    rotydat,daty
          move.l    rotzdat,datz
          jsr       yrot               * rotate
```

```
              move.l      pointx,d1            * add offset
              add.l       plusrot,d1
              move.l      d1,pointx
              move.l      pointy,d1
              add.l       plusrot,d1
              move.l      d1,pointy
              move.l      pointz,d1
              add.l       plusrot,d1
              move.l      d1,pointz
              move.w      yangle,d7
              add.w       plusagle,d7
              move.w      d7,yangle
              move.l      loopc,d0
              dbra        d0,rloop1

              move.w      r1numro,numro
              move.w      r1numpt,numpt
              jsr         rotlin               * Create line array
              jsr         rotsurf              * Create surface array
              rts

rotlin:
              move.w      #1,d7
              move.w      numro,d4             * Number of rotations
              ext.l       d4
              subq.l      #1,d4
              move.w      numpt,d1             * Number of points in def. lin.
              subq.w      #1,d1                * both as counters
              lsl.w       #2,d1                * times two
              ext.l       d1
              move.l      d1,plusrot

rotlop1:      move.w      numpt,d5             * Number of points minus once
              ext.l       d5                   * repeat, last line
              subq.l      #2,d5                * connect points (n-1,n)
              move.l      linxy,a1
              move.w      d7,d6
rotlop2:      move.w      d6,(a1)+             * first line connects
              addq.w      #1,d6                * points (1,2) then (2,3) etc.
              move.w      d6,(a1)+
              dbra        d5,rotlop2
```

```
             move.l     linxy,d1
             add.l      plusrot,d1
             move.l     d1,linxy
             move.w     numpt,d0
             add.w      d0,d7
             dbra       d4,rotlop1

             move.w     numpt,d7
             move.w     d7,delta1
             lsl.w      #2,d7
             ext.l      d7
             move.l     d7,plusrot
             move.w     #1,d6
             move.w     numpt,d0
             ext.l      d0
             subq.l     #1,d0

rotlop3:     move.w     numro,d1
             ext.l      d1
             subq.l     #1,d1
             move.w     d6,d5

rotlop4:     move.w     d5,(a1)+        * generate cross
             add.w      delta1,d5       * connection lines which
             move.w     d5,(a1)+        * connect lines created
             dbra       d1,rotlop4      * by rotation

             add.w      #1,d6
             dbra       d0,rotlop3
             move.w     numro,d1
             add.w      #1,d1

             muls       nummark,d1

             move.w     d1,r1nummark
             move.w     numpt,d1
             muls       numro,d1
             move.w     numpt,d2
             subq.w     #1,d2
             muls       numro,d2
             add.w      d1,d2
```

```
            move.w    d2,r1numline  * store number of lines
            rts


rotsurf:    move.w    numro,d0      * Create surfaces of
            ext.l     d0            * rotation body
            subq.l    #1,d0
            move.w    numpt,d7      * Number of points minus one
            ext.l     d7            * repeat
            subq.l    #2,d7
            move.l    d7,plusrot

            move.l    worldpla,a0   * Address of surface array
            move.w    #1,d1
            move.w    numpt,d2      * Number of points
            addq.w    #1,d2

rotfl1:     move.l    plusrot,d7    * Offset
rotfl2:     move.w    d1,d4
            move.w    d2,d5
            addq.w    #1,d4
            addq.w    #1,d5
            move.w    #4,(a0)+      * Number of lines/surfaces

            move.w    d1,(a0)+      * first surface created here
            move.w    d4,(a0)+
            move.w    d4,(a0)+
            move.w    d5,(a0)+
            move.w    d5,(a0)+
            move.w    d2,(a0)+
            move.w    d2,(a0)+
            move.w    d1,(a0)+
            addq.w    #1,d1
            addq.w    #1,d2
            dbra      d7,rotfl2
            addq.w    #1,d1
            addq.w    #1,d2

            dbra      d0,rotfl1
            move.w    numpt,d1
            subq.w    #1,d1
            muls      numro,d1
```

```
          move.w    d1,r1numsurf
          rts




**********************************************************************
* Pass data and parameters to the link file routines               *
**********************************************************************

wrld2set: move.l    #wrldx,datx
          move.l    #wrldy,daty
          move.l    #wrldz,datz
          move.l    #viewx,pointx
          move.l    #viewy,pointy
          move.l    #viewz,pointz
          move.l    #wlinxy,linxy
          move.w    picturex,x0
          move.w    picturey,y0
          move.w    proz,zobs
          move.w    r1z1,dist
          move.l    #screenx,xplot
          move.l    #screeny,yplot
          move.w    r1numline,numline
          move.w    r1nummark,nummark
          move.w    r1numsurf,numsurf
          rts




**********************************************************************
* Sort surfaces stored in pladress                                 *
**********************************************************************

sortit:   move.l    #pladress,a0
          move.w    surfcount,d7
          ext.l     d7              * for i = 2 to n corresponds to
          subq.l    #2,d7
          bmi       serror          * for i = 1 to n-1 because of
          move.l    #1,d1           * different array structure
sortmain: move.l    d1,d2
          subq.l    #1,d2           * j = i -1
          move.l    d1,d3           * i
          lsl.l     #3,d3
```

```
          move.l    (a0,d3.l),d5       * Comparison value x = a[i]
          move.l    4(a0,d3.l),d6      * Address of surface
          move.l    d5,platz           * a[0] = x = a[-1] in
          move.l    d6,platz+4         * this array
sortlop1: move.l    d2,d4              * j
          lsl.l     #3,d4              * j times 8 for access to array
          cmp.l     (a0,d4.l),d5       * Z-coordinate of surface
          bge       sortw1             * while x < a[j] do

          move.l    (a0,d4.l),8(a0,d4.l)    * a[j+1] = a[j]
          move.l    4(a0,d4.l),12(a0,d4.l)  * Address of  surface array
          subq.l    #1,d2              * j = j-1
          bra       sortlop1


sortw1:   move.l    d5,8(a0,d4.l)      * a[j+1] = x
          move.l    d6,12(a0,d4.l)     * pass address also
          addq.l    #1,d1              * i = i + 1
          dbra      d7,sortmain        * until all surfaces are sorted
sortend:  rts


serror:   rts                          * On error simply return



********************************************************************
* Fill surfaces stored in pladress                               *
********************************************************************


paintit:  jsr       setclip            * GEM clipping routine for Filled Area
          jsr       sortit             * Sort surfaces according to Z-coords.
          move.w    #1,d0              * Write mode to replace
          jsr       filmode
          jsr       filform            * border filled surfaces
          jsr       filcolor           * Fill color is one
          move.w    #2,d0              * Fill style
          jsr       filstyle
          move.l    xplot,a1           * Address of screen coordinates
          move.l    yplot,a2
          move.w    surfcount,d7       * Number of surfaces to be filled
          ext.l     d7                 * as counter
          subq.l    #1,d7              * access to last surface in the array
          move.l    d7,d0              * multiply by eight
          lsl.l     #3,d0
```

```
            move.l      #pladress,a0   * here are the surfaces
            move.l      (a0,d0.1),d5   * largest Z-coordinate
            move.l      #0,d1
            move.l      (a0,d1.1),d6   * first surface in array
            neg.l       d6             * smallest Z-coordinate
            add.l       d6,d5          * subtract from each other
paint1:     move.l      d5,d0
            move.l      (a0,d1.1),d2   * first surface in array
            add.l       d6,d2          * plus smallest Z-coordinate
            lsl.l       #3,d2          * times eight, eight different
            divs        d0,d2          * fill patterns, divide by difference
            neg.w       d2             * leave out last pattern
            add.w       #6,d2
            bpl         paint2
            move.w      #1,d2

paint2:     move.w      d2,d0                   * Set fill index
            jsr         filindex
            move.l      #ptsin,a3               * Enter points here
            move.l      4(a0,d1.1),a6           * Address of surface
            move.w      (a6)+,d4                * Number of lines
            addq.w      #1,d4                   * first point counts double
            move.w      d4,contrl+2
            move.l      (a6)+,d3                * first line of surface
            swap        d3
            subq.w      #1,d3
            lsl.w       #1,d3
            move.w      (a1,d3.w),(a3)+         * transfer to ptsin array
            move.w      (a2,d3.w),(a3)+         * transmit Y-coordinate
            swap        d3
            sub.w       #1,d3
            lsl.w       #1,d3
            move.w      (a1,d3.w),(a3)+         * transmit next point
            move.w      (a2,d3.w),(a3)+         * transmit Y-coordinate
            subq.w      #3,d4                   * two points already transmitted
            ext.l       d4                      * one because of dbra
paint3:     move.l      (a6)+,d3                * next line
            subq.w      #1,d3
            lsl.w       #1,d3
            move.w      (a1,d3.w),(a3)+         * X-coordinate
            move.w      (a2,d3.w),(a3)+         * Y-coordinate
            dbra        d4,paint3               * until all points in ptsin array
```

```
          move.w     #9,contrl          * then call the
          move.w     #0,contrl+6        * function Filled
          move.w     grhandle,contrl+12 * Area
          movem.l    d0-d2/a0-a2,-(a7)
          jsr        vdi
          movem.l    (a7)+,d0-d2/a0-a2
          add.l      #8,d1              * work on next
          dbra       d7,paint1          * surface in pladress
          rts



*********************************************************************
* VDI clipping, used only with VDI functions, also for          *
* filling surfaces.                                             *
*********************************************************************

setclip:  move.w     #129,contrl
          move.w     #2,contrl+2
          move.w     #1,contrl+6
          move.w     grhandle,contrl+12
          move.w     #1,intin
          move.w     clipxule,ptsin
          move.w     clipyule,ptsin+2
          move.w     clipxlri,ptsin+4
          move.w     clipylri,ptsin+6
          jsr        vdi
          rts


          .even



*********************************************************************
*********************************************************************
*   Start of variable area                                      *
*                                                               *
*********************************************************************


*********************************************************************
* Data area for rotation body                                   *
*********************************************************************
          .bss
```

```
numro:      .ds.w     1
numpt:      .ds.w     1

rotxdat:    .ds.l     1
rotydat:    .ds.l     1
rotzdat:    .ds.l     1

rotdatx:    .ds.l     1
rotdaty:    .ds.l     1
rotdatz:    .ds.l     1

r1numline:  .ds.w     1
r1nummark:  .ds.w     1
r1numsurf:  .ds.w     1

plusagle:   .ds.w     1

r1datx:     .ds.w     1540
r1daty:     .ds.w     1540
r1datz:     .ds.w     1540

r1lin:      .ds.l     3200      * 4-Bytes for every line
r1plane:    .ds.l     6600


            .data


r1xdat:     .dc.w 0,40,50,50,20,30,20,30,70,80,80,0

r1ydat:     .dc.w 100,100,80,60,40,30,30,-70,-80,-90,-100,-100

r1zdat:     .dc.w 0,0,0,0,0,0,0,0,0,0,0,0

r1numpt:    .dc.w     12
r1numro:    .dc.w     8       * Number of rotations for creation
```

```
**********************************************************************
*                                                                    *
*                                                                    *
*          Definition of the house                                   *
*                                                                    *
**********************************************************************
```

```
            .data

housdatx:  .dc.w       -30,30,30,-30,30,-30,-30,30,0,0,-10,-10,10,10
           .dc.w       30,30,30,30,30,30,30,30,30,30,30,30

housdaty:  .dc.w       30,30,-30,-30,30,30,-30,-30,70,70,-30,0,0,-30
           .dc.w       20,20,0,0,20,20,0,0
           .dc.w       -10,-10,-30,-30

housdatz:  .dc.w       60,60,60,60,-60,-60,-60,-60,60,-60,60,60,60,60
           .dc.w       40,10,10,40,-10,-40,-40,-10
           .dc.w       0,-20,-20,0

houslin:   .dc.w       1,2,2,3,3,4,4,1,2,5,5,8,8,3,8,7,7,6,6,5,6,1,7,4
           .dc.w       9,10,1,9,9,2,5,10,6,10,11,12,12,13,13,14
           .dc.w       15,16,16,17,17,18;18,15,19,20,20,21,21,22,22,19
           .dc.w       23,24,24,25,25,26,26,23
```

```
**********************************************************************
* here are the definitions of the surfaces for the House            *
*                                                                    *
**********************************************************************
```

```
houspla:   .dc.w       4,1,2,2,3,3,4,4,1,4,2,5,5,8,8,3,3,2
           .dc.w       4,5,6,6,7,7,8,8,5,4,7,6,6,1,1,4,4,7
           .dc.w       4,4,3,3,8,8,7,7,4,4,2,9,9,10,10,5,5,2
           .dc.w       4,10,9,9,1,1,6,6,10,3,1,9,9,2,2,1
           .dc.w       3,5,10,10,6,6,5,4,11,12,12,13,13,14,14,11
           .dc.w       4,15,16,16,17,17,18,18,15,4,19,20,20,21,21,22,22,19
           .dc.w       4,23,24,24,25,25,26,26,23

hnummark:  .dc.w       26      * Number of corner points in the house
hnumline:  .dc.w       32      * Number of lines in the house
hnumsurf:  .dc.w       13      * Number of surfaces in the house
```

```
hxangle:   .dc.w      0     * Rotation angle of house about X-axis
hyangle:   .dc.w      0     *         "         "         "  Y-axis
hzangle:   .dc.w      0     *         "         "         "  Z-axis


xwplus:    .dc.w      0     * Angle increment about X-axis
ywplus:    .dc.w      0     * Angle increment about Y-axis
zwplus:    .dc.w      0     * Angle increment about Z-axis


picturex:  .dc.w      0     * Definition of zero point of display
picturey:  .dc.w      0     * entered by getreso


rotdpx:    .dc.w      0
rotdpy:    .dc.w      0
rotdpz:    .dc.w      0


r1z1:      .dc.w      0
normz:     .dc.w      1500



           .bss

plusrot:   .ds.l      1
first:     .ds.w      1
second:    .ds.w      1
delta1:    .ds.w      1

worldpla:  .ds.l      1

           .data

plag:      .dc.b      1
           .even

           .bss

diffz:     .ds.w      1
```

```
dx:        .ds.w    1
dy:        .ds.w    1
dz:        .ds.w    1

wrldx:     .ds.w    1600    * World coordinate array
wrldy:     .ds.w    1600
wrldz:     .ds.w    1600

viewx:     .ds.w    1600    * View coordinate array
viewy:     .ds.w    1600
viewz:     .ds.w    1600

screenx:   .ds.w    1600    * Screen coordinate array
screeny:   .ds.w    1600


wlinxy:    .ds.l    3200    * Line array



wplane:    .ds.l    6600    * Surface array

vplane:    .ds.l    6600    * Surface array of visible surfaces

platz:     .ds.l    2
pladress: .ds.l     3000    * Surface array

surfcount: .ds.w    1

numsurf:   .ds.w    1

zcount:    .ds.l    1       * Sum of all Z-coord.
zsurf:     .ds.w    1       * Individual Z-coord.of surface

sx:        .ds.w    1
sy:        .ds.w    1
sz:        .ds.w    1

px:        .ds.w    1
py:        .ds.w    1
pz:        .ds.w    1
```

```
rx:        .ds.w      1
ry:        .ds.w      1
rz:        .ds.w      1


qx:        .ds.w      1
qy:        .ds.w      1
qz:        .ds.w      1


kx:        .ds.w      1
ky:        .ds.w      1
kz:        .ds.w      1


           .data

prox:      .dc.w      0        * Coordinates of projection
proy:      .dc.w      0        * center, on the positive
proz:      .dc.w      1500     * Z-axis


           .data

offx:      .dc.w      0        * Transformation through rotation
offy:      .dc.w      0        * to point [offx,offy,offz]
offz:      .dc.w      0


xoffs:     .dc.w      0        * Inverse transformation to point
yoffs:     .dc.w      0        * [xoff,yoffs,zoffs]
zoffs:     .dc.w      0



           .bss

loopc:     .ds.l      1
           .end
```

4.4.1   New things in the main program rotate1.s:

The creation of a surface array during construction of the rotation body is accomplished through the subroutine `rotsurf:`. The array (`r1plane`) is of course passed from the subroutine `makewrld:` into the world system (`wplane`). Furthermore, the subroutines `hideit:`, `setclip:` and `paintit:` as well as the sort routine `sortit:` are new and have already been explained. This sort routine sorts the array `surfaddr`, which contains the Z-coordinates of the visible surfaces as well as the addresses of the visible surfaces, according to increasing Z-coordinates. The subroutine `sortit:` uses the old trick, an additional array index at the beginning of the array. You can recognize this by the variable `space:` in the variable part of the program. The variable `space:` reserves additional space for a data record in the `surfaddr`-arrays. The additional space is used as a marker during sorting. The actual sort algorithm is nothing but a simple insert sort. For better understanding, here is a structogram of the sort algorithm:

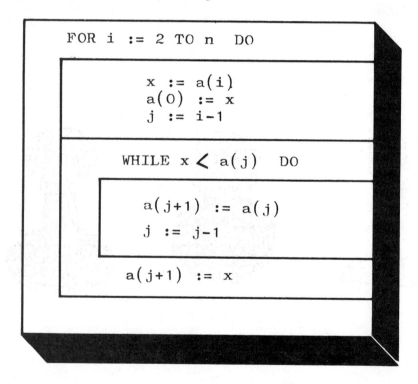

Figure 4.4.4: Structogram of the sort algorithm

4.4.2   Sort algorithm:

In this program too, you should change various parameters to see what they do. Up to now you had to change all the parameters in the program text. This meant that you had to do a lot of assembling and linking just to change a few parameters. The sort algorithm will allow you to change parameters while the program is running. One method to change these parameters is through a menu. See the diagram below. More about this in the next section.

Input	4-Pts	8-Pts	12-Pts	18-Pts	24-Pts	45-Pts	60-Pts	POS	Quit
F-1	F-2	F-3	F-4	F-5	F-6	F-7	F-8	F-9	F-10

  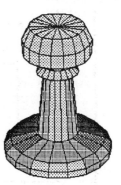

4.5   Entering rotation lines with the mouse

We are now ready to combine the subroutines which we have so far used separately and to construct a little program for creating rotation bodies, including the removal of hidden lines and shading surfaces. Furthermore, we also want to be able to enter the creation lines for the rotation body with the mouse so that we don't have to reassemble the program when we want to use a new definition line. Owners of 520ST's may find themselves running short of memory. The available storage space permits the input of 25 points for a definition line of the rotation body which can then be rotated 60 times about the Y-axis. Thus a maximum of 25*61 = 1525 points and about 3000 lines and almost 1500 surfaces will be created. To store this many parameters as well as the program we need about 190Kbytes of memory, about a third of which is wasted because the object is defined twice (datx, daty, datz, wrldx, wrldy, wrldz). This is done to make things easier, but also in consideration of the next main program which displays several objects at the same time. We also have to keep in mind the memory require by the two screen pages--about 64K

The amount of memory reserved in this program is intended for use on the "smaller" model. Owners of 1 mega byte computers can display larger objects if they want by reserving more space for the individual arrays. The following relationships as are used to calculate the memory requirements:

Number of points:= r1numpt * (r1numo+1)

Number of lines:= ((r1numpt-1)*r1numro) + (r1numpt*r1numro)

Number of surfaces:= (r1numpt-1) * r1numro

The number of lines can be estimated by multiplying the number of points by two. Each point naturally requires two bytes of storage space. You must also remember that every surface of the rotation body, requires 18 bytes of storage space since it is always constructed of four lines. In the surfaddr array every surface requires 8 bytes of additional storage space. With this information you can expand the programs yourself if you have a 1040ST. The introduction of the operating system in ROM will ease the lack of storage space. About 200K of RAM will be released by using the ROM. If you want to generate rotation bodies with more points without RAM enhancement, whether through ROMs or RAM chips, you can change the program so that the rotation body is not duplicated in the arrays `r1datx, r1daty, r1datz,` but generated only in the world system `wrldx, wrldy, wrldz` and the definition of `r1datx, r1daty, r1datz` is completely omitted. This will free about 50 Kbytes of storage which includes the savings from the line array (`r1lin`) and surface array (`r1plane`). This space can be distributed over the world array and thus used to generate larger bodies. The product of the number of points and the number of rotations plus one is limited. You can for example, rotate 16 points 90 times, or 40 points 30 times, etc. The only limits placed are those of your imagination. The number of rotation points to be entered is determined by the variable maxpoint and can be changed there.

The use of this program differs in a few points from the programs presented thus far. After the program start, a menu appears where you can determine the desired number of rotations of a rotation line already defined in the program. After you press one of the function keys F2 to F8, the familiar chess figure appears in the "wire model mode" with the desired number of rotations. The actual rotation parameters such as position of the rotation point and rotation angle increments can be changed with the cursor-keys. To remove hidden lines in this rotation body press the H key on the keyboard (H for Hide). After the visible surfaces have been drawn, you can fill them with a pattern by pressing the P key (P for Paint). In both cases you can obtain a hardcopy by pressing the <Alternate> and <Help> keys at the same time since the surfaces are drawn and in the visible screen page (physical display). The picture drawn on the display remains until the <Return> key is pressed and cannot be changed. As a further option you can fill all the surfaces in the "wire model mode" (P key), not only the visible ones. For hardcopy of a wire model, press Shift D. By pressing the F10 key you return to the main menu and you can enter a new rotation line with F1 and the help of the mouse.

After pressing F1 a small crosshair and a cartesian coordinate system whose origin is the middle of the screen appear. By clicking the left mouse button you can enter up to 25 points for a definition line. The right mouse button ends the definition after which you must press a key to return to the menu. You can set the number of rotations with the function keys. We almost forgot to mention the significance of the F9 function key which displays a mouse pointer when pressed in the wire model mode and allows you to set a new coordinate origin on the screen (left mouse button). Here are some examples of definition lines and the rotation bodies which result.

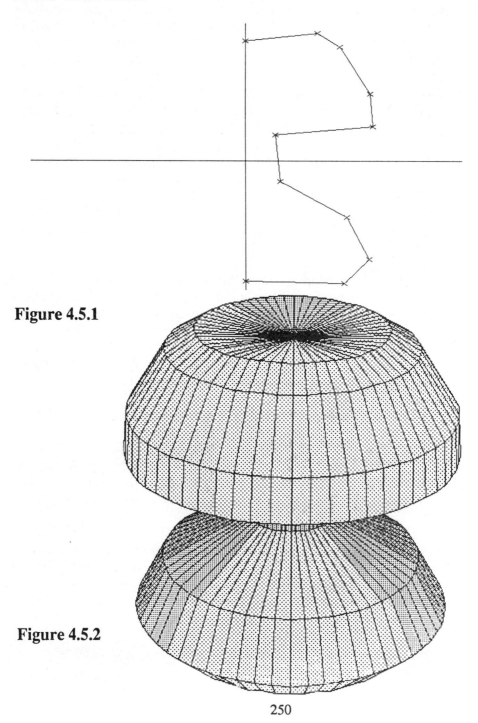

Figure 4.5.1

Figure 4.5.2

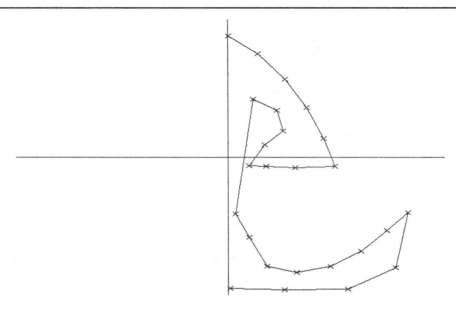

Figure 4.5.3

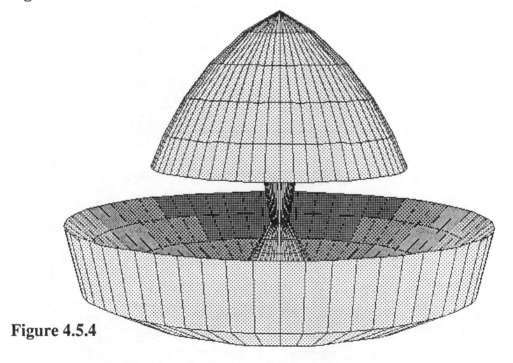

Figure 4.5.4

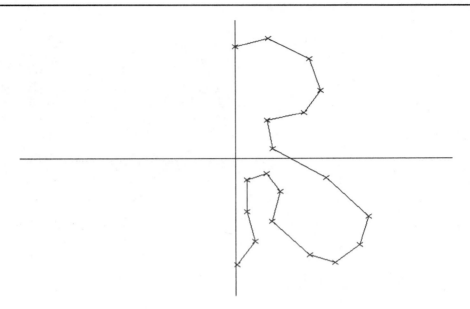

Figure 4.5.5

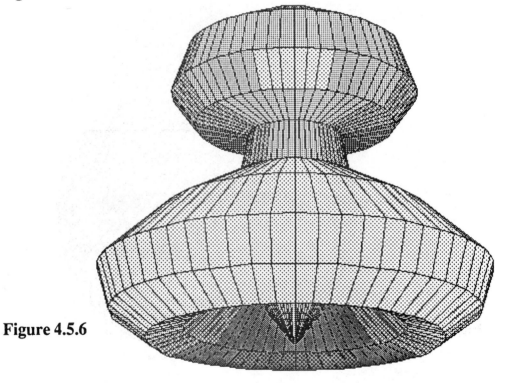

Figure 4.5.6

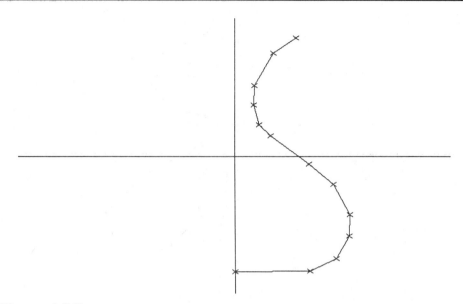

Figure 4.5.7

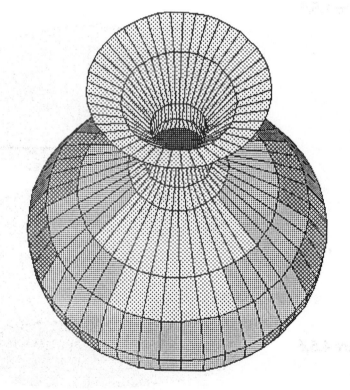

Figure 4.5.8

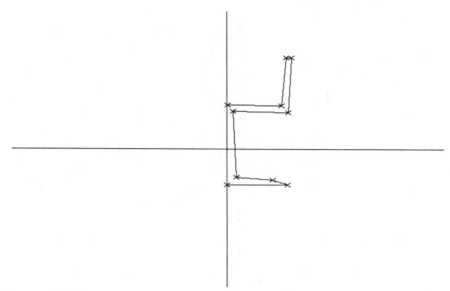

Figure 4.5.9

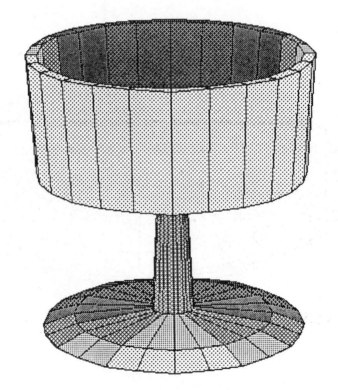

Figure 4.5.10

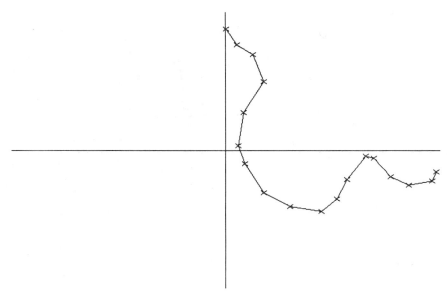

Figure 4.5.11

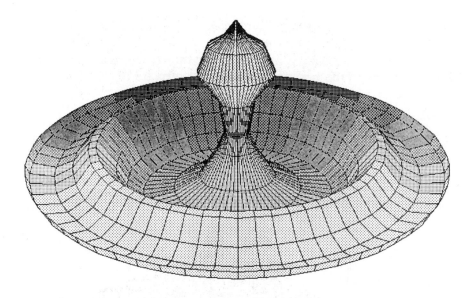

Figure 4.5.12

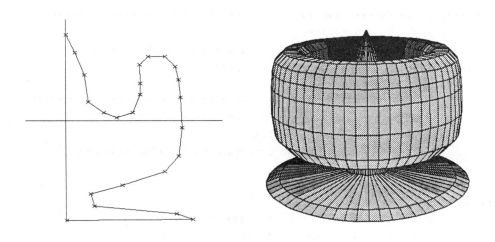

Figure 4.5.13

Don't let the program listing frighten you. First of all, if you have entered the previous programs, all you have to do is enter the new subroutines and change the main loop a bit. Second, you can get a disk containing all of the programs in the book from Abacus Software or your dealer.

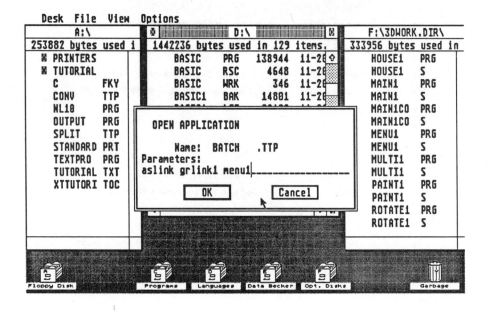

256

```
************************************************************************
*  menu1.s            2/18/1986                                       *
*  Creation of rotation bodies      Uwe Braun 1985  Version 2.2       *
*  with hidden line algorithm and painting                           *
*                                                                     *
************************************************************************
         .globl    main,xoffs,yoffs,zoffs,offx,offy,offz
         .globl    viewx,viewy,viewz
         .globl    wlinxy,mouse_off,setrotdp,inp_chan,pointrot
         .text

main:
         jsr       apinit       * Announce programm
         jsr       grafhand     * Get screen handler
         jsr       openwork     * Display
         jsr       mouse_off    * Turn off mouse
         jsr       getreso      * Display resolution
         jsr       setcocli     * set Cohen sutherland clip.

main1:   jsr       clearbuf
         jsr       menu

         jsr       makerot1     * create rotation body

         jsr       makewrld     * create world system
         jsr       wrld2set     * pass world parameters
         jsr       pageup
         jsr       clwork
         jsr       setrotdp     * initialize observer ref. point
         jsr       pagedown     * Display logical screen page
         jsr       clwork
         jsr       inp_chan

mainlop1:
         jsr       pointrot     * rotate around observ. ref. point
         jsr       pers         * Perspective transformation
         jsr       drawn1

         jsr       pageup       * Display physical screen page
         jsr       testhide
```

```
              jsr      inp_chan     * Input new parameters
              jsr      clwork       * clear page not displayed
              jsr      pointrot     * Rotate around rot ref. point
              jsr      pers         * Transform new points
              jsr      drawn1

              jsr      pagedown     * Display this logical page
              jsr      inp_chan     * Input and change parameters
              jsr      clwork       * erase physical page
              jmp      mainlop1     * to main loop

mainend:  move.l     physbase,logbase

              jsr      pageup       * switch to normal screen page
              rts                   * back to link file and end


*********************************************************************
*  Display menu and selection of menu points                       *
*********************************************************************

menu:     jsr      switch       * Display and draw the same
          move.l   #text2,a0    * screen page
          jsr      printf       * Display menu list
          move.l   #text3,a0
          jsr      printf

menu0:    jsr      inkey        * Read keyboard
          swap     d0
          cmp.b    #$3b,d0      * F1 key pressed ?
          bne      menu1
          jsr      inpmous      * if yes, enter a line
          bra      menu

menu1:    cmp.b    #$3c,d0      * F2 key pressed ?
          bne      menu2
          move.w   #4,r1numro   * if yes, then initial number of
          bra      menend       * rotations to four
```

```
menu2:    cmp.b     #$3d,d0      * F3 key
          bne       menu3
          move.w    #8,r1numro
          bra       menend


menu3:    cmp.b     #$3e,d0      * F4 key
          bne       menu4
          move.w    #12,r1numro
          bra       menend


menu4:    cmp.b     #$3f,d0      * F5 key
          bne       menu5
          move.w    #18,r1numro
          bra       menend


menu5:    cmp.b     #$40,d0      * F6 key
          bne       menu6
          move.w    #24,r1numro
          bra       menend


menu6:    cmp.b     #$41,d0      * F7 key
          bne       menu7
          move.w    #45,r1numro
          bra       menend


menu7:    cmp.b     #$42,d0      * F8 key
          bne       menu8
          move.w    #60,r1numro
          bra       menend


menu8:                           * Room for additional keyboard commands


menu9:    cmp.b     #$44,d0      * F10 key
          bne       menu0
          addq.l    #4,a7
          bra       mainend
menend:   rts
```

```
***********************************************************************
*  Test if removal of hidden surface and shading of surfaces   *
*  is desired                                                  *
***********************************************************************

testhide: jsr        inkey          * Read keyboard
          swap       d0
          cmp.b      #$23,d0        * h key pressed ?
          beq        dohide         * if yes, call hideit
          cmp.b      #$19,d0        * p key pressed ?
          beq        dopaint        * is yes, shade
          rts                       * if not, return


***********************************************************************
*  Call hideit routine to remove hidden Surfaces               *
***********************************************************************

dohide:   jsr        switch         * or you won't see anything
          jsr        clwork         * erase display
          jsr        hideit         * remove
          jsr        surfdraw        * and draw

dohide1:  jsr        inkey          * shade too ?
          swap       d0
          cmp.b      #$19,d0        * if yes, call fill routine
          beq        dopain2
          cmp.b      #$1c,d0        * if not, wait for activation of
          bne        dohide1        * Return key on main keyboard
          jsr        pageup
          rts                       * and back

dopain2:  jsr        paintit        * Shade surfaces
dopain3:  jsr        inkey
          swap       d0
          cmp.b      #$1c,d0        * wait for return key
          bne        dopain3
          jsr        pageup
          rts
```

```
*******************************************************************
*  Shade all surfaces defined in the world system                *
*******************************************************************

dopaint:  jsr       switch
          jsr       clwork
          jsr       paintall    * shade all
dopaint1: jsr       inkey
          swap      d0
          cmp.b     #$1c,d0     * and wait for Return key on the
          bne       dopaint1    * main keyboard
          jsr       pageup
          rts




*******************************************************************
*  Create the rotation body                                      *
*******************************************************************

makerot1: jsr       r1set       * Set parameters of this rot. body
          jsr       rotstart    * Create rot. body
          rts




*******************************************************************
*  Input and change parameters                                   *
*******************************************************************

inp_chan: jsr       inkey       * Read keyboard, key code in
          cmp.b     #'D',d0
          bne       inpwait
          jsr       scrdmp      * Make hardcopy

inpwait:  swap      d0          * Test D0 for
          cmp.b     #$4d,d0     * Cursor-right
          bne       inp1
          addq.w    #1,ywplus   * if yes, add one to Y-angle
          bra       inpend1     * and continue
```

```
inp1:     cmp.b      #$4b,d0       * Cursor-left, if yes, subtract
          bne        inp2          * one from Y-angle increment
          subq.w     #1,ywplus
          bra        inpend1


inp2:     cmp.b      #$50,d0       * Cursor-down, if yes
          bne        inp3
          addq.w     #1,xwplus     * add one to X-angle increment
          bra        inpend1


inp3:     cmp.b      #$48,d0       * Cursor-up
          bne        inp3a
          subq.w     #1,xwplus     * subtract one
          bra        inpend1


inp3a:    cmp.b      #$61,d0       * Undo key
          bne        inp3b
          subq.w     #1,zwplus
          bra        inpend1


inp3b:    cmp.b      #$62,d0       * Help key
          bne        inp4
          addq.w     #1,zwplus
          bra        inpend1


inp4:     cmp.b      #$4e,d0       * plus key on the keypad
          bne        inp5          * if yes, subtract 25 from base of
          sub.w      #25,dist      * projection plane (Z-coordinate)
          bra        inpend1
inp5:     cmp.b      #$4a,d0       * minus key on the keypad
          bne        inp6          *
          add.w      #25,dist      * if yes, add 25
          bra        inpend1


inp6:     cmp.b      #$66,d0       *  * key on keypad
          bne        inp7          * if yes, subtract 15 from rotation
          sub.w      #15,rotdpz    * point Z-coordinate
          bra        inpend1       * make changes
```

```
inp7:       cmp.b       #$65,d0      * Division key on keypad
            bne         inp8
            add.w       #15,rotdpz   * add 15
            bra         inpend1


inp8:       cmp.b       #$43,d0      * F9 pressed ?, if yes,
            bne         inp10
            jsr         newmidd      * display new screen center
            bra         inpend1


inp10:      cmp.b       #$44,d0      * F10 pressed ?
            bne         inpend1
            addq.l      #4,a7        * if yes, jump to new input
            bra         main1


inpend1:    move.w      hyangle,d1   * Rotation angle about the Y-axis
            add.w       ywplus,d1    * add increment
            cmp.w       #360,d1      * if larger than 360, subtract 360
            bge         inpend2
            cmp.w       #-360,d1     * if smaller than 360,
            ble         inpend3      * add 360
            bra         inpend4
inpend2:    sub.w       #360,d1
            bra         inpend4
inpend3:    add.w       #360,d1


inpend4:    move.w      d1,hyangle

            move.w      hxangle,d1   * proceed in the same manner with the
            add.w       xwplus,d1    * rotation angle about the X-axis
            cmp.w       #360,d1
            bge         inpend5
            cmp.w       #-360,d1
            ble         inpend6
            bra         inpend7
inpend5:    sub.w       #360,d1
            bra         inpend7
inpend6:    add.w       #360,d1


inpend7:    move.w      d1,hxangle       *
```

```
          move.w    hzangle,d1
          add.w     zwplus,d1
          cmp.w     #360,d1
          bge       inpend8
          cmp.w     #-360,d1
          ble       inpend9
          bra       inpend10
inpend8:  sub.w     #360,d1
          bra       inpend10
inpend9:  add.w     #360,d1

inpend10: move.w    d1,hzangle
          rts




****************************************************************
* Set the location of the coordinate origin of the screen     *
* system with the mouse                                        *
****************************************************************

newmidd:  jsr       switch
          jsr       mousform    * change mouse form
newmidd1: move.w    x0,d2
          move.w    y0,d3
          jsr       mouspos     * wait for mouse input
          move.w    x0,d2       * must be called for unknown reasons
          move.w    y0,d3       * twice for one input of the
          jsr       mouspos     * Position
          cmp.b     #$20,d1     * left button ? if not, then
          bne       newmidd1    * once more from the beginning
          move.w    d2,x0       * store new coordinates
          move.w    d3,y0
          rts




****************************************************************
*   Determine the current screen resolution                   *
****************************************************************

getreso:  move.w    #4,-(a7)
          trap      #14
          addq.l    #2,a7
```

```
              cmp.w       #2,d0
              bne         getr1
              move.w      #320,picturex    * Monochrome monitor
              move.w      #200,picturey
              bra         getrend
getr1:        cmp.w       #1,d0
              bne         getr2
              move.w      #320,picturex    * medium resolution (640*200)
              move.w      #100,picturey
              bra         getrend
getr2:        move.w      #160,picturex    * low resolution (320*200)
              move.w      #100,picturey
getrend:      rts



**********************************************************************
*    Hardcopy of screen, called by inp_chan                       *
**********************************************************************


scrdmp:       move.w      #20,-(a7)
              trap        #14
              addq.l      #2,a7
              jsr         clearbuf
              rts



**********************************************************************
*    Initialize the rotation reference point to [0,0,0]           *
**********************************************************************


setrotdp:     move.w      #0,d1            * set the initial rotation
              move.w      d1,rotdpx        * ref. point
              move.w      d1,rotdpy
              move.w      d1,rotdpz
              move.w      #0,hyangle       * initial rotation angle
              move.w      #0,hzangle
              move.w      #0,hxangle
              move.w      #0,ywplus
              move.w      #0,xwplus
              move.w      #0,zwplus
              rts
```

```
*****************************************************************
*   Rotation around the rot. ref. point about all three axes      *
*****************************************************************

pointrot: move.w      hxangle,xangle * rotate the world around the
          move.w      hyangle,yangle
          move.w      hzangle,zangle
          move.w      rotdpx,d0       * rotation ref. point
          move.w      rotdpy,d1
          move.w      rotdpz,d2
          move.w      d0,xoffs        * add for inverse transformation
          move.w      d1,yoffs
          move.w      d2,zoffs
          neg.w       d0
          neg.w       d1
          neg.w       d2
          move.w      d0,offx         * subtract for tranformation
          move.w      d1,offy
          move.w      d2,offz
          jsr         matinit         * initialize matrix
          jsr         zrotate         * rotate 'matrix' about Z-axis
          jsr         yrotate         * rotate 'matrix' about Y-axis
          jsr         xrotate         * then rotate about X-axis
          jsr         rotate          * multiply point with matrix
          rts


*****************************************************************
* Set the limit of display window for the Cohen-Sutherland clip   *
* algorithm built into the draw-line algorithm                    *
* The limits are freely selectable by the user which makes the    *
* draw-line algorithm very flexible.                              *
*****************************************************************

setcocli: move.w      #0,clipxule
          move.w      #0,clipyule
          move.w      picturex,d1
          lsl.w       #1,d1           * times two
          subq.w      #1,d1           * minus one equals
          move.w      d1,clipxlri     * 639 for monochrome
          move.w      picturey,d1
          lsl.w       #1,d1           * times two minus one equals
          subq.w      #1,d1           * 399 for monochrome
```

```
        move.w    d1,clipylri
        rts


**************************************************************
* Transfer object data into the world system .              *
**************************************************************

makewrld: move.l   #r1datx,a1      * create the world system through
        move.l    #r1daty,a2
        move.l    #r1datz,a3
        move.l    #wrldx,a4        * copying the point coordinates
        move.l    #wrldy,a5        * into the world system
        move.l    #wrldz,a6
        move.w    r1nummark,d0
        ext.l     d0
        subq.l    #1,d0
makewl1:  move.w   (a1)+,(a4)+
        move.w    (a2)+,(a5)+
        move.w    (a3)+,(a6)+
        dbra      d0,makewl1
        move.w    r1numline,d0     * Number of lines
        ext.l     d0
        subq.l    #1,d0
        move.l    #r1lin,a1
        move.l    #wlinxy,a2
makewl2:  move.l   (a1)+,(a2)+      * Copy lines into world Line
        dbra      d0,makewl2       * array

        move.l    worldpla,a0      * Adress of surface definition
        move.l    #wplane,a1       * of the body,
        move.w    r1numsurf,d0      * Number of surfaces on the body
        ext.l     d0              * as counter
        subq.l    #1,d0

makewl3:  move.w   (a0)+,d1        * All lines in this surface,
        move.w    d1,(a1)+         * and of course the number of
        ext.l     d1              * surfaces copied to world surface
        subq.l    #1,d1            * array

makewl4:  move.l   (a0)+,(a1)+      * copy every line of this surface
        dbra      d1,makewl4       * to the world array
```

```
         dbra      d0,makewl3        * until all surfaces are completed
         rts


wrldset: move.l    #wrldx,datx       * Pass variables for
         move.l    #wrldy,daty       * the rotation routine
         move.l    #wrldz,datz
         move.l    #viewx,pointx
         move.l    #viewy,pointy
         move.l    #viewz,pointz
         move.l    #wlinxy,linxy
         move.w    picturex,x0       * Coordinate source for the
         move.w    picturey,y0       * screen system
         move.w    proz,zobs         * projection center
         move.w    rlz1,dist         * position of projection plane
         move.l    #screenx,xplot
         move.l    #screeny,yplot
         move.w    hnumline,numline
         move.w    hnummark,nummark
         move.w    hnumsurf,numsurf
         rts
```

```
*********************************************************************
*  Enter visible surface into the vplane array                    *
*********************************************************************


hideit:
            move.w      numsurf,d0      * Number of surfaces as counter
            ext.l       d0
            subq.l      #1,d0
            move.l      #viewx,a1       * point coordinates stored here
            move.l      #viewy,a2
            move.l      #viewz,a3
            move.l      #wplane,a0      * here is information for every
            move.l      #vplane,a5      * surface
            move.w      #0,surfcount    * counts the known visible surfaces

            move.l      #pladress,a6    * Address of the surface storage

visible:    move.w      (a0),d1         * start with first surface, number
            ext.l       d1              * of points in this surface in D1
            move.w      2(a0),d2        * Offset of first point of this surface
            move.w      4(a0),d3        * Offset of second point
            move.w      8(a0),d4        * Offset of third point
            subq.w      #1,d2           * Subtract one from current point offset
            subq.w      #1,d3           * for access to point srray
            subq.w      #1,d4
            lsl.w       #1,d2           * then multiply by two
            lsl.w       #1,d3
            lsl.w       #1,d4           * and finally access the current
            move.w      (a1,d3.w),d6    * point coordinates
            cmp.w       (a1,d4.w),d6    * comparison recognizes two points
            bne         doit1           * with some coordinates which can occur
            move.w      (a2,d3.w),d6    * during construction of rotation
            cmp.w       (a2,d4.w),d6    * bodies. If two
            bne         doit1           * points where all point coordinates
            move.w      (a3,d4.w),d6    * (x,y,z) match, the program selects
            cmp.w       (a3,d3.w),d6    * a third point to determine the two
            bne         doit1           * vectors
            move.w      12(a0),d4
            subq.w      #1,d4
            lsl.w       #1,d4
```

```
doit1:
        move.w    (a1,d3.w),d5    * here the two vectors which lie in the
        move.w    d5,kx           * surface plane are detemined by
*                                 *  subtraction
        sub.w     (a1,d2.w),d5    * of coordinates from two points of the
        move.w    d5,px           * points in this surface
        move.w    (a2,d3.w),d5
        move.w    d5,ky           * the direction coordinates of the
        sub.w     (a2,d2.w),d5    * vector are stored in the variables
        move.w    d5,py           * qx,qy,qz and px,py,pz
        move.w    (a3,d3.w),d5
        move.w    d5,kz
        sub.w     (a3,d2.w),d5
        move.w    d5,pz


        move.w    (a1,d4.w),d5    * calculation of vector Q
        sub.w     (a1,d2.w),d5
        move.w    (a2,d4.w),d6
        sub.w     (a2,d2.w),d6
        move.w    (a3,d4.w),d7
        sub.w     (a3,d2.w),d7
        move.w    d5,d1           * qx
        move.w    d6,d2           * qy
        move.w    d7,d3           * qz


        muls      py,d3           * calculation of the cross product
        muls      pz,d2           * of the vector perpendicular to
*                                 * the surface
        sub.w     d2,d3
        move.w    d3,rx
        muls      pz,d1
        muls      px,d7
        sub.w     d7,d1           * the direction coordinates of
*                                 * the vector
        move.w    d1,ry           * which is perpendicular to the
        muls      px,d6           * surface area stored temporarily in
        muls      py,d5           * rx,ry,rz
        sub.w     d5,d6
        move.w    d6,rz


        move.w    prox,d1         * The projection center is used as
        sub.w     kx,d1           * the comparison point for the
```

```
        move.w    proy,d2        * visibility of a surface, which is
        sub.w     ky,d2          * adequate for this viewing
        move.w    proz,d3        * situation. One can also use
        sub.w     kz,d3          * the observation ref. point
        muls      rx,d1          * as the comparison point.
        muls      ry,d2          * Now follows the comparison of the
        muls      rz,d3          * vector R and the vector from
        add.l     d1,d2          * one point on the surface to the
        add.l     d2,d3          * projection center by creating the
        bmi       dosight        * scalar product of the two vectors.
```

* the surface is visible, otherwise continue with next surface.

```
        move.w    (a0),d1      * Number of lines in surface
        ext.l     d1
        lsl.l     #2,d1        * Number of lines times 4 = space for lines
        addq.l    #2,d1        * plus 2 bytes for the number of lines

        add.l     d1,a0        * add to surface array, for access to
sight1: dbra      d0,visible   * next surface. If all surfaces
        bra       hideend      * completed, go to end.


dosight: move.w   (a0),d1      * Number of lines in this surface
         ext.l    d1           * multiplied by two gives result of

         move.l   d1,d2
         lsl.l    #1,d1        * number of words to be transmitted
         move.l   a0,a4
         addq.l   #2,a4        * Access to first line of surface
         move.w   #0,zsurf     * Erase addition storage

sight2: move.l    (a4)+,d6     * first line of surface
        swap      d6           * first point in lower half of D0
        subq.w    #1,d6        * adapt Index
        lsl.w     #1,d6        * adapt Operand size (2-byte)

        move.w    (a3,d6.w),d6 * Z-coordinate of this point
        add.w     d6,zsurf      * add all Z-Coordinates
        dbra      d2,sight2    * until all lines have been processed
```

```
          move.w    zsurf,d6        * Divide sum of all Z-coordinates of
          ext.l     d6              * this surface by the number of lines in
          lsr.l     #2,d6           * the surface. Surfaces created by
          ext.l     d6              * rotation always have four lines


          move.l    d6,(a6)+        * store middle Z-coordinates
          move.l    a0,(a6)+        * followed by address of surface

sight3:   move.w    (a0)+,(a5)+     * transmit the number of lines

          dbra      d1,sight3       * and the individual lines

          addq.w    #1,surfcount    * add one to the number of surfaces
          bra       sight1          * and work on next one

hideend:  rts



************************************************************************
*   Draw all surfaces contained in vplane                             *
************************************************************************


surfdraw:                          * Draws the number of surfaces passed
          move.l    xplot,a4        * in surfcount whose descriptions
          move.l    yplot,a5

          move.l    #vplane,a6      * were entered by hideit in the array
          move.w    surfcount,d0    * at address vplane
          ext.l     d0
          subq.l    #1,d0           * if there are no surfaces in the array
          bmi       surfend         * then end.
surflop1: move.w    (a6)+,d1        * Number of lines in this surface
          ext.l     d1              * as counter of lines to be drawn.
          subq.l    #1,d1

surflop2: move.l    (a6)+,d5        * first line of this surface

          subq.w    #1,d5           * Access to screen array where
          lsl.w     #1,d5           * screen coordinates of points are.
          move.w    0(a4,d5.w),d2
          move.w    0(a5,d5.w),d3   * extract points
          swap      d5              * pass routine.
```

```
              subq.w    #1,d5
              lsl.w     #1,d5
              move.w    0(a4,d5.w),a2    * second point belonging to
              move.w    0(a5,d5.w),a3    * line
              jsr       drawl            * draw line, until all lines in this
              dbra      d1,surflop2      * surface are drawn and repeat
              dbra      d0,surflop1      * until all surfaces are drawn.
surfend: rts                            * finally return.
```

```
*********************************************************************
* Set parameters of this rotation body                             *
*********************************************************************
```

```
r1set:
              move.l    #r1xdat,rotxdat    * Pass parameters of this
              move.l    #r1ydat,rotydat    * rotation body to routine
              move.l    #r1zdat,rotzdat    * for generating the
              move.l    #r1datx,rotdatx
              move.l    #r1daty,rotdaty    * rotation body
              move.l    #r1datz,rotdatz
              move.l    rotdatx,datx       * Array addresses of points
              move.l    rotdaty,daty
              move.l    rotdatz,datz
              move.w    r1numro,numro      * Number of desired rotatations.
              move.w    r1numpt,numpt      * Number of points to be rotated
              move.l    #r1lin,linxy       * Address of line array
              move.l    #r1plane,worldpla  * Address of surface array
              rts
```

```
*********************************************************************
*   and create rotation body                                       *
*********************************************************************
```

```
rotstart: move.w    numpt,d0          * Rotate the def line
          lsl.w     #1,d0             * numro+1 times about the Y-axis
          ext.l     d0
          move.l    d0,plusrot        * Storage space for one line
```

```
          move.w    numpt,nummark      * Number of points
          move.l    rotdatx,pointx     * rotate to here
          move.l    rotdaty,pointy
          move.l    rotdatz,pointz
          move.w    #0,yangle
          move.w    #360,d0            * 360 / numro = angle increment
          divs      numro,d0           * per rotation
          move.w    d0,plusagle        * store
          move.w    numro,d0           * numro +1 times
          ext.l     d0

rloop1:   move.l    d0,loopc           * as loop counter
          move.l    rotxdat,datx
          move.l    rotydat,daty
          move.l    rotzdat,datz
          jsr       yrot               * rotate
          move.l    pointx,d1          * add offset
          add.l     plusrot,d1
          move.l    d1,pointx
          move.l    pointy,d1
          add.l     plusrot,d1
          move.l    d1,pointy
          move.l    pointz,d1
          add.l     plusrot,d1
          move.l    d1,pointz
          move.w    yangle,d7
          add.w     plusagle,d7
          move.w    d7,yangle
          move.l    loopc,d0
          dbra      d0,rloop1

          move.w    r1numro,numro
          move.w    r1numpt,numpt
          jsr       rotlin             * Create line array
          jsr       rotsurf             * Create surface array
          rts

rotlin:
          move.w    #1,d7
          move.w    numro,d4           * Number of rotations
          ext.l     d4
          subq.l    #1,d4
```

```
         move.w   numpt,d1        * Number of points in the def. line.
         subq.w   #1,d1           * both as counter
         lsl.w    #2,d1           * times two
         ext.l    d1
         move.l   d1,plusrot

rotlop1: move.w   numpt,d5        * Number of points minus one
         ext.l    d5              * repeat, last line
         subq.l   #2,d5           * connects the points (n-1,n)
         move.l   linxy,a1
         move.w   d7,d6
rotlop2: move.w   d6,(a1)+        * the first line connects the
         addq.w   #1,d6           * points (1,2) then (2,3) etc.
         move.w   d6,(a1)+
         dbra     d5,rotlop2

         move.l   linxy,d1
         add.l    plusrot,d1
         move.l   d1,linxy
         move.w   numpt,d0
         add.w    d0,d7
         dbra     d4,rotlop1

         move.w   numpt,d7
         move.w   d7,delta1
         lsl.w    #2,d7
         ext.l    d7
         move.l   d7,plusrot
         move.w   #1,d6
         move.w   numpt,d0
         ext.l    d0
         subq.l   #1,d0

rotlop3: move.w   numro,d1
         ext.l    d1
         subq.l   #1,d1
         move.w   d6,d5

rotlop4: move.w   d5,(a1)+        * now generate the cross connections
         add.w    delta1,d5       * which connect the individual lines
         move.w   d5,(a1)+        * created by rotation
         dbra     d1,rotlop4
```

```
        add.w       #1,d6
        dbra        d0,rotlop3
        move.w      numro,d1
        add.w       #1,d1

        muls        nummark,d1

        move.w      d1,r1nummark
        move.w      numpt,d1
        muls        numro,d1
        move.w      numpt,d2
        subq.w      #1,d2
        muls        numro,d2
        add.w       d1,d2
        move.w      d2,r1numline  * Number of lines stored
        rts


rotsurf:  move.w    numro,d0     * create surfaces of the
          ext.l     d0           * rotation body
          subq.l    #1,d0
          move.w    numpt,d7     * Number of points minus one
          ext.l     d7           * repeat
          subq.l    #2,d7
          move.l    d7,plusrot

          move.l    worldpla,a0  * Address of surface array
          move.w    #1,d1
          move.w    numpt,d2     * Number of points
          addq.w    #1,d2
```

```
rotfl1:    move.l     plusrot,d7    * Offset
rotfl2:    move.w     d1,d4
           move.w     d2,d5
           addq.w     #1,d4
           addq.w     #1,d5
           move.w     #4,(a0)+      * Number of lines / surfaces

           move.w     d1,(a0)+      * the first surface is
           move.w     d4,(a0)+      * created here
           move.w     d4,(a0)+
           move.w     d5,(a0)+
           move.w     d5,(a0)+
           move.w     d2,(a0)+
           move.w     d2,(a0)+
           move.w     d1,(a0)+
           addq.w     #1,d1
           addq.w     #1,d2
           dbra       d7,rotfl2
           addq.w     #1,d1
           addq.w     #1,d2

           dbra       d0,rotfl1
           move.w     numpt,d1
           subq.w     #1,d1
           muls       numro,d1
           move.w     d1,r1numsurf
           rts
```

```
*************************************************************************
* Transfer the world parameters and the variables to the link file   *
*************************************************************************

wrld2set: move.l     #wrldx,datx       * transfer the world parameters
          move.l     #wrldy,daty       * and the variables to the
          move.l     #wrldz,datz       * routines in the link file
          move.l     #viewx,pointx
          move.l     #viewy,pointy
          move.l     #viewz,pointz
          move.l     #wlinxy,linxy
          move.w     picturex,x0
          move.w     picturey,y0
          move.w     proz,zobs
          move.w     r1z1,dist
          move.l     #screenx,xplot
          move.l     #screeny,yplot
          move.w     r1numline,numline
          move.w     r1nummark,nummark
          move.w     r1numsurf,numsurf
          rts


*************************************************************************
*   Sort all surfaces entered in pladress                             *
*************************************************************************

sortit:   move.l     #pladress,a0
          move.w     surfcount,d7
          ext.l      d7                * for i = 2 to n corresponds to
          subq.l     #2,d7             * number of runs
          bmi        serror            * for i = 1 to n-1 because of
          move.l     #1,d1             * different array structure
sortmain: move.l     d1,d2
          subq.l     #1,d2             * j = i -1
          move.l     d1,d3             * i
          lsl.l      #3,d3
          move.l     (a0,d3.1),d5      * Comparison value x = a[i]
          move.l     4(a0,d3.1),d6     * address of the surface
          move.l     d5,space          * a[0] = x = a[-1] in this
          move.l     d6,space+4        * array
```

```
sortlop1: move.l    d2,d4              * j
          lsl.l     #3,d4              * j times 8 for access to array
          cmp.l     (a0,d4.1),d5       * Z-coordinate of surface
          bge       sortw1             * while x < a[j] do

          move.l    (a0,d4.1),8(a0,d4.1)    * a[j+1] = a[j]
          move.l    4(a0,d4.1),12(a0,d4.1)  * Address of surface array
          subq.l    #1,d2              * j = j-1
          bra       sortlop1

sortw1:   move.l    d5,8(a0,d4.1)      * a[j+1] = x
          move.l    d6,12(a0,d4.1)     * Pass address also
          addq.l    #1,d1              * i = i + 1
          dbra      d7,sortmain        * Until all surfaces have been sorted
sortend:  rts


serror:   rts                         * On error simply return
```

```
*****************************************************************
* paintall draws all surfaces in world array wplane independent of *
* their visibility; all surface addresses and middle Z-coordinates *
* are entered into the pladress array.                          *
*****************************************************************
```

```
paintall:
          move.w    numsurf,d0         * Number of surfaces
          ext.l     d0
          subq.l    #1,d0              * if no surface present
          bmi       pquit             * then terminate

          move.l    #viewz,a3
          move.l    #wplane,a0
          move.w    #0,surfcount       * Surface counter for surfdraw
          move.l    #pladress,a6       * surfaces are entered here

svisible:
          move.w    (a0),d1            * all surfaces are visible
          ext.l     d1
          subq.l    #1,d1
          move.w    #0,zsurf           * middle Z-coordinate
          move.l    a0,a4
          addq.l    #2,a4
```

```
ssightbl: move.l     (a4)+,d2        * first line of surface
          swap       d2
          subq.w     #1,d2
          lsl.w      #1,d2


ddoit1:   move.w     (a3,d2.w),d6    * add all Z-coordinates of this
          add.w      d6,zsurf        * surface
          dbra       d1,ssightbl
          move.w     zsurf,d6
          ext.l      d6              * then divide by four, shifting
          lsr.l      #2,d6           * is possible only with rotation
          ext.l      d6              * bodies since each surface has
          move.l     d6,(a6)+        * exactly four lines otherwise divide
          move.l     a0,(a6)+        * by number of lines

          addq.w     #1,surfcount  * increment surface counter for surfdraw
          move.w     (a0),d1         * A0 still points to number of lines
          ext.l      d1              * in this surface
          lsl.l      #2,d1           * Number of lines times four (1 long)
          addq.l     #2,d1           * 2 bytes for the number of lines

          add.l      d1,a0           * A0 points to next surface
          dbra       d0,svisible
          move.w     numsurf,surfcount
          jsr        paintit         * Fill surfaces in pladress
pquit:    rts

paintit:  jsr        setclip         * GEM clipping routine for filled area
          jsr        sortit          * Sort surfaces according to Z-coordinates
          move.w     #1,d0           * Write mode to replace
          jsr        filmode
          jsr        filform         * frame filled surface
          jsr        filcolor        * Shading color is one
          move.w     #2,d0           * Fill style
          jsr        filstyle
          move.l     xplot,a1        * Address of screen coordinates
          move.l     yplot,a2
          move.w     surfcount,d7    * Number of surface to be filled
          ext.l      d7              * as counter
          subq.l     #1,d7           * access last surface in array
          move.l     d7,d0           * multiply by eight
```

```
            lsl.l      #3,d0
            move.l     #pladress,a0      * here are largest Z-coordinate
            move.l     (a0,d0.l),d5      * surfaces
            move.l     #0,d1
            move.l     (a0,d1.l),d6      * first surface in array
            neg.l      d6                * smallest Z-coordinate
            add.l      d6,d5             * subtract from one another
paint1:     move.l     d5,d0
            move.l     (a0,d1.l),d2      * first surface in array
            add.l      d6,d2             * plus smallest Z-coordinate
            lsl.l      #3,d2             * times eight, eight different
            divs       d0,d2             * shading patterns, divide by
            neg.w      d2                * difference leave out last
            add.w      #6,d2             * pattern.
            bpl        paint2
            move.w     #1,d2

paint2:     move.w     d2,d0             * set fill index
            jsr        filindex
            move.l     #ptsin,a3         * enter points here
            move.l     4(a0,d1.l),a6     * Address of surface
            move.w     (a6)+,d4          * Number of lines
            addq.w     #1,d4             * first point counted twice
            move.w     d4,contrl+2
            move.l     (a6)+,d3          * first line of surface
            swap       d3
            subq.w     #1,d3
            lsl.w      #1,d3
            move.w     (a1,d3.w),(a3)+   * transfer to ptsin array
            move.w     (a2,d3.w),(a3)+   * pass Y-coordinate
            swap       d3
            sub.w      #1,d3
            lsl.w      #1,d3
            move.w     (a1,d3.w),(a3)+   * transmit next point
            move.w     (a2,d3.w),(a3)+   * transmit Y-coordinate
            subq.w     #3,d4             * already two points transmitted
            ext.l      d4                * and one because of dbra
paint3:     move.l     (a6)+,d3          * next line
            subq.w     #1,d3
            lsl.w      #1,d3
            move.w     (a1,d3.w),(a3)+   * X-coordinate
            move.w     (a2,d3.w),(a3)+   * Y-coordinate
```

```
          dbra      d4,paint3        * until all points in Ptsin-Array
          move.w    #9,contrl        * then call the fill area function
          move.w    #0,contrl+6
          move.w    grhandle,contrl+12
          movem.l   d0-d2/a0-a2,-(a7)
          jsr       vdi
          movem.l   (a7)+,d0-d2/a0-a2
          add.l     #8,d1            * work on next surface in pladress
          dbra      d7,paint1
          rts
```

```
*********************************************************************
* VDI clipping, only needed when VDI functions are used,          *
* for surface filling.                                            *
*********************************************************************
```

```
setclip:  move.w    #129,contrl
          move.w    #2,contrl+2
          move.w    #1,contrl+6
          move.w    grhandle,contrl+12
          move.w    #1,intin
          move.w    clipxule,ptsin
          move.w    clipyule,ptsin+2
          move.w    clipxlri,ptsin+4
          move.w    clipylri,ptsin+6
          jsr       vdi
          rts
```

```
*********************************************************************
* this subroutine allows coordinates to entered with the Mouse    *
* The maximum number of points is in the variable maxpoint, and   *
* is limited only by storage space                                *
*********************************************************************
```

```
inpmous:
          jsr       switch
          move.w    #5,d0
          jsr       setform
          move.w    #1,d0            * set input mode to mouse-request
          move.w    #1,d1            * wait for mouse input which is
          jsr       setmode         * terminated by key activation and
```

```
            jsr       coord        * mouse clicking
            move.l    #0,adressx
            move.w    #5,d0        * set polymarker to diagonal cross
            jsr       marktype


mouslop1:   jsr       mouspos      * For unknown reasons function must
            move.w    picturex,d2  * be called twice to work once.
            add.w     #15,d2
            move.w    picturey,d3
            sub.w     #40,d3
            jsr       mouspos
            cmp.b     #$20,d1      * wait until the left mouse button is
            bne       mouslop1     * pressed
            move.l    #r1xdat,a4   * arrays in which input
            move.l    #r1ydat,a5   * coordinates are entered; enough
            move.l    #r1zdat,a6   * storage must have been reserved

            move.w    d2,newx      * store mouse X and Y positions
            move.w    d3,newy
            jsr       saveit       * and pass line array
            move.w    newx,d2
            move.w    newy,d3
            jsr       markit       * set a polymarker

            add.l     #1,adressx   * increment counter
mous1:      nop

            move.w    newx,altx
            move.w    newy,alty
mouslop2:   move.w    altx,d2      * pass old position of the mouse
            move.w    alty,d3
            jsr       mouspos      * and call again
            jsr       mouspos
            cmp.b     #$21,d1      * if right mouse button, then
            beq       mousend      * end of mouse input
            cmp.b     #$20,d1
            bne       mouslop2
            move.w    d2,newx      * store mouse coordinates
            move.w    d3,newy
            jsr       saveit       * store in array
```

```
        move.w    newx,d2      * draw line from (n-1) n'th point
        move.w    newy,d3
        move.w    altx,a2
        move.w    alty,a3
        jsr       drawl
        move.w    newx,d2
        move.w    newy,d3
        jsr       markit       * and mark point with marker

        add.l     #1,adressx   * increment counter
        move.l    adressx,d7
        cmp.l     maxpoint,d7  * and compare with maximum point count
        bne       mous1        * if not equal, continue

        move.l    adressx,d0
        move.w    d0,r1numpt   * Number of points input
        rts

mousend: move.w   d2,newx
        move.w    d3,newy
        move.w    altx,a2
        move.w    alty,a3
        jsr       markit
        jsr       drawl        * draw last line

        jsr       wait         * and wait for keypress
        jsr       saveit

        add.l     #1,adressx   * also add last point
        move.l    adressx,d0
        move.w    d0,r1numpt   * now store total number of points
        rts                    * finally back to caller



****************************************************************
*  Wait for mouse input, returns also on keyboard input        *
****************************************************************

mouspos: move.w   #28,contrl   * Mouse input, the desired coordinates
        move.w    #1,contrl+2  * where the mouse should appear,
        move.w    #0,contrl+6  * are passed in
```

```
        move.w      grhandle,contrl+12

        move.w      d2,ptsin        * D2 and D3
        move.w      d3,ptsin+2
        jsr         vdi
        move.w      intout,d1       * the result - coordinates
        move.w      ptsout,d2       * are also returned in D2 and
        move.w      ptsout+2,d3     * D3
        rts



***********************************************************************
*  Set the polymarker type                                           *
***********************************************************************

marktype: move.w    #18,contrl           * determines the appearance of
          move.w    #0,contrl+2          * the polymarker, desired
          move.w    #1,contrl+6          * type is passed in D0
          move.w    grhandle,contrl+12
          move.w    d0,intin
          jsr       vdi
          rts




***********************************************************************
*  Set a polymarker, number in contrl+2                              *
***********************************************************************

markit:   move.w    #7,contrl
          move.w    #1,contrl+2          * Number of points, in this
          move.w    #0,contrl+6          * case only one
          move.w    grhandle,contrl+12
          move.w    d2,ptsin
          move.w    d3,ptsin+2
          movem.l   d0-d2/a0-a2,-(a7)
          jsr       vdi                  * draw marker
          movem.l   (a7)+,d0-d2/a0-a2
          rts
```

```
***********************************************************************
*   Set input mode                                                    *
***********************************************************************

setmode:   move.w      #33,contrl          * Set input mode
           move.w      #0,contrl+2
           move.w      #2,contrl+6
           move.w      grhandle,contrl+12
           move.w      d0,intin
           move.w      d1,intin+2          * Parameters in D0 and D1
           jsr         vdi
           rts




***********************************************************************
*   Store coordinates entered in point array                         *
***********************************************************************

saveit:    sub.w       picturex,d2         * Pass mouse coordinates to
           move.w      d2,(a4)+            * rotation line array, with
           sub.w       picturey,d3         * adaptation to coordinate system
           neg.w       d3
           move.w      d3,(a5)+
           move.w      #0,(a6)+
           rts
```

```
*********************************************************************
*  Display and describe the same screen page                       *
*********************************************************************

switch:    move.w     #-1,-(a7)          * Display of Display Page,
           move.l     physbase,-(a7)     * where drawing is made
           move.l     physbase,-(a7)
           move.w     #5,-(a7)
           trap       #14
           add.l      #12,a7
           rts




*********************************************************************
*  Change the mouse form                                           *
*********************************************************************

setform:   move.w     #78,contrl         * Set mouse form, desired shape
           move.w     #1,contrl+2
           move.w     #1,contrl+4        * passed in D0
           move.w     #1,contrl+6
           move.w     #0,contrl+8
           move.w     d0,intin
           jsr        aes
           rts




*********************************************************************
*     Drawing a coordinate system for mouse input                  *
*********************************************************************

coord:     jsr        clwork             * draw coordinate system
           move.w     #0,d2              * for mouse input
           move.w     picturey,d3
           move.w     picturex,d5
           lsl.w      #1,d5
           move.w     d5,a2
```

```
            move.w      d3,a3
            jsr         drawl
            move.w      picturex,d2
            move.w      #0,d3
            move.w      d2,a2
            move.w      picturey,d5
            lsl.w       #1,d5
            move.w      d5,a3

            jsr         drawl
            rts


*******************************************************************
* remove all characters present in the keyboard buffer          *
*******************************************************************

clearbuf: move.w     #$b,-(a7)    * Gemdos fnct. character in Buffer ?
          trap       #1
          addq.l     #2,a7
          tst.w      d0           * if yes, get character
          beq        clearnd      * if no, terminate
          move.w     #1,-(a7)     * Gemdos fnct. CONIN
          trap       #1           * repeat, until all characters
          addq.l     #2,a7        * are removed from the buffer
          bra        clearbuf

clearnd: rts




*******************************************************************
*  Definition of a custom mouse form - Data in mousfor1         *
*******************************************************************

mousform: move.l     #15,d0       * permits the definition of a
          move.l     #mousfor1,a1 * new mouse form, data is
          move.w     #111,contrl  * in mousfor1
          move.w     #0,contrl+2
          move.w     #37,contrl+6
          move.w     grhandle,contrl+12
          move.w     #8,intin
          move.w     #8,intin+2
```

```
            move.w      #1,intin+4
            move.w      #0,intin+6
            move.w      #1,intin+8
            move.l      #intin+10,a5
forlop:     move.l      (a1)+,(a5)+
            dbra        d0,forlop
            jsr         vdi
            rts

            .even


************************************************************************
************************************************************************
*   Beginning of the Variable area                                     *
*                                                                      *
************************************************************************
************************************************************************
* Data area for the rotation body                                     *
************************************************************************
            .bss

numro:      .ds.w       1
numpt:      .ds.w       1

rotxdat:    .ds.l       1
rotydat:    .ds.l       1
rotzdat:    .ds.l       1

rotdatx:    .ds.l       1
rotdaty:    .ds.l       1
rotdatz:    .ds.l       1

r1numline:  .ds.w       1
r1nummark:  .ds.w       1
r1numsurf:  .ds.w       1

plusagle:   .ds.w       1

r1datx:     .ds.w       1600
r1daty:     .ds.w       1600
r1datz:     .ds.w       1600
```

```
r1lin:     .ds.l    3200      * 4-Bytes for every line e
r1plane:   .ds.l    6600



           .data


r1xdat:    .dc.w 0,40,50,50,20,30,20,30,70,80,80,0
           .dc.w 0,0,0,0,0,0,0,0,0,0,0,0,0,0,0,0,0,0,0,0

r1ydat:    .dc.w 100,100,80,60,40,30,30,-70,-80,-90,-100,-100
           .dc.w 0,0,0,0,0,0,0,0,0,0,0,0,0,0,0,0,0,0,0,0

r1zdat:    .dc.w 0,0,0,0,0,0,0,0,0,0,0,0
           .dc.w 0,0,0,0,0,0,0,0,0,0,0,0,0,0,0,0,0,0,0,0

r1numpt:   .dc.w    12
r1numro:   .dc.w    8



****************************************************************************
*                                                                          *
*                                                                          *
*          Definition of the house                                        *
*                                                                          *
****************************************************************************


           .data

housdatx:  .dc.w    -30,30,30,-30,30,-30,-30,30,0,0,-10,-10,10,10
           .dc.w    30,30,30,30,30,30,30,30,30,30,30,30

housdaty:  .dc.w    30,30,-30,-30,30,30,-30,-30,70,70,-30,0,0,-30
           .dc.w    20,20,0,0,20,20,0,0
           .dc.w    -10,-10,-30,-30

housdatz:  .dc.w    60,60,60,60,-60,-60,-60,-60,60,-60,60,60,60,60
           .dc.w    40,10,10,40,-10,-40,-40,-10
           .dc.w    0,-20,-20,0
```

```
houslin:  .dc.w    1,2,2,3,3,4,4,1,2,5,5,8,8,3,8,7,7,6,6,5,6,1,7,4
          .dc.w    9,10,1,9,9,2,5,10,6,10,11,12,12,13,13,14
          .dc.w    15,16,16,17,17,18,18,15,19,20,20,21,21,22,22,19
          .dc.w    23,24,24,25,25,26,26,23
```

```
********************************************************************
* Here is the definition of the surfaces belonging to the house    *
********************************************************************
```

```
houspla:  .dc.w    4,1,2,2,3,3,4,4,1,4,2,5,5,8,8,3,3,2
          .dc.w    4,5,6,6,7,7,8,8,5,4,7,6,6,1,1,4,4,7
          .dc.w    4,4,3,3,8,8,7,7,4,4,2,9,9,10,10,5,5,2
          .dc.w    4,10,9,9,1,1,6,6,10,3,1,9,9,2,2,1
          .dc.w    3,5,10,10,6,6,5,4,11,12,12,13,13,14,14,11
          .dc.w    4,15,16,16,17,17,18,18,15,4,19,20,20,21,21,22,22,19
          .dc.w    4,23,24,24,25,25,26,26,23
```

```
hnummark: .dc.w    26     * Number of corner points in the house
hnumline: .dc.w    32     * Number of Lines in the House
hnumsurf: .dc.w    13     * Number of Surfaces in the House
```

```
hxangle:  .dc.w    0      * Rotation angle of House about the  X-axis
hyangle:  .dc.w    0      *          "           "          "    "   Y-axis
hzangle:  .dc.w    0      *          "           "          "    "   Z-Axis
```

```
xwplus:   .dc.w    0      * Angle increment about the X-axis
ywplus:   .dc.w    0      * Angle increment about the Y-axis
zwplus:   .dc.w    0      * Angle increment about the Z-axis
```

```
picturex: .dc.w    0      * Definition of zero point of screen
picturey: .dc.w    0      * entered by getreso
```

```
rotdpx:   .dc.w    0
rotdpy:   .dc.w    0
rotdpz:   .dc.w    0
```

```
r1z1:      .dc.w    0
normz:     .dc.w    1500



           .bss

plusrot:   .ds.l    1
first:     .ds.w    1
second:    .ds.w    1
delta1:    .ds.w    1

worldpla:  .ds.l    1

           .data

plag:      .dc.b    1
           .even

           .bss

diffz:     .ds.w    1

dx:        .ds.w    1
dy:        .ds.w    1
dz:        .ds.w    1

wrldx:     .ds.w    1600     * World coordinate array
wrldy:     .ds.w    1600
wrldz:     .ds.w    1600

viewx:     .ds.w    1600     * View coordinate array
viewy:     .ds.w    1600
viewz:     .ds.w    1600

screenx:   .ds.w    1600     * Screen coordinate array
screeny:   .ds.w    1600
```

```
wlinxy:     .ds.l    3200      * Line array



wplane:     .ds.l    6600      * Surface array

vplane:     .ds.l    6600      * Surface array of visible surface

space:      .ds.l    2
pladress: .ds.l      3000       * Surface array

surfcount: .ds.w     1

numsurf:    .ds.w    1

zcount:     .ds.l    1         * Sum of all Z-coord.
zsurf:      .ds.w    1         * Individual Z-coord. of surface

sx:         .ds.w    1
sy:         .ds.w    1
sz:         .ds.w    1

px:         .ds.w    1
py:         .ds.w    1
pz:         .ds.w    1

rx:         .ds.w    1
ry:         .ds.w    1
rz:         .ds.w    1

qx:         .ds.w    1
qy:         .ds.w    1
qz:         .ds.w    1

kx:         .ds.w    1
ky:         .ds.w    1
kz:         .ds.w    1
```

```
*******************************************
              .data
              .even

maxpoint: .dc.l     25
mousx:    .dc.w     0
mousy:    .dc.w     0
mousbut:  .dc.w     0
kybdstat: .dc.w     0

altx:     .dc.w     0
alty:     .dc.w     0
newx:     .dc.w     0
newy:     .dc.w     0

adressx:  .dc.l     1
              .data

prox:     .dc.w     0        * Coordinates of the projections
proy:     .dc.w     0        * center on the positive
proz:     .dc.w     1500     * Z-axis

              .data

offx:     .dc.w     0        * Transformation during rotation
offy:     .dc.w     0        * to point [offx,offy,offz]
offz:     .dc.w     0

xoffs:    .dc.w     0        * Inverse transformation to point
yoffs:    .dc.w     0        * [xoff,yoffs,zoffs]
zoffs:    .dc.w     0

text1:    .dc.b     27,'Y',56,61,' (c) Uwe Braun 1985 ',0
text2:    .dc.b     27,'E',27,'p',13,' Input  ',' 4-Pts  ',' 8-Pts  '
          .dc.b     ' 12-Pts '
          .dc.b     ' 18-Pts ',' 24-Pts ',' 45-Pts ',' 60-Pts '
          .dc.b     ' POS    ','  Quit',27,'q',0
text3:    .dc.b     13, 10,'  F-1   ','  F-2   ',',' F-3   ',',' F-4   '
          .dc.b     '  F-5   ','  F-6   ','  F-7   ','  F-8   '
          .dc.b     '  F-9   ','  F-10  ',13,0
```

```
mousfor1: .dc.w      %1111111111111111
          .dc.w      %1111111111111111
          .dc.w      %1111111111111111
          .dc.w      %1111111111111111
          .dc.w      %1111111111111111
          .dc.w      %1111111111111111
          .dc.w      %1111111111111111
          .dc.w      %1111111111111111
          .dc.w      %1111111111111111
          .dc.w      %1111111111111111
          .dc.w      %1111111111111111
          .dc.w      %1111111111111111
          .dc.w      %1111111111111111
          .dc.w      %1111111111111111
          .dc.w      %1111111111111111
          .dc.w      %1111111111111111


mousdat1: .dc.w      %0000001111100000
          .dc.w      %0000110000010000
          .dc.w      %0001001111001000
          .dc.w      %0010010000100100
          .dc.w      %0100100000010010
          .dc.w      %1001000000010100
          .dc.w      %1001000000010100
          .dc.w      %1000100000100101
          .dc.w      %0100011111001001
          .dc.w      %0010000000010010
          .dc.w      %0001111111100101
          .dc.w      %0011111111111001
          .dc.w      %0111111111111111
          .dc.w      %0111111111111111
          .dc.w      %1111111111111110
          .dc.w      %0000000000000000

          .bss

loopc:    .ds.l      1
          .end
```

4.5.1   Description of the new subroutines:

menu: Display a small menu and wait for a function key to be pressed. (F10 returns to Desktop immediately)

testhide: Test if H or P key pressed, branch accordingly to dohide or dopaint.

dohide: Calculate visible surfaces and draw. Then check if filling is required, if not, wait for <Return>.

dopaint: Fill all surfaces of rotation body and wait for <Return>.

paintall: Enter all surfaces of rotation body into surfaddr array, sort and fill.

inpmous: Enter up to 25 points (maxpoint) with the left mouse button. These points are entered through saveit into the point array of the rotation body. Enough space must be reserved in the point array by entering zeros here. For entering fewer than maxpoint points end input with the right mouse button.

mouspos: Wait for mouse input, also returns after keypress. Therefore it checks to see which event occured. This GEM function must be called twice for unknown reasons in order to wait once for an input.

marktype: Determines the appearance of the marker set by function polymarker.

markit: Call the function polymarker to set a marker.

setmode: Set input mode.

saveit: Stores the coordinates entered with the mouse in the point array of the definition line for the rotation body.

saveit: Stores the coordinates entered with the mouse in the point array of the definition line for the rotation body.

switch: Switches the logical page to the displayed page so that the page being drawn is the page being displayed. Otherwise the filling will not be seen and the hardcopy with <Alternate> and <Help> will not function either.

setform: Change mouse form.

coord: Draw a coordinate system.

mousform: Permits the definition of a user-defined mouse form whose data follows after mousfor1. This new mouse form appears after F9 is pressed and looks like a snail. You can change the data in the program according to your own taste.

4.6   Handling several objects

All subroutines discussed up to now really allow the simultaneous display of several objects. The only changes required are limited to the construction of an object definition block for each object, as well as an exchange of the makewrld routine. Let us consider the concrete example of the house from hide1.s and the changes that would be required, to construct a world system with two houses using the existing definition.

The most promising approach appears to be to copy all of the house definitions (housdatx, houslin, houspla, etc.) into the corresponding arrays of the world system several times. The point coordinate arrays housdatx etc. do not present problems. They can be simply appended to the world system. A world system containing two houses would contain 52 points. More difficult is the creation of the world line array since the line definition of the individual objects, here the two houses, always starts at point offset one; the first line of every object starts at point 1 and runs to point 2 for the houses. If the world point array is extended by another house, it becomes apparent that the first line of the second house starts at point 27 of the world point array and runs to point 28, since the first 26 points belong to the first object. The necessary procedure is simple: when constructing the line array from the individual object line arrays, add the total number of points in the first object to each line definition of the second object. Analagously, with three objects the sum of the points of the first two objects is added to the line definitions of the third object during construction of the world line array.

The principle of the construction of the world line array is also used during construction of the world surface array, for example the first surface definition of the second house within the world surface array:

    4,27,28,28,29,29,30,30,27

Furthermore, the total number of all points, lines and surfaces must be calculated and recorded.

If we start with a realistic world description, the positions of the objects in this world system can change continuously--recall the airplane and the tanker truck from Section 4.1. As a consequence of this, it is necessary to

objects belonging to it. The recreation is limited to the coordinate arrays
however, since only they change. The line and surface arrays are not
affected by the position change. The line and surface world arrays are
created only once at the beginning of the program. The coordinate array
is created twice in every main loop pass.

Now to the object definition block, which contains all the information
describing the individual object. The idea was to extend the available
world system by one object through addition of the definition block to the
existing blocks and incrementing the "object counter." Here for
clarification is an object definition block in which N is replaced with the
index of the current object:

```
objectN:
objNxda:    .dc.l   Address  of  the  X-coordinate  array
                    of the obj.
objNyda:    .dc.l   Address  of  the  Y-coordinate  array
                    of the obj.
objNzda:    .dc.l   Address  of  the  Z-coordinate  array
                    of the obj.
objNlin:    .dc.l   Address of the object line array
objNpla:    .dc.l   Address of the object surface array
objmrk:     .dc.w   Number of points in this object
objNali:    .dc.w   Number of lines in this object
objpln:     .dc.w   Number of surfaces on this object
objNx0:     .dc.w   X-position  of  object  in  world
                    system
objNy0:     .dc.w   Y-position  of  object  in  world
                    system
objNz0:     .dc.w   Z-position  of  object  in  world
                    system
objNxw:     .dc.w   Rotation angle of obj. about X-axis
objNyw:     .dc.w   Rotation angle about Y-axis
objNzw:     .dc.w   Rotation angle aboutZ-axis
```

The angles and also the position in the world system relate to the "rotationally neutral" point of the current object, the origin of the object definition coordinate system. As a whole, the block consists of 38 bytes, but can easily be extended with additional information, such as scale factors, etc. If two identical objects are to be created, you write two object definition blocks this is important since the creation routine finds the next block using the distance of 38 bytes between two blocks. Since two identical objects are to be created, the addresses for the two blocks are the same and only the position of the objects and perhaps the rotation angles differ. After the definition has been completed, the total number of objects, in this case two, is placed in the variable numobj: and now the total world system can be generated with a single subroutine call.

Examine the definition blocks in the following listing of multil.s, in which four identical objects are already created through concatenation of four object definition blocks. Naturally, you are not limited to the creation of identical objects. You can define a new object, such as a church, and enter its definition array address and desired position into an object block. Three houses and your church will be displayed.

Description of the new subroutines in multil.s:

The main loop is easily changed. Here the total number of the desired objects, four, is passed and the new subroutines new_wrld and new_mark are called.

new_wrld: The one-time call to the subroutine first creates the entire world system consisting of coordinate, line and surface arrays with corresponding parameter passing of the lines created, etc. Furthermore, the world parameters are passed to the variables of the link file. This assignment was previously performed by subroutine wrldset.

new_mark: Change the position of an object in the world system this subroutine recreates the total coordinate system with the aid of the modified parameters and at the same time passes the world parameters to the variables of the link file.

`new_it:`, `surf_lin:`, `surf_arr:`

These three subroutines are called by `new_wrld` and `new_,mark` and handle the actual creation of the world system from the individual object definitions.

`change:`   Change the object parameters of the individual objects. For simplification, modification is passed to all four objects.

General comments on the program:

Beside being able to display multiple objects, this program offers another novelty: two successive transformations of the same object. First, the four objects are "set" into the world system with `new_mark:` after they have first been rotated about three axes. After all objects have been "rotated" in the world system you can, through control with the keyboard, rotate the entire system consisting of the four houses around a point in the world system, or move the projection plane similar to previous programs. The four houses of the system rotate around different axes of their "rotationally neutral" points at various places in the world system. The display on the screen occurs after the removal of the hidden lines with the familiar subroutine `hideit:`, which is used on the complete world array so that the four houses are not created through mirroring or something similar, but the hidden surfaces of all four objects are calculated in real-time. The `hideit` algorithm of this program does not recognize covering by other visible surfaces so that a house covered by other houses will be drawn.

Control keys are again the cursor, help and undo keys, as well as the / * - + keys on the keypad.

The speed is quite impressive. One enhancement, besides the addition of user-defined objects, is the ability to change an object's parameters in the subroutine `change:` by keyboard input, for example, and to change the position of single objects in the system.

```
*********************************************************************
*   multil.s          22.2.1986                                     *
*   Multiple objects, four houses                                   *
*   with hidden line algorithm                                      *
*                                                                   *
*********************************************************************

            .globl    main,xoffs,yoffs,zoffs,offx,offy,offz
            .globl    viewx,viewy,viewz
            .globl    wlinxy,mouse_off,setrotdp,inp_chan,pointrot
            .globl    wrldx,wrldy,wrldz,gnummark,gnumline,gnumpla
            .globl    viewx,viewy,viewz,wplane
            .globl    new_it,new_wrld,obj2mrk,obj2pln
            .text



*********************************************************************
*    The program starts here--called by link-file                  *
*********************************************************************

main:
            jsr       apinit        * Announce program
            jsr       grafhand      * Get screen handle
            jsr       openwork      * Announce screen
            jsr       mouse_off     * Switch off mouse
            jsr       getreso       * Screen resolution
            jsr       setcocli      * set Cohen-Sutherland clip.

main1:      jsr       clearbuf
            move.w    #4,gnumobj    * announce four objects
            jsr       pageup
            jsr       clwork        * Screen resolution
            jsr       setrotdp      * initialize obs. ref. point.
            jsr       pagedown      * Display logical screen page
            jsr       clwork
            jsr       inp_chan      * Input and change world parameters
            jsr       change        * Change object parameters
            jsr       new_wrld      * create lines and surfaces
```

```
mainlop1:
        jsr     pointrot    * rotate around observ. ref. point
        jsr     pers        * Perspective transformation
        jsr     hideit      * calculate hidden surface
        jsr     surfdraw    * and draw
        jsr     pageup      * Display physical screenpage
        jsr     change      * change object parameters and
        jsr     new_mark    * calculate new coordinates
        jsr     inp_chan    * Input new parameters
        jsr     clwork      * erase page not displayed
        jsr     pointrot    * Rotate around rot. ref. point
        jsr     pers        * Transform new points
        jsr     hideit      * Calculate hidden surfaces
        jsr     surfdraw    * and draw them
        jsr     pagedown    * Display this logical page
        jsr     change      * Change object parameters
        jsr     new_mark    * Calculate new point coordinates
        jsr     inp_chan    * Input and change parameters
        jsr     clwork      * erase physical page
        jmp     mainlop1    * to main loop

mainend: move.l  physbase,logbase
        jsr     pageup      * switch to normal display page
        rts                 * back to link file, and end


*********************************************************************
*    Create the point coordinates of the world array with the      *
*    information from the object parameter block (object1)          *
*********************************************************************

new_mark: move.w  #0,offx
          move.w  #0,offy
          move.w  #0,offz
          jsr     new_it
          move.l  #viewx,pointx
          move.l  #viewy,pointy
          move.l  #viewz,pointz
          move.l  #wrldx,datx
          move.l  #wrldy,daty
          move.l  #wrldz,datz
          move.l  #wlinxy,linxy
```

```
          move.w     gnummark,nummark
          move.w     gnumline,numline
          move.w     gnumpla,numsurf
          rts



************************************************************************
*    Change the object parameter, in this case the rotation angle     *
*    in the object parameter block, which is then taken into account   *
*    when calculating point coordinates with rnew_mark                *
************************************************************************

change:   move.w     obj1yw,d0
          add.w      #4,d0
          cmp.w      #360,d0
          blt        changw1
          sub.w      #360,d0
changw1:
          move.w     d0,obj1yw
          move.w     d0,obj2xw
          move.w     d0,obj3zw
          move.w     d0,obj4xw
          move.w     d0,obj4yw
          move.w     d0,obj4zw
          rts



************************************************************************
*    Set all world parameters for the link file variables and         *
*    create the point, line, and surface arrays of the world system   *
************************************************************************

new_wrld: move.w     #0,d0
          move.w     d0,offx
          move.w     d0,offy
          move.w     d0,offz
          move.w     proz,zobs
          move.w     #0,dist          * Location of projection plane
          move.l     #screenx,xplot   * Address of screen array
          move.l     #screeny,yplot
          move.w     picturex,x0      * Screen center
          move.w     picturey,y0
```

```
        jsr     new_it          * Pass coordinates
        jsr     surf_lin        * Pass lines
        jsr     surf_arr        * Pass surfaces of
        move.w  gnummark,nummark  * all objects to world system
        move.w  gnumline,numline  * Total number of corners, lines
        move.w  gnumpla,numsurf   * and surfaces of world system
        move.l  #wrldx,datx       * Pass parameters of world system to
        move.l  #wrldy,daty       * link file variables
        move.l  #wrldz,datz
        move.l  #viewx,pointx
        move.l  #viewy,pointy
        move.l  #viewz,pointz
        move.l  #wlinxy,linxy
        rts
```

```
******************************************************************
*    Subroutine for creating the world system coordinate array   *
******************************************************************
```

```
new_it:    move.l  #0,mark_it      * Pointer in wrldx,wrldy,wrldz
           move.w  gnumobj,d0      * Total number of objects
           ext.l   d0              * as counter
           subq.l  #1,d0           * Address of first object parameter
           move.l  #object1,a0     * block after A0.
new_lop1:  move.l  (a0),datx       * Object1datx, daty,datz, pass
           move.l  4(a0),daty      * addresses of point array of
           move.l  8(a0),datz      * first object.
           move.l  mark_it,d7      * Offset in point array
           lsl.l   #1,d7           * times two bytes per entry
           move.l  d7,d6
           add.l   #wrldx,d7       * equals offset in world system array
           move.l  d7,pointx       * Target of transmission
           move.l  d6,d7
           add.l   #wrldy,d7
           move.l  d7,pointy
           add.l   #wrldz,d6
           move.l  d6,pointz       * Array of world coordinates
           move.w  20(a0),nummark  * Number of corners in the object
           move.w  26(a0),xoffs    * X-offset
           move.w  28(a0),yoffs    * Y-offset in the world system
           move.w  30(a0),zoffs    * Z-offset
```

```
          move.w      32(a0),xangle      * Rotation angle of object around
          move.w      34(a0),yangle      * the three coordinate axes
          move.w      36(a0),zangle
          movem.l     d0-d7/a0-a6,-(a7)  * Save registers
          jsr         matinit            * Initialize rotation matrix
          jsr         zrotate            * rotate first about the Z-axis, then
          jsr         yrotate            * around Y-axis, and finally
          jsr         xrotate            * around the X-axis (matrix).
          jsr         rotate             * rotate in world coordinate system
          movem.l     (a7)+,d0-d7/a0-a6
          move.w      20(a0),d7          *  Number of corners in the object
          ext.l       d7
          add.l       d7,mark_it         * as offset in point array for
          add.l       #38,a0             * the next object
          dbra        d0,new_lop1        * repeat, until all objects
          move.l      mark_it,d7         * have been pased. After end in
          move.w      d7,gnummark        * mark_it the total number of
          rts                            * points in the world system




*********************************************************************
*    Pass all lines to world system, one-time call at              *
*    program start since nothing changes in the lines              *
*********************************************************************

surf_lin: move.w      gnumobj,d0         * Total of all objects
          ext.l       d0
          subq.l      #1,d0              * as counter
          move.l      #object1,a0        * Address of first Object par. blk.
          move.l      #0,linpntr         * Pointer to line array
          move.w      #0,mark_it         * Pointer to point array
sflnlop1: move.l      linpntr,d7         * Line pointer times four,
          lsl.l       #2,d7              * one lines requires four
          move.l      d7,d6              * bytes.
          add.l       #wlinxy,d7         * Start address of line array, add
          move.l      d7,a2              * to line pointer
          move.l      12(a0),a1          * Address of line array of object
          move.w      22(a0),d1          * Number of lines in this object
          ext.l       d1
          lsl.l       #1,d1              * Number of lines times two equals
          subq.l      #1,d1              * Loop counter for word transmission
```

```
sflnlop2:  move.w    (a1)+,d7        * first point of first line
           add.w     mark_it,d7      * add the offsets of current
           move.w    d7,(a2)+        * objects, and store in world lines
           dbra      d1,sflnlop2     * array, until all lines of this
*                                      object


           move.w    20(a0),d7       * Number of corners of last object
           add.w     d7,mark_it      * add to corner pointer
           move.w    22(a0),d7       * Number of lines
           ext.l     d7
           add.l     d7,linpntr      * Total number of lines
           add.l     #38,a0          * Object offset, distance to next
           dbra      d0,sflnlop1     * object. When all objects are
*                                      completed
           move.l    linpntr,d7      * then store total number of lines
           move.w    d7,gnumline     * in the world system and
           rts                       * back



************************************************************************
*    Create surface array of the world system, one-time call          *
************************************************************************


surf_arr:  move.w    #0,mark_it      * Create the array of surfaces
           move.l    #0,plapntr
           move.w    #0,gnumpla      * Counter of surfaces
           move.w    gnumobj,d0      * Number of objects
           ext.l     d0              * as loop counter
           subq.l    #1,d0
           move.l    #object1,a0     * Address of first object param. blk

sfarlop1:  move.l    plapntr,d7      * Pointer to surface array
           add.l     #wplane,d7      * World surface array
           move.l    d7,a2
           move.w    24(a0),d1       * Number of surfaces on this object
           ext.l     d1              * as loop counter
           subq.l    #1,d1
           move.l    16(a0),a1       * Address of surface array of the object

sfarlop2:  move.w    (a1),d2         * Number of lines of this surface
           ext.l     d2
           lsl.l     #1,d2           * times four (one line = four bytes)
```

```
            move.l    d2,d6
            lsl.l     #1,d6        * complete the mult. by 4
            addq.l    #2,d6        * plus 2 bytes for number of lines
            subq.l    #1,d2        * counter
            add.l     d6,plapntr
            move.w    (a1)+,(a2)+   * Number of lines in this surface
sfarlop3:   move.w    (a1)+,d7      * From the object surface array
            add.w     mark_it,d7    * Add point offset of the object
            move.w    d7,(a2)+      * to world surface array
            dbra      d2,sfarlop3   * until all lines of this surface

            dbra      d1,sfarlop2   * until all surfaces on this object
            move.w    20(a0),d7     * Number of corners
            add.w     d7,mark_it    * add to point offset
            move.w    24(a0),d7
            add.w     d7,gnumpla    * add to total number
            add.l     #38,a0        * Object offset to next object

            dbra      d0,sfarlop1   * until all objects of the world
            rts                     * and return


***********************************************************************
*   Input and change parameters                                      *
***********************************************************************

inp_chan:   jsr       inkey        * Read keyboard, key code in
            cmp.b     #'D',d0
            bne       inpwait
            jsr       scrdmp       * make hardcopy

inpwait:    swap      d0           * D0 , test if
            cmp.b     #$4d,d0      * Cursor-right
            bne       inp1
            addq.w    #1,ywplus    * if yes, add one to Y-angle
            bra       inpend1      * increment and continue

inp1:       cmp.b     #$4b,d0      * Cursor-left, if yes then
            bne       inp2         * subtract one from Y-angle
            subq.w    #1,ywplus    * increment
            bra       inpend1
```

```
inp2:       cmp.b      #$50,d0       * Cursor-down, if yes then
            bne        inp3
            addq.w     #1,xwplus     * add one to X-angle increment
            bra        inpend1


inp3:       cmp.b      #$48,d0       * Cursor-up
            bne        inp3a
            subq.w     #1,xwplus     * subtract one
            bra        inpend1


inp3a:      cmp.b      #$61,d0       * Undo key
            bne        inp3b
            subq.w     #1,zwplus
            bra        inpend1


inp3b:      cmp.b      #$62,d0       * Help key
            bne        inp4
            addq.w     #1,zwplus
            bra        inpend1


inp4:       cmp.b      #$4e,d0       * plus key on the keypad
            bne        inp5          * if yes, subtract 25 from position of
            sub.w      #25,dist      * projection plane (Z-coordinate)
            bra        inpend1
inp5:       cmp.b      #$4a,d0       * minus key on the keypad
            bne        inp6          *
            add.w      #25,dist      * if yes, add 25
            bra        inpend1


inp6:       cmp.b      #$66,d0       * times key on keypad
            bne        inp7          * if yes, then subtract 15 from the
*                                      rotation
            sub.w      #15,rotdpz    * point Z-coordinate
            bra        inpend1       * Make change


inp7:       cmp.b      #$65,d0       * Division key on keypad
            bne        inp8
            add.w      #15,rotdpz    * add 15
            bra        inpend1


inp8:
```

```
inp10:      cmp.b       #$44,d0         * F10 pressed ?
            bne         inpend1
            addq.l      #4,a7           * if yes, jump to
            bra         mainend         * new input

inpend1:    move.w      hyangle,d1      * Rotation angle about Y-axis
            add.w       ywplus,d1       * add increment
            cmp.w       #360,d1         * when larger than 360, then subtract 360
            bge         inpend2
            cmp.w       #-360,d1        * if smaller then 360, then
            ble         inpend3         * add 360
            bra         inpend4
inpend2:    sub.w       #360,d1
            bra         inpend4
inpend3:    add.w       #360,d1

inpend4:    move.w      d1,hyangle

            move.w      hxangle,d1      * proceed in the same manner with
            add.w       xwplus,d1       * Rotation angle about the X-axis
            cmp.w       #360,d1
            bge         inpend5
            cmp.w       #-360,d1
            ble         inpend6
            bra         inpend7
inpend5:    sub.w       #360,d1
            bra         inpend7
inpend6:    add.w       #360,d1

inpend7:    move.w      d1,hxangle

            move.w      hzangle,d1
            add.w       zwplus,d1
            cmp.w       #360,d1
            bge         inpend8
            cmp.w       #-360,d1
            ble         inpend9
            bra         inpend10
inpend8:    sub.w       #360,d1
            bra         inpend10
inpend9:    add.w       #360,d1
```

```
inpend10: move.w      d1,hzangle
          rts



*********************************************************************
*   Determine the current screen resolution                        *
*********************************************************************

getreso:  move.w      #4,-(a7)
          trap        #14
          addq.l      #2,a7
          cmp.w       #2,d0
          bne         getr1
          move.w      #320,picturex    * Monochrome monitor
          move.w      #200,picturey
          bra         getrend
getr1:    cmp.w       #1,d0
          bne         getr2
          move.w      #320,picturex    * medium resolution (640*200)
          move.w      #100,picturey
          bra         getrend
getr2:    move.w      #160,picturex    * low resolution (320*200)
          move.w      #100,picturey
getrend:  rts



*********************************************************************
*   Hardcopy of screen, called by inp_chan                         *
*********************************************************************

scrdmp:   move.w      #20,-(a7)
          trap        #14
          addq.l      #2,a7
          jsr         clearbuf
          rts
```

```
***********************************************************************
*    Initialize the rotation reference point to [0,0,0]            *
***********************************************************************

setrotdp: move.w    #0,d1          * set the initial rotation
          move.w    d1,rotdpx      * reference point
          move.w    d1,rotdpy
          move.w    d1,rotdpz
          move.w    #0,hyangle     * initial rotation angle
          move.w    #0,hzangle
          move.w    #0,hxangle
          move.w    #0,ywplus
          move.w    #0,xwplus
          move.w    #0,zwplus
          rts



***********************************************************************
*   Rotation around the rot. ref. point around all three axes      *
***********************************************************************

pointrot: move.w    hxangle,xangle * rotate the world around
          move.w    hyangle,yangle
          move.w    hzangle,zangle
          move.w    rotdpx,d0      * rotation ref. point
          move.w    rotdpy,d1
          move.w    rotdpz,d2
          move.w    d0,xoffs       * add for inverse transformation
          move.w    d1,yoffs
          move.w    d2,zoffs
          neg.w     d0
          neg.w     d1
          neg.w     d2
          move.w    d0,offx        * subtract for transformation
          move.w    d1,offy
          move.w    d2,offz
          jsr       matinit        * matrix initialization
          jsr       zrotate        * rotate 'matrix' aboutZ-axis
          jsr       yrotate        * rotate 'matrix' about Y-axis
          jsr       xrotate        * then rotate around X-axis
          jsr       rotate         * Multiply points with the matrix
          rts
```

```
******************************************************************
* Set the limits of screen window for the Cohen-Sutherland      *
* clip algorithm built into the draw-line algorithm             *
* The limits can be freely selected by the user, which makes the *
* draw-line algorithm very flexible.                            *
******************************************************************

setcocli: move.w    #0,clipxule
          move.w    #0,clipyule
          move.w    picturex,d1
          lsl.w     #1,d1
          subq.w    #1,d1
          move.w    d1,clipxlri
          move.w    picturey,d1
          lsl.w     #1,d1
          subq.w    #1,d1
          move.w    d1,clipylri
          rts



******************************************************************
*  Entry of visible Surfaces into the vplane array              *
******************************************************************

hideit:
          move.w    numsurf,d0    * Number of surfaces as counter
          ext.l     d0
          subq.l    #1,d0
          move.l    #viewx,a1     * The point coordinates are stored
          move.l    #viewy,a2     * here
          move.l    #viewz,a3
          move.l    #wplane,a0    * here is the information for
          move.l    #vplane,a5    * every surface
          move.w    #0,surfcount  * counts the known visible surfaces.

visible:  move.w    (a0),d1       * start with first surface. Number of
          ext.l     d1            * points on this surface in D1.
          move.w    2(a0),d2      * Offset of first point on this surface
          move.w    4(a0),d3      * Offset of second point
          move.w    8(a0),d4      * Offset of third point
          subq.w    #1,d2         * subtract one for access to point array
          subq.w    #1,d3         * from current point offset.
```

```
        subq.w      #1,d4
        lsl.w       #1,d2        * continue to multiply with two
        lsl.w       #1,d3
        lsl.w       #1,d4        * and then access current
        move.w      (a1,d3.w),d6 * point coordinates
        cmp.w       (a1,d4.w),d6 * Comparison recognizes two points
        bne         doit1        * with matching coordinates, which can
        move.w      (a2,d3.w),d6 * occur during construction of rotation
        cmp.w       (a2,d4.w),d6 * bodies. When two identical points
        bne         doit1        * are found, the program
        move.w      (a3,d4.w),d6 * selects a third point for determination
        cmp.w       (a3,d3.w),d6 * of the two vectors.
        bne         doit1
        move.w      12(a0),d4
        subq.w      #1,d4
        lsl.w       #1,d4

doit1:
        move.w      (a1,d3.w),d5 * here the two vectors which lie in the
        move.w      d5,kx        * surface plane are determined through
        sub.w       (a1,d2.w),d5 * subtraction of the coordinates from
        move.w      d5,px        * two points of the surface
        move.w      (a2,d3.w),d5
        move.w      d5,ky        * The direction coordinates of the
        sub.w       (a2,d2.w),d5 * vectors are stored in the variables
        move.w      d5,py        * qx,qy,qz and px,py,pz.
        move.w      (a3,d3.w),d5
        move.w      d5,kz
        sub.w       (a3,d2.w),d5
        move.w      d5,pz


        move.w      (a1,d4.w),d5 * Calculate vector Q
        sub.w       (a1,d2.w),d5
        move.w      (a2,d4.w),d6
        sub.w       (a2,d2.w),d6
        move.w      (a3,d4.w),d7
        sub.w       (a3,d2.w),d7
        move.w      d5,d1          * qx
        move.w      d6,d2          * qy
        move.w      d7,d3          * qz
```

```
          muls      py,d3          * Calculate of the cross product
          muls      pz,d2          * of the vector perpendicular
          sub.w     d2,d3          * to the current surface
          move.w    d3,rx
          muls      pz,d1
          muls      px,d7
          sub.w     d7,d1          * the direction coordinates of the
vector
          move.w    d1,ry          * standing vertically to the surface
          muls      px,d6          * are temporarily stored in rx,ry,rz
          muls      py,d5
          sub.w     d5,d6
          move.w    d6,rz


          move.w    prox,d1    * The projection center serves as
*                              the comparison
          sub.w     kx,d1      * point for the visibility of a surface,
          move.w    proy,d2    * which is acceptable for the viewing
          sub.w     ky,d2      * situation chosen here. One can also
          move.w    proz,d3    * use the observation ref. point as
          sub.w     kz,d3      * comparison point.
          muls      rx,d1      * Now follows the comparison of vector
          muls      ry,d2      * R and the vector from one point of the
          muls      rz,d3      * surface to the projection center
          add.l     d1,d2      * by creation of the scalar product
          add.l     ,d2,d3     * of the two vectors.
          bmi       dosight


* the surface is visible, otherwise continue with next surface.


          move.w    (a0),d1    * Number of lines of the surface
          ext.l     d1
          lsl.l     #2,d1      * Number of lines times 4 = space for Lines
          addq.l    #2,d1      * plus 2 bytes for the number of lines.

          add.l     d1,a0      * add to surface array for access
sight1:   dbra      d0,visible * to next surface. If all surfaces
          bra       hideend    * are completed, then end.
```

```
dosight:   move.w     (a0),d1      * Number of lines in this surface,
           ext.l      d1           * multiplied by two equals the

           move.l     d1,d2
           lsl.l      #1,d1        * number of words to be passed
           move.l     a0,a4
           addq.l     #2,a4        * Access to first line of the Surface

sight3:    move.w     (a0)+,(a5)+  * Pass the number of the lines

           dbra       d1,sight3    * and the individual lines

           addq.w     #1,surfcount * the number of surfaces plus
           bra        sight1       * one, and work on next one


hideend:   rts



***********************************************************************
*   Draw surfaces entered in vplane                                   *
***********************************************************************

surfdraw:                         * draw surfaces with the count
           move.l     xplot,a4     * of surfaces passed in surfcount
           move.l     yplot,a5

           move.l     #vplane,a6   * Description in array at address
           move.w     surfcount,d0 * vplane, was entered by routine hideit
           ext.l      d0
           subq.l     #1,d0        * if no surface was entered in array,
           bmi        surfend      * then end.
surflop1:  move.w     (a6)+,d1     * Number of lines on this surface
           ext.l      d1           * as counter of lines to be drawn.
           subq.l     #1,d1

surflop2:  move.l     (a6)+,d5     * first line of this surface

           subq.w #1,d5            * Access to screen array, which contains
           lsl.w  #1,d5            * display coordinates of the
           move.w 0(a4,d5.w),d2    * points.
           move.w 0(a5,d5.w),d3    * extract points, pass from
           swap   d5               * the routine.
```

```
          subq.w   #1,d5
          lsl.w    #1,d5
          move.w   0(a4,d5.w),a2   * second point belonging to the the line
          move.w   0(a5,d5.w),a3
          jsr      drawl           * draw line, until all lines of this
          dbra     d1,surflop2     * surface have been drawn and repeat
          dbra     d0,surflop1     * until all surface have been drawn.
surfend: rts                       * finally return.



*********************************************************************
*********************************************************************
*  Display and description of the same screen page                 *
*********************************************************************


switch:   move.w    #-1,-(a7)       * show display page in which
          move.l    physbase,-(a7)  * drawing is being made
          move.l    physbase,-(a7)
          move.w    #5,-(a7)
          trap      #14
          add.l     #12,a7
          rts



*****************************************************************
* remove all characters present in the keyboard buffer         *
*****************************************************************


clearbuf: move.w    #$b,-(a7)    * Gemdos function. character in buffer ?
          trap      #1
          addq.l    #2,a7
          tst.w     d0           * if yes, get character
          beq       clearnd      * if no, terminate
          move.w    #1,-(a7)     * Gemdos function  CONIN
          trap      #1           * repeat until all characters have
          addq.l    #2,a7        * been removed from the buffer
          bra       clearbuf

clearnd:  rts
          .even
```

```
************************************************************************
************************************************************************
*                    Start of variable area                          *
*                                                                     *
************************************************************************



************************************************************************
*                                                                     *
*                                                                     *
*         Definition of the house                                     *
*                                                                     *
************************************************************************


          .data

housdatx: .dc.w       -30,30,30,-30,30,-30,-30,30,0,0,-10,-10,10,10
          .dc.w       30,30,30,30,30,30,30,30,30,30,30,30

housdaty: .dc.w       30,30,-30,-30,30,30,-30,-30,70,70,-30,0,0,-30
          .dc.w       20,20,0,0,20,20,0,0
          .dc.w       -10,-10,-30,-30

housdatz: .dc.w       60,60,60,60,-60,-60,-60,-60,60,-60,60,60,60,60
          .dc.w       40,10,10,40,-10,-40,-40,-10
          .dc.w       0,-20,-20,0

houslin:  .dc.w       1,2,2,3,3,4,4,1,2,5,5,8,8,3,8,7,7,6,6,5,6,1,7,4
          .dc.w       9,10,1,9,9,2,5,10,6,10,11,12,12,13,13,14
          .dc.w       15,16,16,17,17,18,18,15,19,20,20,21,21,22,22,19
          .dc.w       23,24,24,25,25,26,26,23
```

```
***********************************************************************
* here is the definition of the surfaces belonging to the house       *
***********************************************************************


houspla:   .dc.w      4,1,2,2,3,3,4,4,1,4,2,5,5,8,8,3,3,2
           .dc.w      4,5,6,6,7,7,8,8,5,4,7,6,6,1,1,4,4,7
           .dc.w      4,4,3,3,8,8,7,7,4,4,2,9,9,10,10,5,5,2
           .dc.w      4,10,9,9,1,1,6,6,10,3,1,9,9,2,2,1
           .dc.w      3,5,10,10,6,6,5,4,11,12,12,13,13,14,14,11
           .dc.w      4,15,16,16,17,17,18,18,15,4,19,20,20,21,21,22,22,19
           .dc.w      4,23,24,24,25,25,26,26,23

hnummark:  .dc.w      26     * Number of corner points of the house
hnumline:  .dc.w      32     * Number of lines of the house
hnumpla:   .dc.w      13     * Number of surfaces of the house

hxangle:   .dc.w      0      * Rotation angle of house about X-axis
hyangle:   .dc.w      0      *         "        "          "   Y-axis
hzangle:   .dc.w      0      *         "        "          "   Z-axis

xwplus:    .dc.w      0      * Angle increment about X-axis
ywplus:    .dc.w      0      * Angle increment about Y-axis
zwplus:    .dc.w      0      * Angle increment about Z-axis

picturex:  .dc.w      0      * Definition of zero point on the screen
picturey:  .dc.w      0      * entered by getreso


rotdpx:    .dc.w      0
rotdpy:    .dc.w      0
rotdpz:    .dc.w      0


r1z1:      .dc.w      0
normz:     .dc.w      1500



           .bss
```

```
plusrot:    .ds.l    1
first:      .ds.w    1
second:     .ds.w    1
delta1:     .ds.w    1


worldpla:   .ds.l    1


            .data


plag:       .dc.b    1
            .even


            .bss


diffz:      .ds.w    1


dx:         .ds.w    1
dy:         .ds.w    1
dz:         .ds.w    1


wrldx:      .ds.w    1600    * world coordinate array
wrldy:      .ds.w    1600
wrldz:      .ds.w    1600


viewx:      .ds.w    1600    * view coordinate array
viewy:      .ds.w    1600
viewz:      .ds.w    1600


screenx:    .ds.w    1600    * screen soordinate array
screeny:    .ds.w    1600



wlinxy:     .ds.l    3200    * line array



wplane:     .ds.l    6600    * surface array

vplane:     .ds.l    6600    * surface array of visible surfaces
```

```
space:      .ds.l     2
pladress:   .ds.l     3000      * surface array

surfcount:  .ds.w     1
numsurf:    .ds.w     1

zcount:     .ds.l     1         * Sum of all Z-coordinates
zsurf:      .ds.w     1         * Individual Z-coordinates of the surface

*********************************************************************
            .data

gnumobj:    .dc.w     2

gnummark:   .dc.w     0
gnumline:   .dc.w     0
gnumpla:    .dc.w     0

mark_it:    .dc.l     0
linpntr:    .dc.l     0
plapntr:    .dc.l     0

object1:
obj1xda:    .dc.l     housdatx
obj1yda:    .dc.l     housdaty
obj1zda:    .dc.l     housdatz
obj1lin:    .dc.l     houslin
obj1pla:    .dc.l     houspla
obj1mrk:    .dc.w     26
obj1ali:    .dc.w     32
obj1pln:    .dc.w     13
obj1x0:     .dc.w     150
obj1y0:     .dc.w     100
obj1z0:     .dc.w     0
obj1xw:     .dc.w     20
obj1yw:     .dc.w     0
obj1zw:     .dc.w     0

object2:
obj2xda:    .dc.l     housdatx
obj2yda:    .dc.l     housdaty
obj2zda:    .dc.l     housdatz
```

```
obj2lin:    .dc.l     houslin
obj2pla:    .dc.l     houspla
obj2mrk:    .dc.w     26
obj2ali:    .dc.w     32
obj2pln:    .dc.w     13
obj2x0:     .dc.w     -150
obj2y0:     .dc.w     100
obj2z0:     .dc.w     0
obj2xw:     .dc.w     0
obj2yw:     .dc.w     20
obj2zw:     .dc.w     0


object3:
obj3xda:    .dc.l     housdatx
obj3yda:    .dc.l     housdaty
obj3zda:    .dc.l     housdatz
obj3lin:    .dc.l     houslin
obj3pla:    .dc.l     houspla
obj3mrk:    .dc.w     26
obj3ali:    .dc.w     32
obj3pln:    .dc.w     13
obj3x0:     .dc.w     -150
obj3y0:     .dc.w     -100
obj3z0:     .dc.w     0
obj3xw:     .dc.w     0
obj3yw:     .dc.w     20
obj3zw:     .dc.w     0


object4:
obj4xda:    .dc.l     housdatx
obj4yda:    .dc.l     housdaty
obj4zda:    .dc.l     housdatz
obj4lin:    .dc.l     houslin
obj4pla:    .dc.l     houspla
obj4mrk:    .dc.w     26
obj4ali:    .dc.w     32
obj4pln:    .dc.w     13
obj4x0:     .dc.w     150
obj4y0:     .dc.w     -100
obj4z0:     .dc.w     0
```

```
obj4xw:    .dc.w      0
obj4yw:    .dc.w      0
obj4zw:    .dc.w      0
           .bss


sx:        .ds.w      1
sy:        .ds.w      1
sz:        .ds.w      1

px:        .ds.w      1
py:        .ds.w      1
pz:        .ds.w      1

rx:        .ds.w      1
ry:        .ds.w      1
rz:        .ds.w      1

qx:        .ds.w      1
qy:        .ds.w      1
qz:        .ds.w      1

kx:        .ds.w      1
ky:        .ds.w      1
kz:        .ds.w      1

*******************************************
           .data
           .even

maxpoint:  .dc.l      25
mousx:     .dc.w      0
mousy:     .dc.w      0
mousbut:   .dc.w      0
kybdstat:  .dc.w      0

altx:      .dc.w      0
alty:      .dc.w      0
newx:      .dc.w      0
newy:      .dc.w      0
```

```
addrssx:    .dc.l    1
            .data


prox:       .dc.w    0          * Coordinates of Projection
proy:       .dc.w    0          * Center on the positive
proz:       .dc.w    1500       * Z-axis


            .data


offx:       .dc.w    0          * transformation during Rotation
offy:       .dc.w    0          * to Point [offx,offy,offz]
offz:       .dc.w    0


xoffs:      .dc.w    0          * Inverse transformation to point
yoffs:      .dc.w    0          * [xoff,yoffs,zoffs]
zoffs:      .dc.w    0


            .bss


loopc:      .ds.l    1


.end
```

```
Desk  File  View  Options
┌─────────────────────┐ ┌───────────────────────────┐ ┌──────────────────────┐
│        A:\          │ │           D:\             │ │   F:\3DWORK.DIR\     │
│ 253882 bytes used i │ │ 1442236 bytes used in 129 items. │ │ 333956 bytes used in │
│  ▓ PRINTERS         │ │   BASIC    PRG  138944  11-26 ⬆ │ │   HOUSE1    PRG      │
│  ▓ TUTORIAL         │ │   BASIC    RSC    4648  11-26 │ │   HOUSE1    S        │
│    C        FKY     │ │   BASIC    WRK     346  11-26 │ │   MAIN1     PRG      │
│    CONV     TTP     │ │   BASIC1   BAK   14801  11-26 │ │   MAIN1     S        │
│    NL10     PRG     │ │                              │ │   MAIN1CO   PRG      │
│    OUTPUT   PRG   ┌─────────────────────────────┐   │ │   MAIN1CO   S        │
│    SPLIT    TTP   │  OPEN APPLICATION           │   │ │   MENU1     PRG      │
│    STANDARD PRT   │                             │   │ │   MENU1     S        │
│    TEXTPRO  PRG   │     Name:  BATCH   .TTP     │   │ │   MULTI1    PRG      │
│    TUTORIAL TXT   │  Parameters:                │   │ │   MULTI1    S        │
│    XTTUTORI TOC   │  aslink grlink1 multi1|____  │   │ │   PAINT1    PRG      │
│                   │    ┌──────┐   ┌────────┐    │   │ │   PAINT1    S        │
│                   │    │  OK  │   │ Cancel │    │   │ │   ROTATE1   PRG      │
│                   │    └──────┘  ▸└────────┘    │   │ │   ROTATE1   S        │
│                   └─────────────────────────────┘   │ │                      │
└─────────────────────┘                              │ └──────────────────────┘
```

Suggestions for additional development

5. Suggestions for additional development

One application of this program module for manipulating three-dimensional objects that will occur to almost everyone is a flight simulator. The last program can in fact be used as a basis for a flight simulator. We are missing the description of the position of the airplane in the world system as well as a modified `pointrot` routine. The modified `pointrot` routine, after rotation around the reference point, should not transform all of the world coordinates back to the old coordinate origin, which occurred in the old `pointrot` routine by adding the reference point coordinates after the rotation. Furthermore, houses do not change position in the world system of a flight simulator and for an airport other structures must be developed (hangar, tower). In addition, fields, forests, and landing strips can be simulated with simple rectangular surfaces.

The position of the airplane, or to be exact, the center of its cockpit windshield, in the the reference point in the world system for all transformations to follow, especially that of the creation of the view system. For simulation of airplane movement, the reference point must be manipulated with keyboard input. This input must affect both the point coordinates as well as the orientation of the plane in space. The orientation of the airplane in space is described with the three angles (hxangle,hyangle,hzangle) so that even adventurous flight situations (spins) can be simulated. For adjustment of the world system to the airplane system the following operations are required:

1. Move the coordinate origin of the world system to the cockpit center by subtracting the cockpit windshield center-coordinates from all point coordinates.

2. Rotate of the displaced world system about the three rotation angles which describe the position of the airplane in relation to its three axes.

3. Remove hidden surfaces with `hideit`, noting that the reference point for the calculation of the vector S through point [0,0,0], the cockpit center-point (coordinate origin of the view system) is chosen and not the projection center, which of course can also be freely selected in this observation model. From the endpoint of vector S the direct result: all objects outside the cockpit window are, if they satisfy the criteria for visibility, visible.

4. Projection on the screen through the perspective transform routine.

After the observed world is displayed, the parameters such as the position of the airplane in the world system or the position of other objects in the world system, such as a second airplane, can be changed. Now the procedure described above is called again and this cycle repeated continually.

5.1 Light and Shadow

To enhance the program module to correctly define a light source, as in section 2.8, it is necessary to have the vectors L, i.e. the vector, which points from each surface to the observation reference point as well as the vector N, which points from the light source to the current surface, as unit vectors of length one. One should divide the vector coordinates (x, y, z) by the root of the sum of its squares $\sqrt{(x^2+y^2+z^2)}$. Furthermore, the data structure of the objects must be changed since you want to shade the surfaces according to the light intensity and not according to their Z-coordinates. It is possible to enter the intensity of every surface in the extended `surfaddr` array and give each surface an individual shading pattern, either through comparison of the light source vectors or completely at random.

5.2   Animated Cartoons

In principle even this application has already been realized in program
`multi.s`. You simply create more objects in a world system and then
changes their position and place in the system continuously. The world
line and surface arrays, as we have seen, need be created only once while
the coordinate array is created with every pass through the main loop.
After the line surface array has been constructed, you have free choice in
the number of displayed objects, i.e. you can define, for example, ten
objects through object definition blocks but at the creation of the corners
you could only actually create and display. One possible application is
moving text where the letters are three dimensional objects. You could
have several letters "fly" together from various directions and assemble
them on the screen into a word. The complete word could then be rotated
around some point. The individual letters could even be constructed with
the mouse.

Appendices

Appendix A: Number systems

Every number, in any number system, is represented by a sequence of digits. This sequence may be interrupted by a decimal point. We can write the following for the digit sequence:

$$(...a_4a_3a_2a_1a_0.a_{-1}a_{-2}a_{-3}a_{-4}...)b =$$
$$+ a_4*b^4 + a_3*b^3 + a_2*b^2 + a_1*b^1 + a_0*b^0 + a_{-1}*b^{-1} + ...$$

Here the coefficients a_{-4} to a_4 represent the individual digits of the number and b is the number base. Here is an example of the most commonly used number system, the decimal system:

$$(3423.87)10 =$$
$$3*10^3 + 4*10^2 + 2*10^1 + 3*10^0 + 8*10^{-1} + 7*10^{-2} =$$
$$3000 + 400 + 20 + 3 + 0.8 + 0.07 = 3423.87$$

Two number systems often encountered, in computer programming, are the binary (base 2) and the hexadecimal systems (base 16). Binary uses only the two numbers 0 and 1 as digits. An example:

$$1110010010010 = 1*2^{12}+1*2^{11}+1*2^{10}+1*2^7+1*2^4+1*2^1 =$$
$$4096 + 2048 + 1024 + 128 + 16 + 2 = 7314$$

Numbers in the hexadecimal system with base 16 are generally indicated by a leading dollar sign ($). For representation of numbers in this format, the standard ten digits from 0 to 9 are not enough. For this reason the first six characters of the alphabet are added (A through F). A has the value of 10, and F means 15. It is especially easy to convert between binary and hexadecimal. Four binary digits (4 bits) are grouped together, starting from the decimal point, to form one hexadecimal digit.

The unwieldy binary number 1110010010010 becomes the hexadecimal number $1C92. The conversion into the Decimal system is done in the same manner as for the binary system. $1C92 means therefore:

$1*16^3 + 12*16^2 + 9*16^1 + 2*16^0 =$

$1*4096 + 12*256 + 9*16 + 2*1 = 7314$

Appendix B: Analytical geometry of planes and space

The cartesian coordinate system is defined as a system of perpendicular lines in which the horizontal line is designated as the X-axis (abscissa) and the line perpendicular to it is called the Y-axis (ordinate). The intersection of the two lines is the origin of the system. Now all points within the system can be defined unambiguously by specifying their coordinate values (x,y).

A line in such a system is defined by two points which belong on the line. All points on the line can be ascertained with the following equation.

$$\frac{y-y1}{x-x1} \quad = \quad \frac{y2-y1}{x2-x1} \quad \text{for } (x2-x1) <> 0$$

In this two point format, the expression (y2-y1)/(x2-x1) gives the slope m of the straight line, which simultaneously represents the tangent of the angle between the line and the X-axis (phi).

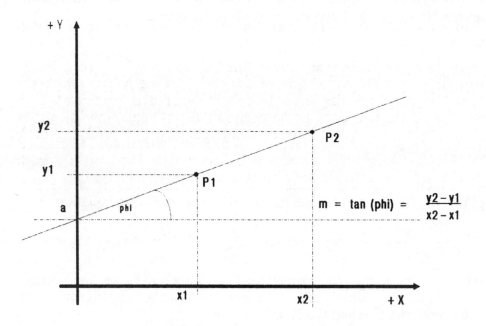

Figure B.1: Line in the plane

With the definition of the slope m as well as the axis intersection a, the
intersection of the line with the Y-axis, we get what is called the normal
form of the straight line equation.

$$y = m*x + a$$

With this equation you can calculate all points on the line by introducing
various X values into the above equation, knowing the slope m and axis
intersection a.

For the middle-point of a straight line which connects two points (P1,
P2), we can easily calculate the coordinates of this segment:

$$Xm = \frac{x1+x2}{2} \qquad Ym = \frac{y1+y2}{2}$$

The two equations above are used in the Cohen-Sutherland clipping algorithm.

The geometry of a plane is just a special case of the geometry of space and therefore the same laws apply to a straight line in space as to a straight line in a plane, i.e. two points are also sufficient to define a point in space. One difference from the plane is the Z-axis which, if one leaves the X and Y axis unchanged, can point in different directions. Depending on the direction used, this system is called a right-hand or left-hand system. They differ therefore only in the orientation of the Z-axis.

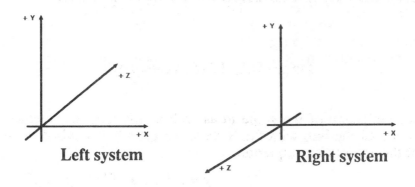

Left system   **Right system**

Figure B.2

An easy way to distinguish between the right- and left-hand systems as well as all operations within the system is possible with the aid of a screw (imagine simply a normal screw inside the system). The screw transfers a rotating motion into a movement along the rotation axis and there are basically two types of screws: those with left-handed threads and those with right-handed threads. For a complete system description, we still need to know how positive angles are measured and for equalization of both coordinate systems the following definition is agreed upon:

Rotation about the: positive angle is measured:

Z-axis	from +X to +Y axis
Y-axis	from +Z to +X axis
X-axis	from +Y to +Z axis

With the aid of this definition we can say for the system and the screw: If a screw is placed in such a system (in the direction of a coordinate axis) and the screw is turned about a positive angle (see above definition), then the screw moves in the direction of a positive coordinate axis. You can determine the position axis of a coordinate system through the definition of the positive angle as well as the selection of the screw, or you can recognize the type of an existing coordinate system. As an explanation, in a right-hand system the right-handed screw moves in the direction of a positive coordinate axis when rotated about a positive angle. On the other hand, a left handed screw in a left-hand system rotated about a positive angle will also move in the direction of positive coordinate axis. Since in our country, screws with right-handed threads are most common, we shall follow the positive rotations of a right-handed screw in a right-hand system.

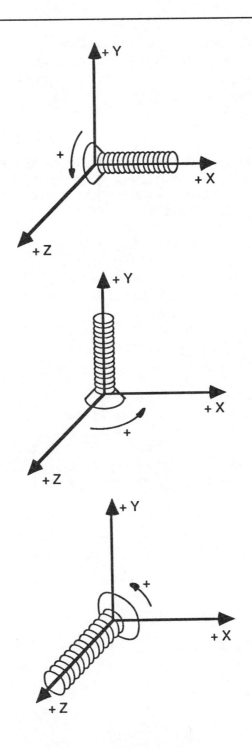

Figure B.3: Screws in a right-hand system

Two points in space or in a plane are sufficient to describe a line. Under consideration of Z-coordinates the following relationships hold:

$$\frac{y-y1}{x-x1} = \frac{y2-y1}{x2-x1} \qquad \frac{z-z1}{x-x1} = \frac{z2-z1}{x2-x1}$$

Using a parameter u, which can assume real values between -infinity and +infinity, all points on a line running through points P1[x1,y1,z1] and P2[x2,y2,z2] can be determined. For individual coordinates the values are:

```
x = (x2-x1) * u + x1
y = (y2-y1) * u + y1
z = (z2-z1) * u + z1
```

If we use only u real numbers between 0 and 1, all points on the line between P1 and P2 can be calculated. The line would not run beyond P1 and P2, but would be cut off at the two points. From the lines we get a vector, which has a definite direction in space. In our example it points from P1 to P2.

A vector is a directional line, the connecting line between two points in a coordinate system. The coordinates of the vector are calculated by subtracting the point coordinates. The vector is therefore indicated by the vector coordinates and its direction. The direction is shown in the illustration by an arrow. A vector can be moved along its axis without consequences for the total system, since only the length and direction are of significance.

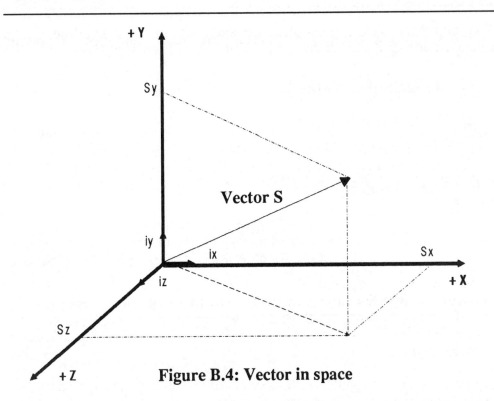

Figure B.4: Vector in space

The vector S in Figure 6.3.4 is given by its vector coordinates
$S[sx,sy,sz] = [x2-x1,y2-y1,z2-z1]$ and its value, the length
of the distance S, can be determined as follows:

$$\text{Value } S = |S| = \sqrt{(sx^2 + sy^2 + sz^2)}$$

A unit vector is a vector whose value is one. If you want to generate a
unit vector to a given vector S, a vector which points in the same
direction as S but has a value of one, the vector coordinates of the unit
vector are I $[ix,iy,iz]$:

$$ix = \frac{sx}{|S|} \qquad iy = \frac{sy}{|S|} \qquad iz = \frac{sz}{|S|}$$

Dividing the individual vector coordinates of vector S $[sx,sy,sz]$ by
the length of vector S results in the vector coordinates of the unit vector.

Various operations can be performed on the vectors and those important for our purposes are:

1. The scalar product (A·B)

2. The cross product (A×B)

B.1   Scalar Product

The scalar product is the sum of the products of the individual vector coordinates and is important to determine angles (phi) between two vectors (A,B).

$$A \cdot B = ax*bx+ay*by+az*bz = |A|*|B|*\cos(phi)$$
$$A \cdot B = \sqrt{((ax^2+ay^2+az^2)*(bx^2+by^2+bz^2))}*\cos(phi)$$

See also Figure 2.7.5.

B.2   Cross Product

The cross product (A×B), in contrast to the scalar product, is not a real number but another vector (C). The resultant vector stands perpendicular to the plane between the vectors A and B and together with them forms a new coordinate system. The rule of the screw helps us again in the determining the direction of the resulting vector:

In a right-hand system the result vector (C = [cx,cy,cz]) of the cross product points in the same direction in which a screw with right-handed threads would move from A to B when turned. The vectors A, B, and C form a right-hand system. Similarly for a left-hand system: if one turns a left-threaded screw from A to B, then C points in the direction in which the screw would move. This connection can be seen easily in Figure 6.3.5 and in our program is responsible for the recognition of visible surfaces.

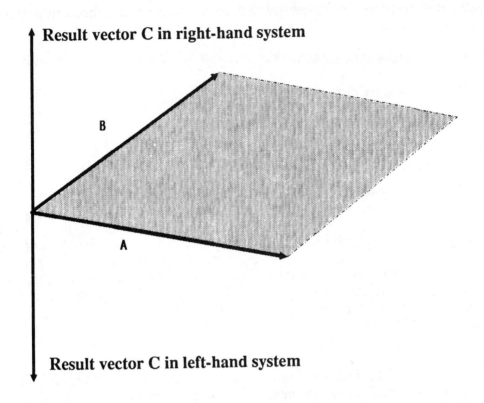

Result vector C in right-hand system

B

A

Result vector C in left-hand system

Figure B.5

To determine the result vector C [cx,cy,cz] one proceeds as follows:

A·B = [ax*bz-az*by, az*bx-ax*bz, ax*by-ay*bx]

Appendix C: Matrix calculations

A matrix (m,n) is a square number system consisting of m by n numbers.

$$A = \begin{matrix} a_{11} & a_{12} & a_{13} & ... & a_{1n} \\ a_{21} & a_{22} & a_{23} & ... & a_{2n} \\ a_{31} & a_{32} & a_{33} & ... & a_{3n} \\ . & . & . & . & . \\ . & . & . & . & . \\ . & . & . & . & . \\ a_{m1} & a_{m2} & a_{m3} & ... & a_{mn} \end{matrix}$$

The numbers a_{ik} where $i = 1,2...m$ and $k = 1,2...n$ are the elements of the matrix A. The elements a_{i1}, a_{i2},...a_{in} form the i-Line, and the elements a_{1k},a_{2k},...a_{mk} form the kth column of the matrix. If the number of columns is equal to the number of rows (m=n), A is called a square matrix. A few rules can be stated for matrix calculation.

1. Matrices are designated with uppercase letters (A-Z). The individual elements of a matrix carry the corresponding lower case letter (a-z).

2. The element a_{ik} is located in the ith row, kth column of matrix A. i is the row index and k is the column index.

3. The matrix A(m,n) is of the type (m,n) and is defined as a two-dimensional matrix with m rows and n columns.

4. Matrices with one row and any number of columns, of the type (1,n), are called row vectors and those of type (n,1) are called column vectors.

C.1 Adding matrices

The addition of matrices is defined only for matrices of the same dimensions. Here is an example with two (3,3) matrices, A with the elements a_{ik} and the matrix B with the elements b_{ik}. During addition, the sum matrix S is created with elements s_{ik}. S=A+B.

$$A = \begin{matrix} 1 & 2 & 3 \\ 4 & 5 & 6 \\ 7 & 8 & 9 \end{matrix} \qquad B = \begin{matrix} 1 & 2 & 3 \\ 4 & 5 & 6 \\ 7 & 8 & 9 \end{matrix}$$

$$C = A+B = \begin{matrix} 2 & 4 & 9 \\ 8 & 10 & 12 \\ 14 & 16 & 18 \end{matrix}$$

The elements of the sum matrix result from: $s_{ik} = a_{ik} + b_{ik}$ for i,k from 1 to 3. The limits of the variables i and k are written in mathematical form: i,k = 1(1)3. The value in front of the parentheses is the start value, the value in the parenthesis is the increment and the last number designates the final value of the variables. In this example, i and k take values of one through three with an increment of one. These are the numbers 1,2,3. During matrix addition, one adds the elements which are in the same place in each matrix, to obtain the elements of the sum matrix S. One proceeds in the same manner when multiplying of matrix A with a constant factor fac. The elements of the product matrix P are calculated by multiplying each element in A by the factor.

$$p_{ik} = fac * a_{ik} \quad i,k=1(1)3$$

C.2   Multiplying Matrices

The multiplication of two matrices A and B is somewhat more complex than addition and has some limitations. The product of two matrices is only defined when the number of columns of A matches the number of rows in B. For two square matrices with i=k=constant, the multiplication is always defined. The product of two matrices A (a_{ij}) and B (b_{jk}) is defined as follows: A is a matrix of type (m,l) and B is of type (l,n), then the product of the matrices A and B is A*B, the result matrix P is (p_{ik}), whose elements are calculated in the following manner:

$$p_{ik} = \text{sum of } j=1 \text{ to } l \text{ over } a_{ij}*b_{jk}$$
$$\text{with } i = 1(1)m \text{ and } j = 1(1)n.$$

This connection can be recognized in the following example.

$$A= \begin{matrix} 1 & 2 \\ 3 & 4 \end{matrix} \qquad B = \begin{matrix} 5 & 6 \\ 7 & 8 \end{matrix}$$

$$C = A*B = \begin{matrix} 1*5 + 2*7 & 1*6 + 2*8 \\ 3*5 + 4*7 & 3*6 + 4*8 \end{matrix} =$$

$$\begin{matrix} 19 & 22 \\ 43 & 50 \end{matrix}$$

The result matrix P therefore contains the same number of lines as the multiplicand A and the same number of rows as the multiplier B. In regard to matrix multiplication there is a neutral element, i.e. for every matrix A there is a matrix N with which A can be multiplied without changing the original matrix. A*N=A. N is called the unit matrix and the elements of the diagonal are one. All others have the value zero. Moreover, the associative and the distributive law are valid during multiplication.

$$A*(B*C) = (A*B)*C \qquad \text{Associative Law}$$
$$A*(B+C) = (A*B)+(A*C) \qquad \text{Distributive Law}$$

The commutative law does not hold for matrix multiplication. This means A*B is not necessarily equal to B*A. The order of the multiplication is not arbitrary, as you see, and must be observed.

Appendix D: Bibliography

[1]   Foley James D., van Dam A., Fundamentals of Interactive Computer graphics, Addison Wesley Publishing Company (1984)

[2]   Harrington Steven, Computer Graphics, McGraw-Hill (1983)

[3]   Newman William M., Principles of Interactive Computer Graphics, McGraw-Hill (1984)

[4]   Knuth Donald E., The Art of Computer Programming Volume 2 Seminumerical Algorithms, Addison-Wesley Publishing Company (1981)

[5]   Kane Gerry, Hawkins Doug, Leventhal Lance, 68000 Assembly Language Programming, McGraw-Hill (1981)

[6]   Bruckmann, Englisch, Gerrits, Atari ST Internals, Abacus Software (1986)

[7]   Szczepanowski, Gunther, Atari ST GEM Programmer's Reference, Abacus Software (1986)

INDEX

Optional Diskette

For your convenience, the program listings contained in this book are available on an Atari ST formatted floppy disk. You should order the diskette if you want to use the programs, but don't want to type them in from the listings in the book.

All programs on the diskette have been fully tested. You can change the programs for your particular needs. The diskette is available for $14.95 plus $2.00 ($5.00 foreign) for postage and handling.

When ordering, please give your name and shipping address. Enclose a check, money order or credit card information. Mail your order to:

Abacus Software
5370 52nd Street SE
Grand Rapids, MI 49508

Or for fast service, call **616/698-0330**.

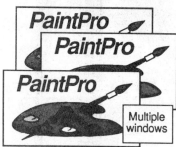
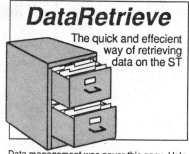

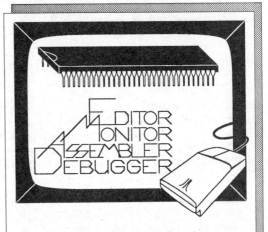
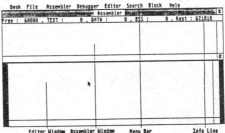
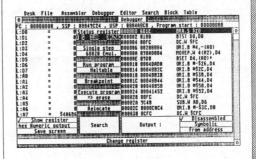
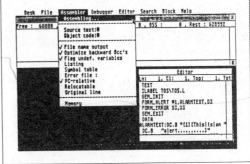

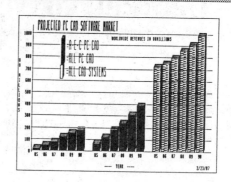
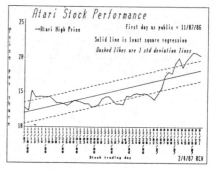
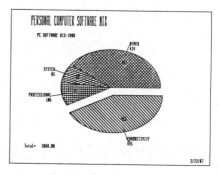
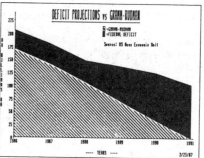

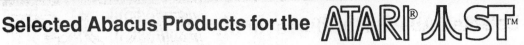
DataRetrieve

(formerly FilePro ST)

Database management package for the Atari ST

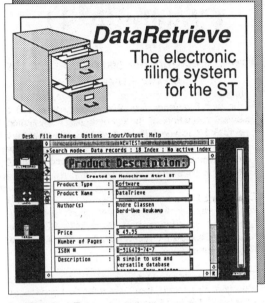

"DataRetrieve is the most versatile, and yet simple, data base manager available for the Atari 520ST/1040ST on the market to date."

—Bruce Mittleman
Atari Journal

DataRetrieve is one of Abacus' best-selling software packages for the Atari ST computers—it's received highest ratings from many leading computer magazines. **DataRetrieve** is perfect for your customers who need a powerful, yet easy to use database system at a moderate price of $49.95.

DataRetrieve's drop-down menus let the user quickly and easily define a file and enter information through screen templates. But even though it's easy to use, **DataRetrieve** is also powerful. **DataRetrieve** has fast search and sorting capabilities, a capacity of up to 64,000 records, and allows numeric values with up to 15 significant digits. **DataRetrieve** lets the user access data from up to four files simultaneously, indexes up to 20 different fields per file, supports multiple files, and has an integral editor for complete reporting capabilities.

DataRetrieve's screen templates are paintable for enhanced appearance on the screen and when printed, and data items may be displayed in multiple type styles and font sizes.

The package includes six predefined databases for mailing list, record/video albums, stamp and coin collection, recipes, home inventory and auto maintenance that users can customize to their own requirements. The templates may be printed on Rolodex cards, as well as 3 x 5 and 4 x 5 index cards. **DataRetrieve**'s built-in RAM disks support lightning-fast operation on the 1040ST. **DataRetrieve** interfaces to **TextPro** files, features easy printer control, many help screens, and a complete manual.

DataRetrieve works with Atari ST systems with one or more single- or double-sided disk drives. Works with either monochrome or color monitors. Printer optional.

DataRetrieve Suggested Retail Price: **$49.95**

DataRetrieve Features:

- Easily define your files using drop-down menus
- Design screen mask size to 5000 by 5000 pixels
- Choose from six font sizes and six text styles
- Add circles, boxes and lines to screen masks
- Fast search and sort capabilities
- Handles records up to 64,000 characters in length
- Organize files with up to 20 indexes
- Access up to four files simultaneously
- Cut, past and copy data to other files
- Change file definitions and format
- Create subsets of files
- Interfaces with **TextPro** files
- Complete built-in reporting capabilities
- Change setup to support virtually any printer
- Add header, footer and page number to reports
- Define printer masks for all reporting needs
- Send output to screen, printer, disk or modem
- Includes and supports RAM disk for high-speed 1040ST operation
- Capacities: max. 2 billion characters per file
  max. 64,000 records per file
  max. 64,000 characters per record
  max. fields: limited only by record size
  max. 32,000 text characters per field
  max. 20 index fields per file
- Index precision: 3 to 20 characters
- Numeric precision: to 15 digits
- Numeric range $\pm 10^{-308}$ ti $\pm 10^{308}$

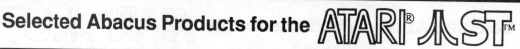
Forth/MT

Powerful Multi-tasking Language for the Atari ST

Forth is not only a programming language, but also an operating environment—the user can program, assemble and edit. Since Forth is fast, compact, flexible and efficient., it's particularly well-suited to the solution of real time problems. In use for more than fifteen years in industrial and scientific applications, Forth dramatically reduces program development time compared to programming in assembly language or other higher-level languages.

The powerful multi-tasking **Forth/MT** package was designed to make the fullest use of the ST's features for Forth programming.

Forth/MT features include:

- Over 750 words in the Kernal
- Complete TOS and LINE-A commands available
- Over 1500 words (disk accessible)
- Complete 32-bit implementation based on Forth-83 standard
- Machine language sections added for speed
- Many utilities: full screen editor, monitor, disk monitor and Forth macro assembler
- Utility descriptions stored on disk-you can change them to suit your needs
- Multitasking capability
- Machine language sections added for high-speed operation

Forth programmers will love the ease of use of this excellent package. **Forth/MT** the perfect tool for unleashing the power of the Forth programming language on the Atari ST line of computers.

Forth/MT   Suggested retail price: **$49.95**

```
POINTER NEW-MOUSE <CR> (DEFINE BUFFER HEADER )
0 W, ( MASK COLOR ) 1 W, (MOUSE COLOR ) <CR>
BIN 0000000000000000 W, <CR>  ( 1ST MASK LINE )
    0000000000000000 W, <CR>  ( 2ND MASK LINE )
    0001111001111000 W, <CR>  ( 3RD MASK LINE )
    0001111001111000 W, <CR>  ( 4TH MASK LINE )
    0001001001001000 W, <CR>  ( 5TH MASK LINE )
    0001001001001000 W, <CR>  ( 6TH MASK LINE )
    0001001001001000 W, <CR>  ( 7TH MASK LINE )
    0000001000001000 W, <CR>  ( 8TH MASK LINE )
    0000000000000000 W, <CR>  ( 9TH MASK LINE )
    0000101010100000 W, <CR>  ( 10TH MASK LINE )
    0000011111100000 W, <CR>  ( 11TH MASK LINE )
    0000001001000000 W, <CR>  ( 12TH MASK LINE )
    0000000000000000 W, <CR>  ( 13TH MASK LINE )
    0000000000000000 W, <CR>  ( 14TH MASK LINE )
    0000000000000000 W, <CR>  ( 15TH MASK LINE )
    0000000000000000 W, <CR>  ( 16TH MASK LINE )
    0000000000000000 W, <CR>  ( 1ST MOUSE LINE )
    0001111001111000 W, <CR>  ( 2ND MOUSE LINE )
    0010000110000100 W, <CR>  ( 3RD MOUSE LINE )
    1010000110000101 W, <CR>  ( 4TH MOUSE LINE )
    1110110110110111 W, <CR>  ( 5TH MOUSE LINE )
    1110110110110111 W, <CR>  ( 6TH MOUSE LINE )
    1110110110110111 W, <CR>  ( 7TH MOUSE LINE )
    0111110111110110 W, <CR>  ( 8TH MOUSE LINE )
    0111111111111110 W, <CR>  ( 9TH MOUSE LINE )
    0011010101011100 W, <CR>  ( 10TH MOUSE LINE )
    0001100000011000 W, <CR>  ( 11TH MOUSE LINE )
    0001110110111000 W, <CR>  ( 12TH MOUSE LINE )
    0000111111110000 W, <CR>  ( 13TH MOUSE LINE )
    0000001111000000 W, <CR>  ( 14TH MOUSE LINE )
    0000001111000000 W, <CR>  ( 15TH MOUSE LINE )
    0000000000000000 W, <CR>  ( 16TH MOUSE LINE )
NEW-MOUSE TRANSFORM <CR>   ( SET NEW MOUSE )
SHOW <CR>                  ( AND DISPLAY )
```

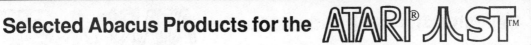
PaintPro

Design and graphics software for the ST

PaintPro is a very friendly and very powerful package for drawing and design on the Atari ST computers that has many features other ST graphic programs don't have. Based on GEM™, **PaintPro** supports up to three active windows in all three resolutions—up to 640x400 or 640x800 (full page) on monochrome monitor, and 320 x 200 or 320 x 400 on a color monitor.

PaintPro's complete toolkit of functions includes text, fonts, brushes, spraypaint, pattern fills, boxes, circles and ellipses, copy, paste and zoom and others. Text can be typed in one of four directions—even upside down— and in one of six GEM fonts and eight sizes. **PaintPro** can even load pictures from "foreign" formats (ST LOGO, DEGAS, Neochrome and Doodle) for enhancement using **PaintPro**'s double-sized picture format. Hardcopy can be sent to most popular dot-matrix printers.

PaintPro Features :

- Works in all 3 resolutions (mono, low and medium)
- Four character modes (replace, transparent, inverse XOR)
- Four line thicknesses and user-definable line pattern
- Uses all standard ST fill patterns and user definable fill patterns
- Max. three windows (dependng on available memory)
- Resolution to 640 x 400 or 640x800 pixels (mono version only)
- Up to six GDOS type fonts, in 8-, 9-, 10-, 14-, 16-, 18-, 24- and 36-point sizes
- Text can be printed in four directions
- Handles other GDOS compatible fonts, such as those in **PaintPro Library # 1**
- Blocks can be cut and pasted; mirrored horizontally and vertically; marked, saved in LOGO format, and recalled in LOGO
- Accepts ST LOGO, DEGAS, **Doodle & Neochrome** graphics
- Features help menus, full-screen display, and UNDO using the right mouse button
- Most dot-matrix printers can be easily adapted

PaintPro works with Atari ST systems with one or more single- or double-sided disk drives. Works with either monochrome or color ST monitors. Printer optional.

PaintPro   Suggested Retail Price: **$49.95**

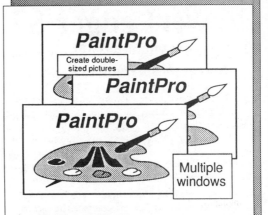

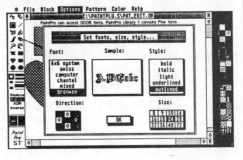

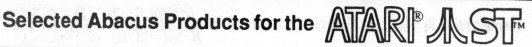
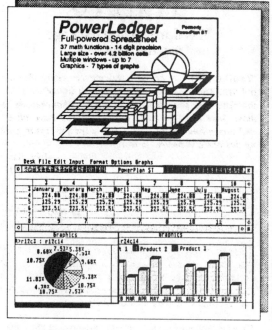

Selected Abacus Products for the  ATARI ST™

TextPro
Wordprocessing package
for the Atari ST

"TextPro seems to be well thought out, easy, flexible anf fast. The program makes excellent use of the GEM interface and provides lots of small enhancements to make your work go more easily... if you have an ST and haven't moved up to a GEM word processor, pick up this one and become a text pro."

—John Kintz
ANTIC

"TextPro is the best wordprocessor available for the ST"
—Randy McSorley
Pacus Report

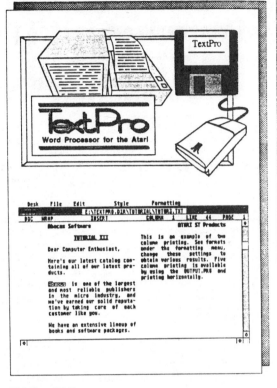

TextPro is a first-class word processor for the Atari ST that boasts dozens of features for the writer. It was designed by three writers to incorporate features that they wanted in a wordprocessor—the result is a superior package that suits the needs of all ST owners.

TextPro combines its "extra" features with easy operation, flexibility, and speed—but at a very reasonable price. The two-fingered typist will find **TextPro** to be a friendly, user-oriented program, with all the capabilities needed for fine writing and good-looking printouts. **Textpro** offers full-screen editing with mouse or keyboard shortcuts, as well as high-speed input, scrolling and editing. **TextPro** includes a number of easy to use formatting commands, fast and practical cursor positioning and multiple text styles.

Two of **TextPro**'s advanced features are automatic table of contents generation and index generation —capabilities usually found only on wordprocessing packages costing hundreds of dollars. **TextPro** can also print text horizontally (normal typewriter mode) or vertically (sideways). For that professional newsletter look, **TextPro** can print the text in columns—up to six columns per page in sideways mode.

The user can write form letters using the convenient Mail Merge option. **TextPro** also supports GEM-oriented fonts and type styles—text can be **bold**, underlined, *italic*, superscript, outlined, etc., and in a number of point sizes. **TextPro** even has advanced features for the programmer for development with its Non-document and C-sourcecode modes.

TextPro   Suggested Retail Price: **$49.95**

TextPro ST Features:

- Full screen editing with either mouse or keyboard
- Automatic index generation
- Automatic table of contents generation
- Up to 30 user-defined function keys, max. 160 characters per key
- Lines up to 180 characters using horizontal scrolling
- Automatic hyphenation
- Automatic wordwrap
- Variable number of tab stops
- Multiple-column output (maximum 5 columns)
- Sideways printing on Epson FX and compatibles
- Performs mail merge and document chaining
- Flexible and adaptable printer driver
- Supports RS-232 file transfer (computer-to-computer transfer possible)
- Detailed 65+ page manual

TextPro works with Atari ST systems with one or more single- or double-sided disk drives. Works with either monochrome or color ST monitors.

TexPro allows for flexible printer configurations with most popular dot-matrix printers.